Orthodox Women Speak

Orthodox Women Speak

Discerning the "Signs of the Times"

Edited by

Kyriaki Karidoyanes FitzGerald

With a Foreword by
Aruna Gnanadason

WCC Publications, Geneva

Holy Cross Orthodox Press,
Brookline, Massachusetts

Cover design: Edwin Hassink
Cover illustration: An icon depicting Jesus' appearance in the garden to two women following his resurrection from the dead – the good news to which the women were the first witnesses.

ISBN 2-8254-1317-8

150 route de Ferney, 1211 Geneva 2, Switzerland
Website: http://www.wcc-coe.org

Printed in Switzerland

With profound appreciation and respect
for a woman who has been faithfully bearing witness
to the fullness of the "life in abundance" (John 10:10)
extended to both women and men,
this volume is lovingly dedicated to

Elisabeth Behr-Sigel

Contents

Preface

Perhaps the image that best captures the Ecumenical Decade – Churches in Solidarity with Women (1988-1998) has been the round table. It reflects the longing of concerned women to bring their voices together at a common table for dialogue leading to common action, a desire to deepen the conversation across boundaries and to learn to listen rather than simply speak. The round table invites everyone into its space as equals. It is an ecumenical space where all those at the table are welcome, and where there is always room for more people to join. At this welcoming table women theologians, women in different positions in the church and women in the pew – all the women who keep alive the faith and life of the church – are respected and valued.

The longing for solidarity which has grown among women has been one of the gifts and continuing challenges of the Decade. There have been many events, many common concerns that have transcended regional and denominational boundaries as women have drawn together for refuge. Over these ten years efforts have been made to bring women together to the round table, for dialogue and reflection on issues that concern them. These events have often been ecumenical – allowing for women to bring their varying perspectives, anxieties and visions together.

This attempt at coming to a common table is not without its difficulties. No transformation comes about without labour and pain; and if we come to the table with honesty and commitment, we must also come with the realization that this new way of being together is neither easy nor comfortable – nor should it be! The Decade has made us painfully aware of the many challenges which remain to our solidarity with each other as women. We are divided as women – and we need to face up to this and in the years beyond the Decade to work more intentionally for dialogue and reflection so that we can grow closer together.

If diversity – of culture, regional background, race and denomination – is no more than an ecumenical slogan, it will quickly be submerged.

Differences in the way we live our faith are God-given and add beauty and grace to our common witness. Regrettably, we are not always able to handle diversity. We assume that women and groups of women who do not think or act as we do are a threat and discord to our community.

In the ecumenical movement, we often speak of "ecumenical spaces". This is about a "spirituality of connectedness", as US theologian Letty Russell describes it. When we come to the round table we make a choice for connectedness – with God, with ourselves and with the sisters who join us there. It is the Spirit of God who moves us this way – disturbing us and the old ways in which we perceived each other and lived with each other, and yet at the same time filling us with the power of God's unconditional love. It moves us into deeper and deeper dimensions of connectedness. This yearning for connectedness is symbolic of the deep sense we have as churches together of God's love and hospitality towards us as children of God.

But it is possible to create ecumenical spaces only when all those who come to the table come with the confidence of their self-worth, their integrity and their spiritual strength. They come with their marvellous gifts and they offer these at the table, in faith and with hope. The challenge for all of us who come to the table is to receive each other's gifts with grace. There is need for a prioritization of politeness, deference and sometimes silence as the basic requirements for authentic learning across boundaries of difference.

It is in this context that I would place the work that the World Council of Churches has done with Orthodox women during the course of this Decade, culminating in the two gatherings of Orthodox women in Damascus (1996) and Istanbul (1997), which are covered in this publication. It was my privilege to be part of these Orthodox women's meetings. I learned from my Orthodox sisters what it means for us as women to love the church and to respect its great traditions and yet speak with courage and conviction when something there disturbs us. All the women I met at these meetings are indeed gifts to the ecumenical movement. The Orthodox women spoke with sensitivity and respect and yet with boldness. It taught me that women can speak from within the tradition, yet also speak to the tradition and be a part of the transformation of tradition. I thank them for all this and more!

As we grew together in mutual trust and respect, we recognized that it was all well worth the effort, as this volume will so ably demonstrate. It was important to have Dr Kyriaki Karidoyanis FitzGerald as the theological consultant to work on the content of the meetings. She brought to the process her insights and knowledge of what is the best way to gather together the theological and experiential aspects of Orthodox women in their faith. We are grateful to her for her indispensable contribution, and I am personally thankful to her for her understanding and patience with me as we organized the events.

Holding the two meetings in two different regions was important, because this allowed us to be deeply influenced by the histories and contexts of the places and the churches where we met. Perhaps the greatest blessing of all was to have the full support of the four Patriarchs who accompanied us in the process and supported us all the way. We are grateful too for the active engagement of the churches in officially naming the women to attend. This was a sign of the respect that our Orthodox sisters receive from their churches and the genuine longing within these churches to let the women participate in discerning the signs of the times.

And so our journey together to come to the round table continues. It is not without its difficulties and challenges. It is not without its irritants and risks. But the round table signifies an open circle of love and compassion to which we hope all women will come, so that we can move forward in faith and offer to the church a new model of being the church as an embodiment of God's love.

ARUNA GNANADASON
Women's Programme
Justice, Peace and Creation Team
World Council of Churches

Introduction

KYRIAKI KARIDOYANES FITZGERALD

"Discerning the 'Signs of the Times' (Matt. 16:3): Women in the Life of the Orthodox Church" was the theme for two international Orthodox women's conferences in 1996 and 1997. The first, in Damascus from 4-10 October 1996, brought together Orthodox and Oriental Orthodox women representing churches in Asia, Africa and the Middle East. Most of the 65 participants were official representatives of the churches. The host of the gathering was His Beatitude Ignatius IV, Greek Orthodox Patriarch of Antioch and All the East. Participants also enjoyed the hospitality and active participation of His Beatitude Ignatius Zakka II, Syrian Orthodox Patriarch of Antioch and All the East.

Ecumenical Patriarch Bartholomew of Constantinople hosted the second conference, which was held in Istanbul, from 10-17 May 1997. It brought together women representing the churches from North and South America, Eastern and Western Europe and Russia; again, most of the more than 50 participants were delegates officially appointed by their churches. His Beatitude Patriarch Karekin II of the Armenian Orthodox Patriarchate of Constantinople also extended his hospitality and participated actively in the conference.

The delegates to both conferences were sent by their churches at the invitation of the World Council of Churches. The conferences were organized and sponsored through the WCC's office of the Ecumenical Decade – Churches in Solidarity with Women.

The two official statements which resulted from these proceedings are presented at the beginning of this volume. Here we should underscore the seriousness with which these texts and the meetings which produced them were taken by church leadership. Four patriarchs, as noted above, and a number of regional bishops were actively involved in the progress of the work. They were very committed to learning more about what Orthodox women had to say. Furthermore, there is an official quality to these statements, as they reflect the concerns of formally appointed delegates from the regional Orthodox churches. The representatives were appointed by their presiding hierarchs, who themselves were acting on behalf of their regional synods.

To be sure, these results only reflect preliminary considerations. Nevertheless, we have now for the first time in history a consensus regarding some of the most important issues which concern Orthodox women – and this global consensus is discerned *from the perspective of Orthodox women.* It is hoped that the information presented here regarding who Orthodox women experience themselves to be, as well as their concerns, may prove helpful both in the life of the Orthodox churches and in ecumenical dialogue.

In addition to the two final texts, this volume includes a selection of the presentations and study papers offered to the delegates for their consideration and discussion. These appear with no additional commentary, as they speak for themselves and solely reflect the perspectives of the authors. Nevertheless, the variety of expertise and experiences reflected in all of the presentations assisted tremendously in both formal and informal exchanges and made an obvious impact on the final formulation of the statements.

It is appropriate at the outset to offer thanks. First of all, we thank and give glory to God for the miracle of these two conferences. Because of this, profound appreciation and gratitude is expressed to Ecumenical Patriarch Bartholomew and Patriarch Ignatius IV for their kind and even enthusiastic invitations to host these events. Each manifested his commitment to our efforts by delegating personnel and making available resources which facilitated the success of these conferences. Deepest thanks are also expressed to Patriarch Ignatius Zakka II and Patriarch Karekin II. The personal openness and thoughtful generosity demonstrated by these four presiding hierarchs was not only a wonderful expression of the Orthodox ethos and Eastern hospitality but also bore witness to their commitment to our collaboration together as Orthodox women.

Sincere gratitude is expressed to the regional synods and the presiding hierarchs who appointed the delegates to the conferences. The formal and informal discussions and the deep commitment to setting priorities made it obvious that some of the best regional representatives of the church had been sent. It also indicated that church officials cared deeply about discerning and responding to the real issues which affect Orthodox women. The delegates were not afraid to engage some very difficult challenges with other Orthodox sisters.

Heartfelt thanks for initiating and supporting this effort is expressed to the World Council of Churches, especially to the director of its women's programme Aruna Gnanadason, to Nicole Fischer, who extended herself personally, professionally and administratively for the Damascus meeting, and to Claire Tierney for her expert administrative collaboration and support at the Istanbul meeting.

Aruna Gnanadason was kindly available to offer advice from her vast experience in the difficult art of balancing content and practical logistics in international conferences. Sensitive to the need that these conferences reflect and address the concerns of Orthodox women, she was always accessible to offer constructive advice and criticism but entrusted all final decisions concerning the theological content of the programme to me as Orthodox theological consultant.

Profound appreciation must be now extended to the consultants and official observers invited by the WCC as well as the local visitors who participated in these programmes. The consultants and observers represented a diversity of experience and opinion. A small number of delegates from the Damascus conference were also invited to serve as consultants to the meeting in Istanbul, providing an extra measure of continuity between the two meetings.

The context

Planning the programme was indeed challenging. The WCC women's programme was strongly committed to respecting the regional contexts in designing these two meetings. My additional concern as an Orthodox woman was to strive to offer "a singular event in two different contexts". Within the limited resources available, we attempted to develop such a programme. We intentionally worked without pre-conceptions about the type of final statements the representatives would produce at each meeting.

The theme for the conferences – "Discerning the Signs of the Times" emerged during the official visit to the Geneva offices of the WCC by the Ecumenical Patriarch Bartholomew in December 1995. During a news conference the patriarch was asked about the possibility of rejuvenating the ministry of women deacons. After displaying openness to the possibility, he concluded by stating:

> It is important to watch for "the signs of the times" (Matt. 16:3) and to fine-tune our ears to the stirring and calls of the Spirit as recommended in the Apocalypse, "he who has an ear, let him hear what the Spirit says to the churches" (Rev. 2:7).[1]

Apparently, the Ecumenical Patriarch believes that the ministry of women is an important issue which merits "discerning" during our present "times". Furthermore, the source of this process is not male or female human persons, central as they may be, but rather the "*calls of the Spirit*".

In Matthew 16:3, the biblical story associated with this theme, Jesus confronts the religious hypocrites of his day after they try to trap him by asking for a sign from heaven. Within his response, he also exposes their pride, malice, inertia and profound *lack* of authority by simply revealing their unwillingness and inability to discern the "signs of the times" in which they lived. Orthodox Christianity teaches that the "signs" of our own times, just as of those times, point to the risen Lord Jesus Christ himself.

The sub-theme, "Women in the Life of the Orthodox Church", was intended to encourage the delegates to consider deeply the nature of their own presence and participation in the life of the church. Orthodox theology and spirituality teach that we are responsible for discerning the will of God for our own circumstances. The ancient Christian liturgical greeting "Christ is in our midst" affirms that in each generation every aspect of life is called to reflect this reality with integrity.

Discernment is an ongoing task. The Greek term *diakrisis* connotes an often subtle and sometimes virtually imperceptible dynamic which requires a clear and lasting division in cutting through a crisis. *Compromises fail miserably when* diakrisis *is necessary*. According to Orthodox spirituality, discernment in its fullness occurs among persons who "know God", who live in communion with God.[2] They are the holy ones, the saints, both male and female. No matter how short of this the vast majority of us fall, we are called to discern to the best of our ability, even as we acknowledge our limitations.

This call is to an ongoing, life-long process, marked by increasing congruency, integrity and ultimately transparency between personal "interior" experience and "external" expression. Accounts from the lives of the saints attest to the value this congruency gives to the unique situation of every human being. God respects our personal circumstances, and loves us from where we are. On the basis of these assumptions, Orthodox spirituality asserts that how we live, act and relate with others is somehow expressive of our innermost relationship with God. At the same time, how we live, act and relate with others offers countless opportunities to experience the mercy, love and presence of God outside our own selves – provided that we are ready and open to this.

For these reasons, we cannot be passive, letting others live our lives for us. There are innumerable choices to make within the context of our own lives. We are accountable to God for each of these choices. Like the wise bridesmaids in Jesus' parable (Matt. 25:13), we are called to "keep awake", consciously awaiting the presence of the Bridegroom within the context of daily events, relationships and responsibilities. Like the good servants entrusted with a gift of talents (Matt. 25:14-30), we are called judiciously and creatively to use and even increase the good we have been given. And, like the faithful followers at the second coming of our Lord, we too are to discern the presence of Christ in the needs of our neighbours (Matt. 25:31-46). In this manner and as part of a living, "holy" people, Christians are continuously compelled faithfully to "discern".

The outcome: unity in diversity

While this summarizes the theory, belief and hope undergirding the rationale for these meetings, there was no way to know what would actually transpire. We did not know whom the churches would send or how they would work together.

In fact, the churches sent a rich variety of devoted women. And they came ready to work. We did not anticipate the remarkable amount of congruency which would emerge between the final texts of the two conferences. The Orthodox participants came from countries, cultures and regions which are vastly different from each other. Many of them had never before left home.

In general, the delegates did not identify their unity solely in terms of a gathering of women from numerous contexts. Rather, the unity experienced within each conference seemed to be based on a deeper foundation. This was shown by the profound level of interest, patience and active listening which the participants extended to each other in both formal and informal discussions. This quality of compassionate, focused attention is too rare a commodity in theological and ecumenical settings. This concentrated discipline perhaps assisted in the mysterious process of discerning the "one Orthodox faith" in the other. Once the delegates experienced the "orthodoxy" of their sister representatives, they appeared to encounter "the one church" in each other as well. Once "the church" was discerned in the sister delegate, enthusiasm about the nature of the work to be accomplished emerged almost immediately. Within this indispensable overarching contact, participants could turn readily to the immediate concerns of the church, differing regional practices and personal experience.

At the same time, each meeting displayed its own unique personality. Despite the vast diversity of regional, cultural and social settings and the abundant variety of personal histories, the delegates to the Damascus meeting appeared to be fairly homogeneous regarding their experience of and concerns for the church. They accomplished their work in a fluid manner and quickly approved the draft of their statement with a unanimous and resounding voice.

The Istanbul meeting began more slowly. At first a number of the representatives seemed tentative about who their Orthodox sister was. Trust had to be earned. Nevertheless, a powerful bond of love and collaboration was soon forged among participants and generated an almost electric energy and enthusiasm in the writing of the statement. The delegates experienced the document as theirs and devoted undivided attention to it. By the end of the conference, several delegates were speaking of the meeting as a personal miracle for them. It marked a process of discovering who their Orthodox sisters truly were and the importance of expressing their concerns together as women of the church.

Both final documents reflect the fact that the delegates regarded themselves as full members of the church. There is even an apparent ease and comfort about their identity as Orthodox women. But this way of taking their membership for granted also created a deep sense of responsibility among the participants "to speak the truth in love" (Eph. 4:15) in the formal and informal discussions. This sense of accountability compelled them to call attention to certain practices in the church which compromise the gospel and impede the mission and witness of the church. The ramifications of sexism as a sin were discussed at both conferences. The text from Damascus, for example, states:

> We note with tremendous sadness, how easy it is for the presence of women to be forgotten... There are some occasions when the role and presence of women, as well their work, is not always validated for the value it has... Rather, women may be seen by some as more readily dispensable...
>
> Women have also been dismissed in other ways as well. We recognize with deep concern how social injustices such as poverty, illiteracy and invisibility may affect Orthodox women and women in general in our part of the world. Wherever possible, we must strive to assist them and open our lives and our hearts to them, as our Lord would have us do.

The Istanbul text takes this a step further to suggest that sexism be taken up programmatically by the church, observing that "the church would benefit from theological and soteriological reflection on this issue, especially through the medium of consultations, workshops and informal study".

Almost ten years earlier, the inter-Orthodox consultation on the place of women in the Orthodox church in Rhodes emphasized the need to

> confess in honesty and humility that, owing to human weakness and sinfulness, the Christian communities have not always and in all places been able to suppress effectively ideas, manners and customs, historical developments and social conditions which have resulted in practical discrimination against women. Human sinfulness has thus led to practices which do not reflect the true nature of the church of Jesus Christ.[3]

Both the Damascus and Istanbul discussions and documents also voiced concern about certain liturgical practices associated with the presentation of infants, particular prayers related to miscarriage, abortion, post-partum mothers, and the assumptions which in some places still prohibit women from receiving communion for biological reasons. These concerns were discussed openly, yet with great sensitivity. The delegates recognized the need to examine more thoughtfully the relationship between theology and praxis. Indeed, a focus on *orthopraxia* as the theologically correct application of practice, was reflected in the discussions at each conference.

The Synod of the Greek Orthodox Patriarchate of Antioch, under the leadership of Patriarch Ignatius IV, immediately responded to these issues, which had also been identified a few weeks earlier by a regional meeting of Orthodox women from the Middle East. The Synod "affirmed the God-given value of women in the church and ordered that liturgical texts which imply otherwise be corrected". Furthermore,

> The Holy Synod discussed certain matters which touched the lives of women and decided that women and men should be treated equally concerning their participation in divine services and receiving sacraments. *Whatever references are in the liturgical books that women are unclean and tainted should be abolished...* This necessitates a new look at liturgical texts.[4]

Thus a beginning was made on implementing the recommendation from the Rhodes consultation that the Orthodox

> are bound to affirm in the strongest possible way the dignity of the human person, both the female and the male. Any act which denies the dignity of the human person and any act which discriminates against women and men on the basis of gender is a sin. It is therefore the task of the church to affirm before the world the dignity of the human person, created in the image and likeness of God (Gen. 1:26).[5]

This essential discussion was seen within the context of an even deeper issue: commitment to the unity of the church. Just as the practices mentioned above may distort the relationship between men and women and thus threaten the unity between male and female members within the same Orthodox family, so, too, the absence of eucharistic communion between our two Orthodox families, despite more than 30 years of unofficial and official dialogues, discussions and agreements, was viewed as a scandal and a threat to the unity of the whole church. A commitment to unity between the two Orthodox families seemed to be the highest priority among the delegates.[6]

The Damascus meeting stated quite powerfully that "as we prayed, discussed the themes and met together, we recognized that we serve the same Lord and share in the same Orthodox faith. It is our common faith which has guided our reflection and which has inspired us to deepen our service to the Orthodox church and our witness in the world." The Istanbul meeting also echoed the concerns they heard from church hierarchs, who "eagerly anticipate the final reconciliation and restoration of ecclesiastical communion between the two families". The vast majority of delegates seemed painfully aware that it was not the will of Christ which is impeding the restoration of full communion between the two Orthodox families.

The participants at both meetings were also well aware that most of their recommendations had been expressed by others before them in some manner. Two previous conferences – in Agapia, Romania, in 1976, and in Crete in 1990 – had been sponsored on behalf of the Orthodox churches at the invitation of the WCC. Much of what these two consultations called for was also recommended by the Rhodes consultation. The lack of enthusiasm for and commitment to applying these earlier recommendations was experienced as a source of frustration and even embarrassment by many from within the churches. Noting that some recommendations from previous meetings of Orthodox women have been addressed and others have not, the Istanbul text says: "We are concerned about the reception of this document and recommend our churches make this statement available for women either through general publications or correspondence to parishes." Speaking of the expansion of the scope of the ministries of women, the Damascus meeting similarly emphasizes "that we still wait for the application of the recommendations" from Rhodes. In part perhaps due to these concerns, participants in both meetings affirmed the importance of Orthodox spirituality, which serves to deepen one's relationship with Christ and others. Because of this spiritual foundation, the delegates demonstrated a strong commitment "to stimulate a desire in our people to take an active role in the life of the church. This may happen with the realization, on the part of Orthodox Christians, of their own royal priesthood" (Istanbul). The participants in Damascus acknowledged with gratitude the chance "to learn from each other about the many forms of ministry in which women in our churches are already engaged".

Whether in the aftermath of the cataclysmic changes in Eastern Europe or, more generally, in the face of the onslaught of challenges raised by modernity, a new concern was articulated for the lapsed Orthodox. "In some of our churches, Orthodox Christians have lost interest and joined social, cultural and para-church organizations," Istanbul said. "We are looking for ways to bring Orthodox Christians back to the church." Some women attending the Istanbul meeting came from areas which have recently experienced the tragedy of war. With this in mind, the delegates spoke of women as "peacemakers" and called on all the churches to make "a greater commitment to support our sister Orthodox churches in crisis situations... and to support refugees and those in war-torn situations. Often in these situations, women and children suffer most."

A particularly strong desire was expressed for more communication among Orthodox women regarding theological, spiritual and practical concerns which affect them in particular. There was a strong call for more resources and materials which can be used in church schools throughout the Orthodox world to help Christians live their faith from day to day. Some delegates from Eastern Europe stressed that in addition to receiving food and clothing there is a deeply felt need to be fed spiritually and theologically. They looked to Orthodox Christians in other parts of the world for assistance.[7]

Both meetings placed a surprisingly strong emphasis on the serious lack of opportunity for women in far too many situations to study Orthodox theology. Noting that "in families and schools, women are the primary educators", Istanbul said that "theologically-educated women have a particular ministry in teaching our faithful", making "Orthodox theological education for women... a priority". Damascus expressed "deep disappointment" that many women "have not had the chance to study theology in a formal setting", which "hinders our role and work in the church". The statement added that women should receive both spiritual and financial support to pursue studies in theological education. At both meetings those women present who have pursued formal studies in Orthodox theology were publicly recognized and encouraged. Both meetings also benefited from the presence of a number of participants who have experienced the spiritual and theological formation afforded by monastic life; and appreciation was often expressed for the importance of the gift of monasticism to the life of the church, both historically and today. Istanbul in particular encouraged the development of monastic vocations for women.

Both conferences echoed earlier meetings in stressing the importance of the role of the laity within the church. On this point, it is evident that the practices of Orthodox communities vary widely. In some churches laymen and laywomen are actively involved in various forms of leadership and influence in a virtually analogous manner; elsewhere, this is clearly not the case. The Istanbul delegates stated that "women are able to and should be invited to offer guidance to the church on issues that specifically concern them". The Damascus representatives recommended "that our leaders encourage women's involvement and participation in the everyday decision-making process of our local churches".

Both meetings expressed a desire for the development of ministries in theology, education and mission, ecumenical relations, and pastoral care. The latter was a particular focus at the Damascus meeting, which called on church leaders to

> encourage women's formal and informal ministries in pastoral care, so as to reach out to others who may have been spiritually isolated, in material need, grieving the loss of a loved one, survivors of abuse or violence, etc. These persons deserve particular attention, as they require the healing presence and assistance of the church through her prayer, counselling and support.

The participants recommended that the churches take more positive actions in affirming and supporting the various vocations to which women may be called. Many examples of women serving the church actively were shared by the participants, a number of whom were themselves involved in such ministries as spiritual direction, pastoral counselling, Christian education, theological education, hospital visitations, medical missions, philanthropy, and caring for orphaned children, the destitute and the elderly in their communities.

Questions about ordination

Discussions about the rejuvenation of women in the diaconate occurred at both conferences. The participants at Damascus recognized "the ministry of deaconesses as a response to the Holy Spirit for various needs of this present age" and recommended "that our church leaders discern prayerfully and courageously the presence of the Holy Spirit in those many places where the ministry of ordained deaconesses, as well as other forms of ministry, are needed". The Istanbul delegates stated: "Many of us believe the incorporation of deaconesses in the life of the church will help contribute to the atmosphere of love and learning, and to the life of the church."

While not all participants were familiar with this tradition of ministry, encouragement to reflect on it came in the welcoming address at Istanbul of Patriarch Bartholomew. He reminded the participants that "since the earliest days of the church, faithful Christian women and men have lived in this city... Here, at the Great Church of Agia Sophia a number of devoted women, such as St Olympias, served as deaconesses... To both women and men, to both clergy and laity, these women saints continue to be a source of inspiration, for it is written: 'God is revealed in his saints!'" Contemporary discussions about the ordination of women deacons in the Orthodox church have their origins in the early 1800s. This is not, as some have claimed, a new issue initiated from "outside", though the pastoral challenges of the contemporary world have certainly renewed a sense of urgency about it among many Orthodox Christians all around the world. The 1988 Rhodes consultation said that the rejuvenation of the ancient ministry of the order of women deacons would "represent a positive response to many of the needs and demands of the contemporary world in many spheres. This would be all the more true if the diaconate in general (male as well as female) were restored in all places in its original manifold services... in response to the increasing specific needs of our time."

That the women deacon has been ordained through the laying on of hands has been well established. The eucharistic context of the woman deacon's ordination was central, reflecting an ecclesiology which is built on active participation in the life of the Triune God. Especially during the Byzantine period, deaconesses were ordained within the sanctuary and in front of the holy altar. The rite occurred during the celebration of the eucharist and began at the same time as the ordination of the deacon.

As is characteristic with Byzantine ordinations to the "higher orders", this rite included the ancient proclamation of "the divine grace", two ordination prayers and the diaconal "Litany of Peace". The deaconess was vested with the diaconal stole and received communion with the clergy.

From the perspective of Orthodox ecclesiology, the ordination service and prayers for the woman deacon testify to the genuine ordination she received. Furthermore, both the rite and prayers witness to the fact that all ordinations are a gift to the worshipping church community from the living God. Ordination is neither a "right" to be demanded nor a "commodity" anyone can "possess". Rather, it is a profound mystery to be humbly and joyfully received by the church. Like the mysteries of baptism and chrismation, which mark the process of Christian initiation, ordinations are "Pentecostal" events. For this reason, ordinations are not to be hidden from the living Christian community.

The Byzantine ordination rite is part of a larger tradition of the church which bears witness to the existence of women deacons and their ministry in the life of the early church, especially in the Christian East. Exegesis of St Paul's reference to women deacons was done by Origen, St John Chrysostom and Theodoret of Cyrus. Mention of women deacons can be found in the *Syriac Didascalia* and *Apostolic Constitution* as well as in the canons of the early Ecumenical Councils. Several stories of women deacons appear in the magnificent collection known as the *Meterikon*, a rich hagiographical series edited by Prof. Dimitrios Tsamis of the University of Thessaloniki.

Historically, the ministerial activities of woman deacons could perhaps be summarized into three broad expressions. First, women deacons often had a dynamic, evangelical ministry of *teaching the Christian faith* – instructing believers in the faith, guiding others in their growth in holiness, leading pagan and heretical women and men into the church. Because of their gift of discernment, many women deacons were renowned as spiritual mothers whose intercession, advice and guidance were sought by both women and men, even ranking members of the clergy.

Second, many women deacons had a dynamic, evangelical ministry in the areas of what would be called today *pastoral care and social work*. Some devoted their efforts to providing food and shelter for the poor; others attended to the physically ill and disabled; still others had a ministry of providing a safe haven to foreign travellers. Women deacons ministered to the homeless and hospitalized, the orphans and the prisoners, both Christians and non-Christians. People from all walks of life would come to these holy women seeking hope, inspiration and assurance of the love of God during times of trouble and need.

Women deacons would also bring holy communion to those members of the community who were unable to participate in the eucharist. Acting as the ambassador of the bishop, they became the vehicle of the church's care for the needy and those who appeared to be on the edges of society.

Finally, a number of women deacons exercised a dynamic, evangelical ministry directly related to the life of *monastic community*. The order of women deacons became associated with monasticism especially during the middle ages. Some women deacons founded monastic communities; others were elected abbesses of an established community.

The contemporary rejuvenation of the ministry of deaconesses has been strongest within the Oriental Orthodox family. In the Armenian Orthodox Church of Constantinople, for example, *the same prayers of ordination are employed for both the male and female deacon*. While other prayers are used for the blessing of a deaconess in the Coptic Orthodox tradition,[8] the Coptic Church has begun to enjoy the ministry of deaconesses to a greater extent than many other parts of the Orthodox world which are actively engaged in academic debate about deaconesses.

The ordination of women as presbyters (priests) and bishops was not brought up at any of the discussions. But even if this is not an issue for many Orthodox women, there was a common appreciation expressed by the delegates that this has become an important ecumenical issue coming from traditions originating in the West. For this reason, the findings of Constantine Yokarinis, a member of the theological faculty of the University of Athens, were included for consideration during one of the panel discussions at the Istanbul meeting. (He was one of three men to have offered presentations at either of the conferences.)

Of their own accord, participants organized extra discussion time in order to consider his research more carefully; and more than a third of the delegates attended this meeting. This may indicate that Orthodox women are comfortable considering and discussing this issue – at least with other Orthodox women – even when they are not themselves proponents of the ordination of women as presbyters and bishops.

The church must be the church

These statements from these two meetings reflect a number of global concerns relevant to Orthodox women. They also demonstrate that Orthodox women see themselves as full members of the church. For them, this experience of church is more than a mere intellectual affiliation. A subtle yet pervasive sense of "the one faith" and "the one church" seemed to saturate their being, as well as undergird interpersonal exchanges. This may be an indicator of what Orthodox refer to in Greek as the living *phronema* of the faith. It may have been this deep, almost palpable sense which grounded the delegates' ease when discussing inconsistencies, shortcomings, sins and abuses which have occurred within the contemporary life of the church. And it is from this foundation where they offer their written observations and recommendations. Because of this living foundation in the *phronema* of the faith, these statements offer a focused and resounding call for "the church to be the church".

Sadly, inertia threatens the application of *orthopraxia*. These conferences have also demonstrated that Orthodox women from around the world are still waiting – for the implementation of proposals from previous conferences, for the application of recommendations which seek to reflect better the theology of the church (some of them now over 20 years old).

"The church must be the church" on issues related to women. The longer inertia dominates, the more the integrity of the church's mission in the world is compromised. At some level, every Orthodox Christian is affected. The witness of laymen and laywomen, and especially that of hierarchs, clergy and those in leadership, is seriously undermined whenever we fail the church in this manner.

Now is the time aggressively to apply the lesson taught in Matthew 16:3. We too must avoid the temptation to which the Pharisees and Scribes succumbed, the temptation of looking the other way instead of to Christ. Now is the time for us as members of the church to seek out the will of God and respond.

Now is the time to discern the "signs of the times". Discernment, while often subtle, requires a clear, active and courageous response to the will of God. In being accountable to this process, we also discover for ourselves what is depicted in the gospel story: that "the signs of the times", including our own times, point to the risen Lord Jesus Christ himself.

NOTES

[1] Terres des Femmes, 1995, cited in *MaryMartha*, Vol. 4, no. 1, Winter 1995, p.23.

[2] This refers to the "experience of God" usually called theosis in Greek, rendered in English by such terms as "deification", "glorification", "sanctification".

[3] Gennadios Limouris, ed., *The Place of Woman in the Orthodox Church and the Question of the Ordination of Women*, Katerini, Greece, Tertios, 1992, p.29. About one-third of the participants invited to this consultation in 1988 were Orthodox women theologians.

[4] *The St Nina Quarterly*, Vol. 1, no. 4, Fall 1997, p.20 (italics added); thanks to Tarek Mitri for the English translation of these decisions.

[5] *The Place of Woman in the Orthodox Church*, p.28.

[6] On relations between the Eastern Orthodox and Oriental Orthodox, see for example, Thomas FitzGerald, "Toward the Reestablishment of Full Communion: The Orthodox-Oriental Orthodox Dialogue", *The Greek Orthodox Theological Review*, Vol. 36, no. 2, 1991, pp.169-83.

[7] It should be noted here that this meeting did not choose to address a statement to the World Council of Churches as such, although invited to do so. The delegates seemed to feel deeply the urgency of time constraints and preferred at this first meeting of such a diversity of Orthodox women to maintain their focus as Orthodox women on pressing matters affecting the church which they believed had to be directly communicated to their own communities.

[8] Prayers from the rite used by the Coptic Orthodox Church include versions of the ancient ordination prayer for the woman deacon from the Apostolic Constitutions, and prayers from ancient and other sources. Even though presently modified, ancient versions of the ordination rite designate ordination *(cheirotonia)*; cf. K. Fitzgerald, *Women Deacons in the Orthodox Church*, Brookline MA, Holy Cross, 1999.

Address to the Istanbul Meeting

H.A.H. ECUMENICAL PATRIARCH BARTHOLOMEW

Christ is risen!

Beloved children in Christ:

We welcome you very warmly to the Ecumenical Patriarchate and to this historic centre of Orthodox Christianity. It is a great joy for us to host this important inter-Orthodox conference for Orthodox women on the topic "Discerning the Signs of the Time". At this time we should like to express our appreciation to the World Council of Churches for providing so much support for this conference.

Our risen Lord and Saviour is the one who richly blesses us. And you have been blessed by him with the opportunity to come to this special city and to the Ecumenical Patriarchate not simply as participants in a conference, but as holy pilgrims, always seeking out those sacred centres of inspiration and spiritual nourishment which enable you to more fully serve the Lord and others in his name.

As you know, this city and the Church of Constantinople is rich in Christian history. Tradition tells us that St Andrew the Apostle and the First-Called preached the gospel of salvation in this region in the years following the coming of the Holy Spirit on Pentecost. Since the earliest days of the church, faithful Christian women and men have lived in this city. Here some of Christianity's greatest theologians and our predecessors on the venerable throne of Andrew, such as St Gregory the Theologian and St John Chrysostom honoured God both with their lives and their words. Here at the great church of Agia Sophia, a number of devoted women, such as St Olympias, served as deaconesses. Here, in this city and in the nearby cities, many of the great councils of the early church were held. At these councils, the fundamental convictions of our faith were affirmed and defended for the sake of our salvation. And it was from the Church of Constantinople that dedicated missionaries, such as St Cyril and St Methodios, whose memories we celebrated yesterday

[11 May], went out to preach the gospel to many peoples and to guide them to salvation.

Here we also remember the example of the countless martyrs and saints who bore witness to Christ. When you visit the patriarchal cathedral of St George the great martyr, you will find the sacred relics of three women saints: Euphemia, Theophano and Solomone. These pious women lived in different periods and different places. They had different stations in society. Yet they are united in their faith in Christ and in their devotion to his holy gospel. To both women and men, to both clergy and laity, these women saints continue to be a source of inspiration, for it is written: "God is revealed in his saints!"

Indeed, this city is well known for its historic churches as well as for its great treasures of Byzantine architecture and iconography. But most importantly, we honour the Church of Constantinople as the centre of Orthodox Christian life and witness. It is a church of saints and martyrs, a church of missionaries and theologians, a church with a history, but one with a future too. The examples of holiness and of service continue to guide us and to nurture us as we seek to serve our Lord in this day and age and in the dawning millennium.

Today it is our duty and honour to serve the few thousand faithful Christian men and women who live here in this city. Like the generations before them, the faithful stewards here continue to bear witness to their faith by keeping lit the *phanar* which is the beacon of Orthodoxy, by honouring their sacred heritage and by serving others in the name of our Lord Jesus Christ. We ask that you remember in your prayers, especially this week, all the faithful of the Church of Constantinople.

Trusting in God's grace, it is also our responsibility as Ecumenical Patriarch to be a servant of the unity of our holy Orthodox church throughout the world. While always respecting the dignity and rights of all the holy patriarchates and autocephalous churches, the archbishop of Constantinople and Ecumenical Patriarch is the "first among equals" of all the bishops of the church. Because of this we, humbly occupying the venerable throne of St Andrew, have a particular ministry through which we encourage and strengthen the unity of the holy Orthodox church. We seek to strengthen the "bond of peace" among the sister churches. We do not do this for our own honour and glory. Rather, we do this for the sake of the church's mission and witness in the world. We do this for the glory of God!

We are especially happy that your conference has brought together official delegates from both the autocephalous Orthodox churches and the Oriental Christian churches. As you know, our churches are presently engaged in official theological dialogue. The goal of this dialogue is to restore communion between our two families of churches. Although we have been divided for many centuries, our theologians have clearly affirmed that we share the same apostolic faith.

We pray fervently that the two families of churches will soon be able to resolve all outstanding differences and to act formally and in a canonical manner to restore ecclesiastical communion. We believe that this is the will of our common Lord. With God's grace, your conference and the previous one in Damascus will contribute in a very important way to the process of reconciliation and unity.

The Ecumenical Patriarchate has received with much appreciation the report of the conference of Orthodox women held in Damascus under the leadership of His Beatitude Patriarch Ignatius of Antioch and all the East, our beloved brother and co-celebrant. The report is a positive and inspiring one. It reminds all of us of the devotion and the piety of the many faithful who serve their church and society in the name of our Lord. It expresses faithfulness to the Orthodox tradition and the desire to respond to the challenges of today.

Among the many important recommendations of the Damascus conference is the call for the full restoration of the order of women deacons. This recommendation echoes a similar one coming from the inter-Orthodox consultation in Rhodes in 1988. The order of women deacons is an undeniable part of the tradition coming from the early church. Now, in many of our churches, there is a growing desire to restore this order so that the spiritual needs of the people of God may be better served. There are already a number of women who appear to be called to this ministry.

Beloved in the Lord:

Yesterday, you began your conference by participating in the divine liturgy offered at the historic shrine and monastery of the Life-Giving Fountain. There in that holy place we gathered together on the Sunday dedicated to the memory of the holy Myrrh-Bearing Women. The reading of the holy gospel reminded us once again of those devoted women whose names were Mary Magdalene, Mary the mother of James, and Salome. Disheartened and troubled, they went to the tomb to anoint the body of Christ on the first day of the week. Upon reaching the tomb, their sorrow was changed to joy when they learned that the Lord had risen from the dead. From the place of the dead, they rushed to Jerusalem to proclaim the life-giving message of the resurrection. They became, as our hymns say, the "apostles to the apostles". They were the proto-evangelists of the good news.

The example of the Myrrh-Bearing Women is important for all of us. Throughout the world, many people desire to hear the good news of salvation. There is a desire among many people to come to a deeper relationship with the living God. There is a longing for spiritual growth and an even greater longing for salvation. There is a desire for holiness and healing and forgiveness which comes from God alone.

Truly, the Orthodox faith has much wisdom to offer to all people. Like the Myrrh-Bearing Women, we are called to proclaim the living Lord who is risen from the dead. Through the Holy Spirit, Christ continues to offer us the love, the healing and the mercy of the heavenly Father. Because of Christ, we know that we belong to God, and that he loves each of us and that indeed we are his daughters and sons. Because of Christ, we know that we are most fully human when we live our lives in communion with him. Salvation is communion with God and with his people.

Through his gospel, our Lord also teaches us that we cannot grow in our relationship with the triune God apart from one another. We are bonded together through the mystery of God's goodness. And because of this, the followers of our Lord are obliged to oppose all forms of injustice, discrimination or abuse. As women and men of faith, we must not only pray for one another, we also must do all that we can to honour, preserve and protect the dignity of the human person who is created in the "image and likeness" of God.

Finally, we must remember that we grow closer to God and to one another in the midst of creation. Creation comes to us as a blessing and a gift. It is our common inheritance which is entrusted to us by God. Because we are stewards of this creation, we also have an obligation to honour and to preserve all that we have received from the Creator of heaven and earth.

Beloved in Christ:

We pray that your conference is one filled with all the blessings of the risen Lord and that your pilgrimage to this city and to the Ecumenical Patriarchate will be a source of blessing for your life and for our churches. We further pray that our risen Lord, through the intercession of his mother and the holy Myrrh-Bearing Women, will always guide you and protect you.

To him be glory, honour and worship, together with the eternal Father and the all-holy, good and life-giving Spirit, now and forever, and unto ages of ages. Amen.

Address to the Damascus Meeting

H.B. IGNATIOS IV

I am pleased that this meeting is being held here in Syria. From this part of the world, the cradle of apostolic mission, Christianity extended to Turkey and Greece; and the Western world was subsequently Christianized. Christianity is an Eastern reality. We interpret it here in its Eastern context. It is not bound to a Western identity.

Ecumenical dialogue is rooted in an understanding of Christianity which takes the plurality of our cultures and historical experiences very seriously. The search for such dialogue motivated our participation in the World Council of Churches since its early history. Our church expresses its ecumenical commitment in many different ways. Our openness to others is part of our being as Christians. We cannot isolate ourselves nor accept being isolated. As someone who for many years was involved in the life of the World Council of Churches and other ecumenical organizations, I can bear witness to this spirit of openness prevalent in our church. Together with sister churches in the region, we founded the Middle East Council of Churches. We are also involved with the Catholic Church and other churches in various bilateral dialogues.

The encounter of Christians in dialogue does not mean that we are in agreement. We do disagree, but we are called to love each other. Christianity in the East tries to be faithful to its apostolic tradition. We have rediscovered together with our non-Chalcedonian Orthodox sister churches what brings us very close to each other. We are not seeking only an agreement on Christian doctrines, for we are called to be witnesses of the one faith. Our faith cannot be reduced to belief in the Book. We often say to our Muslim neighbours that we are not a religion of the Book. We are a community of faith, a faith in a person. Scriptures are a way that leads us to the person of Christ, true God and true man.

I am also very pleased to see this women's meeting held in Syria. We are proud of our women, of the riches they have offered and continue to offer to the church. There is no discrimination against women in the church. There may have been failures in recognizing the role of women. We are aware of many questions which invite a serious effort of interpretation. We need to be faithful to the true Tradition and discern what is essential. We have to reconsider critically ideas that may absolutize traditional norms and practices. Such an effort is incumbent not only on women in the church but on us all. Your meeting as Orthodox women has, I am sure, much to contribute in this respect. May God bless your lives and your encounter.

Report of the Damascus Meeting

We are grateful to God the Father, Son and Holy Spirit for the special opportunity we have had to meet together as Orthodox women. The theme of our conference was "Discerning the 'Signs of the Times' (Matt. 16:3): Women in the Life of the Orthodox Church". We met together in Damascus, Syria, from 4-10 October 1996.

Most of the 65 participants were official women delegates sent by their churches at the invitation of the World Council of Churches. This meeting took place in the context of the Ecumenical Decade – Churches in Solidarity with Women. It focused especially on the concerns of women from the Orthodox churches of the Middle East, Africa and Asia. A small number of lay and ordained Orthodox men also attended the conference. Their support and encouragement of our efforts were a welcomed resource.

We benefited greatly from the rich hospitality of His Beatitude Ignatius IV, Greek Orthodox Patriarch of Antioch and all the East. He graciously received the participants and opened the conference with an address. He affirmed that the church in Syria wanted this event to be an important one, a significant one, so that we can understand more and do more for women.

We were also graciously received by His Beatitude Ignatius Zakka II, Syrian Orthodox Patriarch of Antioch and all the East. He also offered the closing message for the conference. In his presentation, he affirmed the many important ministries women have had and continue to have in the life of the church.

The fact that we were so warmly greeted by both patriarchs not only greatly enriched our meeting, but also reminded us of the growing reconciliation between our two families of Orthodox churches. Since our meeting included participants from both families of churches, we believe that we have also made a contribution to this reconciliation.

We gathered in a land rich in Christian history. In addition to our regular opportunity for worship, we visited the women's monasteries of

Saydnaya and Maaloola, the men's monasteries of St George and St Ephraim, as well as the famous site of the Krak des Chevaliers. During our stay here, we were reminded of St Paul's baptism in the city and the witness of so many saints, especially St Thekia and St John of Damascus.

Our conference focused on a variety of topics about women in the life of the Orthodox church. Each day had its own theme, which was articulated in the presentations and panel discussions. Among our topics, we reflected on "The Holy Spirit in the Life of the Church", "Discerning the Tradition Today" and "Reflecting on *Orthopraxia*".

The good news

We have been richly blessed by our time together. As we prayed, discussed the themes and met together, we recognized that we serve the same Lord and share the same Orthodox faith. It is our common faith which has guided our reflection and which has inspired us to deepen our service to the Orthodox church and our witness in the world.

We were very happy to learn from each other about the many forms of ministry in which women in our churches are already engaged. We witnessed to a wide range of ministries from the women present at our meeting. Some women, for example, are active in monastic life. Others are active as single women, wives or mothers. A number are serving within their local parish or diocese, other participants are active in the ecumenical movement. Some are involved with the study or teaching of theology, and many are involved in philanthropic, medical or educational service in association with either the church or a respected regional or national institution.

Undergirding this variety, we observed a high level of competency, intelligence, dynamism, commitment and, most of all, a deep love of the church and of God. This range of ministries manifested among us was truly inspiring. This variety reminded us how, throughout the history of the church, women have been active in many forms of ministry in response to the same Lord, in the Holy Spirit.

At the same time, we came to see that the church continues to need the service of faithful women as well as men, who feel called to serve the Lord and his church. These women, as well as men, deserve the support and encouragement of our church leaders. These women, as well as men, deserve to receive appropriate theological education and spiritual formation which will assist them in their ministry. These women, as well as men, deserve to have their vocations recognized and blessed.

In our discussions together, we also came to appreciate more deeply the ministry of the wife of the priest. We believe this ministry is tantamount to the ministry of the priest himself. The wives of priests especially deserve the recognition of the church, as well as our encouragement and support. This support is necessary so that the ministry of priests' wives may continue to be life-giving to their communities and families.

Concerns

Through the intercessions of the Holy Theotokos, who is our role model, we recognize that all Christians are invited to emulate her example as a person of faith. We are all, women and men, called by the Lord himself to grow in our relationship with him and others, so that there is integrity between our faith and our actions.

In our discussions we came to affirm the importance of the witness of the church in today's world. We also came to sense the challenge of relating more directly our theology with our church practice.

Through our discussions together, we recognize that some of our churches have made a concerted effort to involve women in the different ministries in the church. Others have indeed made significant progress in this direction. Yet, there are still some churches who have not yet considered the needs of their women and therefore the whole church itself.

We are concerned that some women have expressed deep disappointment that they have not had the chance to study theology in a formal setting such as a seminary or theological school. This hinders our role and work within the church. Furthermore, we feel that we must encourage Orthodox women theologians especially to study the interpretation of the Scriptures so as to be able to discern their meaning more fully.

We also recognize there are sacramental practices which need study in depth by both men and women, as they appear to run contrary to our theological affirmations regarding the dignity of women. We specifically call to mind here certain liturgical practices which need immediate attention, as we believe they do indeed diminish the dignity of women. We note, for example, the practice of churching female babies differently from male babies, and the practice of depriving women of the eucharist during their period of menstruation, which continues to exist in some of our churches.

We note as well, with tremendous sadness, how easy it is for the presence of women to be forgotten. From our discussions together we realize that there are some occasions when the role and presence of women, as well as their work, is not always validated for the value it has in the everyday life of the church. Rather, women may be seen by some as more readily dispensable. Women have also been easily dismissed in other ways as well. We recognize with deep concern how social injustices such as poverty, illiteracy and invisibility may affect both Orthodox women and women in general in our part of the world. Wherever possible, we must strive to assist them and open our lives and our hearts to them, as our Lord would have us do.

This conference also recognizes the important ministry of deaconesses as a response to the Holy Spirit for various needs of this present age. Nevertheless, we must emphasize that we still wait for the application of the recommendations from the 1988 inter-Orthodox consultation in Rhodes, on "The Place of Woman in the Orthodox Church", to rejuvenate this order of ordained ministry.

Recommendations

In light of the above, we prayerfully recommend to the leadership of our churches:

- that our leaders encourage women's involvement and participation in the everyday decision-making process of our local churches; we note this after having recognized the differing practices regarding women among the various Orthodox churches;
- that efforts begin which will raise the theological and spiritual awareness among women concerning their role in the church, their families and society – through spiritual retreats, ongoing study groups, seminars, lectures and workshops;
- that women receive both spiritual and financial support in order to pursue studies in theological education; relatedly, that more informal opportunities to study and grow in the theology of the church be created;
- that more research, presentations and community-wide discussions on the Theotokos be encouraged, so that we will grow in authentic relationship and appreciation of her;
- that the sacramental practices which appear to diminish the dignity of women be studied in depth and changed whenever necessary, in order to reflect the fuller Orthodox understanding regarding women;
- that lay theologians (women and men) be encouraged to direct Bible studies in local parishes, as this form of adult education may help inspire confidence to witness to the Orthodox faith;
- that a space in the life of the church be provided where Eastern and Oriental Orthodox women may regularly come together, so they may learn from each other; perhaps they may also be invited to attend some of the suggested activities listed above;
- that our leadership encourage women's informal and formal ministries in pastoral care, so as to reach out to others who may be spir-

itually isolated, in material need, grieving the loss of a loved one, survivors of abuse or violence, etc.; these persons deserve particular attention, as they require the healing presence and assistance of the church through prayer, counselling and support;

- that our leadership develop more ways for the wives of priests to come together for support and opportunities for enrichment;
- that more frequent dialogue take place, both formal and informal, with our surrounding societies, as this will facilitate more focused and appropriate pastoral care and witness; this dialogue also involves taking seriously the presence of Orthodox Christian women who are engaged in various forms of work and service in the world; we desire the ongoing support and encouragement of our leadership in this effort; similarly, as society changes, we recommend that extra care must be paid to understanding the concerns of our young people;
- that a qualified woman spiritual advisor and/or canonist be included as an advocate on the spiritual courts of all our churches;
- that our church leaders discern prayerfully and courageously the presence of the Holy Spirit in those many places where the ministry of ordained deaconesses, as well as other forms of ministry, is needed;
- that more opportunities for ecumenical dialogue and relationships be encouraged; this would be both beneficial for Orthodox witness and for the strengthening of our relationships with other Christian women in our common work;
- that more clergymen (and male lay leaders) be encouraged to attend these conferences in order to increase their pastoral awareness regarding women's concerns;
- that valuable conferences such as "Discerning the Signs of the Times" be sponsored, making participation open to all women in our churches.

Conclusion

In conclusion, we affirm that holding and participating in this conference on "Discerning the Signs of the Times" is a direct result of the work of the Holy Spirit and our response to his call. We understand that through baptism and chrismation (confirmation), women also are called to be a vital part of the church. Women also are called to communion with God, and women also have the vocation of manifesting the presence of the kingdom even in this life. The church comprises both men and women called to continue the saving acts of Jesus Christ for the salvation of humanity and the whole of creation. "There is one body and Spirit... but to each one of us grace was given, according to the measure of Christ's gift. And he himself gave some to be apostles, some prophets, some evangelists, and some pastors and teachers...; every part does its share, causes growth of the body for the edifying of itself in love" (Eph. 4:4, 11, 16). Therefore, we believe we have a responsibility to fulfill our calling as disciples and apostles, which is to communicate the gospel to the whole inhabited earth and strive towards the sanctification and well being of the Body.

Finally, we bear witness to the fact that each member of the Body of Christ is essential for the proper functioning of his church. We hold fast to the holy Tradition of our Orthodox church in which clergy and laity have constituted an organic whole since the time of the apostles. Throughout the history of the church, we have the testimony of countless women saints who responded to Christ in many ways, such as apostles, evangelists, confessors, martyrs, ascetics and nuns, teachers, mothers, spiritual and medical healers and deaconesses. We Orthodox women of today, inspired through the prayers and example of these women saints, now endeavour to continue in their footsteps, as we too strive to respond to our Lord's call: "Follow me". *Amen.*

Report of the Istanbul Meeting

You have destroyed death by your Cross
You have opened Paradise to the thief.
You have changed a lamentation of the Myrrh-Bearers into joy,
and you have commanded your apostles to proclaim
that you, O Christ our God,
Have risen and granted the world the great mercy.

(Troparion, Tone 7)

Christ is risen!

We thank our God, the life-giving Trinity, Father, Son and Holy Spirit, for the opportunity to celebrate this joyful season of the resurrection with our sisters from Europe, North and South America, Australia and the Middle East.

We gathered together in Istanbul, Turkey, for this conference on women in the life of the Orthodox Church entitled, "Discerning the Signs of the Times". Over 50 women and men from the Eastern and Oriental Orthodox churches met from 10-17 May 1997 as participants officially delegated by their churches, as observers and as resource people to represent the concerns of Orthodox women from Eastern and Western Europe and North and South America, coming from Albania, Armenia, Brazil, Bulgaria, Chile, the Czech Republic, Finland, France, the Republic of Georgia, Germany, Great Britain, Greece, Poland, Romania, Russia, Serbia, Switzerland and the United States of America. This meeting took place within the context of the Ecumenical Decade – Churches in Solidarity with Women.

It has been a tremendous blessing to meet and get to know one another, learning more about each other's histories and traditions. We have rejoiced in the commitment to seeking God's will in loving and costly service which has so often been clear in presentations and conversations. While at times we differed in thinking and acting, we have learned that the respect and love which exists among us, which is a gift from Jesus Christ, is one of the most important characteristics of this conference. We have come to realize more deeply the importance of committing ourselves to a community united in diversity.

This is the last of three WCC-sponsored meetings within the Ecumenical Decade for Orthodox women (the others being Crete 1990 and Damascus 1996). We realize the need to deepen our reflection on many topics and themes, and we are grateful for this conference in that it has helped us to continue this reflection.

We had the opportunity to visit and worship at some of the most historic and ancient Christian sites of this city. We toured Agia Sophia, the Great Church of Constantinople, the monastery at Chora, where we were inspired by the beautiful iconography of the 11th century, and the Theological School at Halki, where we felt as if we had entered a modern-day garden of Paradise. Also, we had the honour of attending the divine liturgy celebrated by His All-Holiness Bartholomew I at the monastery of Zoodochos Pege, the burial site of the ecumenical patriarchs, and drank from the spring whose water has been known for centuries as a source of healing. We believe Christ, who is the place (*chora*) of Life, revealed himself through the deep spiritual and prayer experiences of our daily worship at Holy Trinity Church, and throughout the entire week. The name of Mother Maria Skobtsova came up repeatedly during the conference, and we felt as the week progressed that she was very close to us. Her utter self-giving for the care and salvation of everyone who came her way in France during the second world war was especially inspiring: Russian students needing a mother, homeless women needing a place to stay, Jews and many others fleeing persecution needing shelter and a hiding place – all came under the wing of her love and compassion. In the end, she gave her life for her friends. She is a holy woman of our day, a model for us, one who lived in our century and in a culture and under conditions that are familiar to us.

Thanksgiving

We thank you, O Lord our God, for bringing us together in this holy city and granting us the opportunity to worship and partake of your heavenly blessings. We thank you for bestowing your divine grace upon us for these few days and ask to keep in our hearts the desire to live for you, our Lord and Benefactor. We thank you for this time together, for being the silent partner in every conversation and the ever-present guest at each meal.

We are exceedingly grateful for the generous hospitality of the Ecumenical Patriarch, His All-Holiness Bartholomew I, Archbishop of Constantinople and New Rome. In his opening address, the Ecumenical Patriarch spoke of the desire on the part of many people to achieve a more meaningful relationship with the living God; there is a deep longing for spiritual growth and an even greater longing for holiness, healing and forgiveness, which come from God alone. He blessed not only our conference but our pilgrimage to this holy city, a centre of inspiration and spiritual nourishment, and asked us to keep the local community in our prayers.

We were also very warmly received at the Armenian Patriarchate of Constantinople by His Beatitude Patriarch Karekin II. We took part in morning prayers and were encouraged to take the initiative in the important ministry work of our church, given the many gifts women offer. His Beatitude mentioned that the Armenian Apostolic Church has taken the initiative in ordaining women to the order of the diaconate, an order in which both men and women are ordained and perform similar duties.

Both patriarchs addressed the current official theological dialogue taking place between the Eastern and Oriental Orthodox churches, and both eagerly anticipate the final reconciliation and restoration of ecclesiastical communion between the two families.

It is equally important to thank the World Council of Churches' women's programme for sponsoring this historic event. This conference and so many that have gone before are of vital importance for Orthodox women, the Orthodox church and worldwide ecumenical dialogue.

Finally, we must thank all who have gone before us, women and men, laity and clergy, who have initiated and contributed to the inter-Orthodox dialogue, without whose dedication and love for our church we would not be here today. Their work, specifically over the last twenty years, has been a source of encouragement and hope for many of us. The consultations of Agapia (1976), Rhodes (1988), Crete (1990) and Damascus (1996) have laid the foundations for the work we are doing here.

Concerns

This consultation studied the statement that emerged from the Damascus consultation and has affirmed many of the concerns there. In addition, we offer the following:

There is a need to stimulate a desire in our people to take an active role in the life of the church. This may happen with the realization on the part of Orthodox Christians of their own royal priesthood.

There is a need for new workers in the church, including children and young people, to be nurtured and educated to play a more active role in the various ministries. We must call upon all people to bring their gifts forward, the gifts which have been bestowed upon the laity through the

Holy Spirit for the life and growth of the church. We must stimulate the interest of lay people who feel that they have been excluded in the past and remind them of their individual responsibilities as members of "a chosen race, a royal priesthood, a holy nation" (1 Pet. 2:9).

In some of our churches, Orthodox Christians have lost interest and have joined social, cultural and para-church organizations. We are looking for ways to bring Orthodox Christians back to the church.

Recommendations

As members of the church we feel ready to carry out our responsibility to promote the welfare of the church, particularly by encouraging the various ministries of women.

1. Theological education

A. Many women seek deeper knowledge of the church through theological study. In families and schools, women are the primary educators. Women share this task and learn well from one another. Thus, theologically-educated women have a particular ministry in teaching our faithful. For these reasons, Orthodox theological education for women is a priority and should be facilitated on all levels.

B. We recommend that the churches encourage the present efforts of women who are engaged in producing journals, both academic and for the community, in order to inform and educate women and men on the Orthodox faith. There is a real need on the part of women for the creation of a forum where women are able to reflect upon their experiences and engage in theological research. Women need to be notified of publications, theological seminars and other events and materials that are of benefit to them.

C. There is a tremendous need for resources and materials in the following areas:

- for church schools;
- in multiple languages to address the increasingly multinational nature of our churches;
- on how to live one's faith daily;
- providing up-to-date translations of ancient Christian liturgical and patristic texts specifically dealing with the Theotokos and other women saints.

2. Liturgical life

A. The perception and interpretation of some of the practices pertaining to liturgical life need to be addressed. We ask for a re-evaluation of certain liturgical customs, for example, the presentation of infants and the 40-day rule for childbirth, the prayer for miscarriages, abortions and post-partum mothers, and expectations pertaining to the reception of communion. Some of us feel these practices and prayers do not properly express the theology of the church regarding the dignity of God's creation of women and their redemption in Christ Jesus. We realize that the practices in the various local communities may differ.

B. We recommend the incorporation of the lives of the martyrs, both women and men, and the new experiences of the people in this century into the hymnography of the church. While this may be happening in some churches, we recommend a universal incorporation of the new martyrs of this century into the life of our church. Perhaps the best forum for such a recommendation is the upcoming Great and Holy Council.

3. The diaconate

A. Many of us believe the incorporation of deaconesses in the life of the church will help contribute to the atmosphere of love and learning in the church. Deaconesses are able to work as helpers to the priests and counsellors to the people, providing an important link and thereby strengthening relationships within the body of the church.

B. In our discussion we realized we came to this conference with differing assumptions regarding the role of the deaconess. While some see the diaconate for women as a sacramental ministry which takes place by ordination, for others this ministry is not sacramental and described as a church ministry. This question has become for some more academic than practical. Therefore while some may affirm the work of our sisters from the previous meetings of Orthodox women regarding the importance of the re-emergence of the order of the deaconess, for others there is still work to be done in order to come to a fuller understanding.

C. With the re-emergence of the order of deaconesses, we would not want this ministry in any way to diminish the other ministries of the laity in the church. Rather, vocations to this ministry may be experienced as another response to the Holy Spirit who fills and guides the church. We call to mind the words of St Paul: "It is he who gave apostles, prophets, evangelists, pastors and teachers in roles of service for the faithful to build up the body of Christ, until we become one in faith and in the knowledge of God's Son" (Eph. 4:11-13).

4. Priests' wives

The ministry of the priest's wife is very specific and unique. We recommend the church offer a special blessing on women who undertake this ministry and provide instruction and guidance for their role.

5. Spiritual life

A. There is a thirst for spirituality in many of our countries and a rediscovery of the Orthodox living experience. We recommend the development of materials and programmes to help our people grow in their spiritual lives. We feel that the gifts of women may be of service to the churches specifically in this area. Women need concrete teaching in Orthodox spirituality which includes biblical reflection and study.

B. We encourage the development of monastic vocations for women. Historically, Orthodox monastic communities have been a source for theological education and spiritual life. The very presence of monastics witnesses to "the one thing necessary" (Luke 10:42) to which all are called.

C. We recognize that the churches have been helping one another by sending missionary teams and providing materials in local languages. We recommend that the churches incorporate the experiences of women in their teaching materials. These experiences will enrich the spiritual life of the people.

D. Women benefit from sharing spiritual experiences with one another. Opportunities for such sharing should be provided and supported by our churches. This has begun with meetings organized by the WCC for Orthodox women, such as the present one in Istanbul. Networking and sharing should continue on international, national and parish levels. We recommend the appointment of women delegates as representatives of the Orthodox church to the various gatherings and bodies of the ecumenical movement, whether on the international, national or local level.

6. Community life

A. We feel that women, quite naturally, are peacemakers. Therefore we recommend that our churches make a greater commitment to support sister Orthodox churches in crisis situations, for example, during natural disasters, and to support refugees and those in war-torn countries. Often in these situations women and children suffer most.

B. We recommend that our people support, spiritually and materially, the Christians of our churches who are still suffering in various ways, socially, politically and economically. We are also aware of the current climate of increased religious fundamentalism, which is affecting the lives of people in all our countries. Some churches need educational materials to help develop programmes for the faithful to combat erroneous teachings.

C. We recommend that the issue of sexism be seriously considered. The church would benefit from theological and soteriological reflection on this issue, especially through the medium of consultations, workshops and informal study.

7. Youth

A. We recommend the development of programmes for the spiritual growth of the youth, the hope of our churches. Because we are one body, their concerns affect the entire church and their spiritual well-being is vital to the health of our church.

B. We recommend the development of youth and church school exchange programmes between our churches through national or regional councils of churches.

8. Church polity

A. As stated in previous meetings of Orthodox women, we recommend that the role of the laity in the decision-making processes be evaluated. There is a variety of practices in the Orthodox church regarding this process, and this recommendation pertains only to churches in which voting takes place. In those circumstances where there is a need to determine change in church polity or practice by voting, each man and woman should have an equal opportunity. Women are able to and should be invited to offer guidance to the church on issues that specifically concern them, for example, family life, social needs, education and charity. Women have unique gifts to offer with regard to these issues.

B. With the advent of a more technologically oriented society, we are finding that our world is changing at a very rapid pace. It is important for our churches to become aware and stay abreast of these changes, because at times they can contribute to the life of the church. Women must also find a way to become better informed and learn to cope with these changes. We believe this will happen with better educational opportunities.

C. With regard to the various offices within the churches we recommend the churches encourage the participation of women on the local and higher levels.

9. Inter-Orthodox concerns

A. We recommend that our churches continue the theological dialogue regarding the restoration of communion between the Eastern and Oriental Orthodox churches.

B. We support and look forward to a resolution to the calendar differences among all Orthodox churches. We realize that the differences which exist are a result of certain historical difficulties. However, we await the day when our churches will celebrate the liturgical year together.

10. And the future...

A. We ask our churches to consider seriously the request by the World Council of Churches for 50 percent participation by women at its upcoming assembly in Harare, Zimbabwe, in December 1998. We also ask our churches to bestow their blessings on the women planning to take part in the Ecumenical Decade Festival which takes place a few days prior to the Assembly.

B. We recommend the establishment of a resource centre where theological research and writings by Orthodox women and the reports from conferences such as this will be made available for all.

C. We hope and pray that Orthodox theological institutions which have been closed, such as the Theological School at Halki, will shortly be re-opened, and we ask that women be able to participate in theological studies and research at all theological institutions.

D. Some participants at the consultation welcome the idea of organizing an inter-Orthodox conference on the ordination of women to the priesthood. We realize that for some this question is not an issue and will not be discussed. Any study and examination of the issue in no way presupposes a commitment to move in this direction. This would simply provide the opportunity for women and men to examine this topic in greater depth from both the theological and spiritual perspectives. This conference would include attendance by clergy, laity and monastics.

E. Many recommendations have emerged from previous meetings of Orthodox women. While some recommendations have been addressed, others have not. We are concerned about the reception of this document and recommend that our churches make this statement available for women either through general publications or correspondence to parishes.

F. We have gained considerable knowledge and great benefit from the present conference. It is our hope from now on and into the coming millennium that our churches will continue to sponsor conferences for women where we can come together to enjoy fellowship, share our concerns and learn from one another.

Conclusion

We began our consultation with the celebration of the Holy Myrrh-Bearers at the women's monastery at Balukli. The spirit of these missionary women, which is the same spirit that has inspired the Ecumenical Decade – Churches in Solidarity with Women, comforted us and accompanied us in our prayers and work during this week.

Our spiritual experience was enriched by our visit to the important monuments of the Orthodox heritage, St Sophia and the monastery at

Chora. The mosaic of the Incarnate Word of God, which is the embodiment of living human beings, reassured us of the spiritual reality that salvation is for all.

Finally, the fresco of the resurrection depicting the risen Christ pulling both man and woman from the grave shows us, once again, that our common faith and expectation is the central theme of this consultation on "Discerning the Signs of the Times".

Women in the Life of the Orthodox Church

SOPHIE DEICHA

In recent years the ecumenical movement has shown a growing interest in the Orthodox tradition, motivated by the fact that Orthodoxy can offer solutions to many of the problems facing Christianity in the modern world. This is the context for bringing together the theme of "discerning the signs of the times" with the issue of the place of women in the churches, a context which is characterized by the progress of knowledge in a wide variety of disciplines, especially the scientific study of human beings and their environment.

First witnesses of the resurrection

But these ecumenical studies sometimes quote the expression "discerning the signs of the times" out of context. In Matthew 16:3, this phrase has a precise theological meaning: it refers explicitly to the mystery of the resurrection. Addressed to those who refuse to believe the word of God and to acknowledge the Christ, the expression has the character of a revelation, transcending time and turning every chronology upside down. The Pharisees and Sadducees, as a test, demand a sign from Christ. He replies that he will give them no miracle except the sign of Jonah, who was thrown into the sea and on the third day emerged from the belly of the fish. This passage from ancient reality to the absolutely new, experienced in the joy of Easter, takes place in the midst of unbelief.

This unbelief was the crucial paradoxical test which later had to be endured by the women returning from Jesus' tomb. The Myrrh-Bearing Women, carrying the ancient spices, proclaimed the news of Jesus' resurrection:

> ... returning from the tomb, they told all this to the eleven and to all the rest. Now it was Mary Magdalene, Joanna, Mary the mother of James and the other women with them who told this to the apostles. But these words seemed to them an idle tale, and they did not believe them (Luke 24:9-11).

The apostles did not believe these women; yet it is first of all because of their words that the reality of the resurrection became the central affirmation of Christianity.

We may ask whether contemporary ecumenical research takes the reality of Easter sufficiently into account. Within the ecumenical movement, Orthodox theology has never stopped insisting on explaining its ecclesiological vision by beginning with the mystery of the resurrection. Here it is appropriate to recall the view of Fr Serge Bulgakov that the unity of the church is not an institution, but rather a new life with Christ and in Christ, under the guidance of the Holy Spirit. The light of Christ's resurrection shines on the church, and it is filled with the joy of the resurrection, which triumphs over death. Across the millennia the witness of the women returning from the tomb has indeed spread throughout the world, and has taken its place at the heart of Orthodox church life in liturgical celebration.

As the liturgical refraction of the light of Easter, the Orthodox hymns can shed light on this theological and also ecumenical reflection. Like a ray of light passing from one transparent medium to another, a diffraction occurs between historical chronology and the Easter event, which is conveyed by the richness of Orthodox liturgical celebrations. In the liturgical tradition, the interpretation, no longer of signs but of the Sign for all time, is indissolubly linked to the message of the Myrrh-Bearing Women.

The presence of these women attests to the Easter unity of the Passion and resurrection of Christ. What is extraordinary about them is their faithfulness to Christ. It is this which can assure Christian unity in times when everything seems to be pushing towards dispersal and denial. Through the wealth of hymns dedicated to the Myrrh-Bearing Women, the realization of the unity of the Easter mystery shapes the inner life of the believer. Orthodoxy has always affirmed that it was women who were the first to see and proclaim the gospel of the resurrection, the Sign of the times.

Christians from other traditions are sometimes struck by the paradox of a reverse chronology in the Orthodox liturgy. For example, during the Vespers service for Good Friday, at the very moment when the *epitaphion*, the holy shroud representing Christ in the tomb, is placed in the centre of the church, the witness of the women is already affirmed by the hymn for the beginning of Easter: "The angel of the Lord came to the Myrrh-Bearing Women at the tomb and said, 'Myrrh is fitting for the dead; but Christ has shown himself a stranger to corruption.'" In praise of the Mother of God, during the Easter period, the twofold angelic annunciation – at the birth of her Son and at his resurrection – is proclaimed: "The angel cried to the one full of grace, 'Rejoice, O pure Virgin, again I say, Rejoice. Your Son is risen from his three days in the tomb.'"

It remains to be studied how these ecclesiastical traditions might influence the contemporary development of ecumenical reflections on the role of women in the churches.

The cosmic dimension of the incarnation and the resurrection, "source of life of the universe", leads to new visions of the human person and the place of human beings in the world, relativizing the classical schemes imposed on humanity from ancient times. The old order is reversed, and the Orthodox church sings: "Rejoice, you who were the first to see Christ's resurrection and who proclaimed to his apostles the restoration of the whole world." We celebrate the Myrrh-Bearing Women as "apostles of the apostles", and the joining in of all the disciples: "the chorus of your disciples unites in joy with the chorus of the Myrrh-Bearing Women".

This uniting in joy is indissolubly linked with the coming of the Holy Spirit promised by Christ before his passion. The women had received from the risen Christ the mission to go and tell the disciples that the time had come: "But go to my brothers and say to them, 'I am ascending to my Father and your Father, to my God and your God'" (John 20:17). The hymns go beyond human chronology, telescoping it theologically by bringing together the resurrection and the gift of the Holy Spirit.

Women saints in history and today

This manifestation of the trinitarian mystery in the light of Easter should constantly illumine our search for unity. Recent church history, marked by the witness of martyrs as in the first centuries, has shown that the human person plays a part in the mystery of Easter and constitutes a new source for ecclesiastical tradition. In the second century, the figure of St Blandine of Lyons tied to the stake represented the icon of Christ on the cross, thus giving courage to the other Christians of Fourvière. In the 20th century the church has again seen the witness of innumerable martyrs, but sufficient account has not yet been taken of these in the development of theological reflection. In Western Europe, for example, we might mention Mother Marie Skobtsova, who is only beginning to be known ecumenically.

The church benefits from a luminous heritage of Easter joy, indissolubly linked to the witness of many generations of Christians. It is to be hoped that this witness can take its place in the memory of the church in a modern, creative doxology. The visibility of women in the church can increase within an ecclesial tradition that is richer and more diverse than we sometimes think. This tradition has room for openness to wholly new initiatives.

Contemporary theological reflection has begun to move in this direction. The first theological discipline to take into consideration the place of women as such and the breadth of their commitment has been the study of sainthood and the saints. As early as the latter half of the 1920s, Georges Fedotov carried out some statistical studies which led him to suggest that, in the Russian church at least, there was a marked lack of knowledge of saints other than priests. This disparity worked to the disadvantage of the laity and notably of women. The question of the place of women in relation to the changing times had already been of concern to the members of the preparatory commissions at the Council of Moscow in 1917-1918. This was an acknowledgment not only of the historical place of women in the church, but also of the new perspectives of modern times.

Some of the colleagues of Georges Fedotov at the St Sergius Institute of Orthodox Theology in Paris, including Metropolitan Eulogius, Fr Serge Bulgakov and Antoine Kartachev, all of whom had participated in the Council of Moscow, shared his concerns. Their successors, including Archbishop Georges, Fr Alexis Kniazeff and Fr Nicholas Koulomzine, encouraged theological engagement by women.

There is every evidence that the study of the saints provides obvious examples of recognition by the church of equality between women and men. But the study of the saints as a theological discipline has not developed very far in the Western churches; and its importance for ecumenical reflection is only beginning to be rediscovered – for example, at the meeting of the plenary commission of Faith and Order in Moshi, Tanzania, in August 1996.

The equality of women and men is theologically self-evident, since every human being is called to exercise a "royal priesthood". This ministry corresponds to God's general invitation to "be holy as I am holy". The broad and open concept of holiness or sainthood precludes the deviations of scholastic anthropology which sometimes make ecumenical dialogue such a delicate process.

Women's roles in the church

A spiritual openness makes it possible to compare – both in present-day realities and in the prospects for the future – those factors which are invoked to minimize the role of women in the Christian churches with those which exalt women's role. These factors are closely woven together, and each person gives them importance according to his or her degree of social and cultural, spiritual, intellectual and personal development. In brief outline we may distinguish the following:

- *Economic factors* have often in history exerted a pressure which works to the detriment of women, for example with regard to their rights.
- *Political factors*, developing differently in the history of different countries, both Orthodox and non-Orthodox, have often created and maintained inequalities for women. For example, women have been excluded from participation in government, sometimes *de jure*, as under certain dynasties, sometimes *de facto*, as is still the case in certain democracies.
- *Educational factors* – specifically the undereducation of women. While Byzantine civilization had women scholars, access to schools – and later university degrees – in the West was restricted to men for a long time.

These distinctions were not only the consequence of socio-economic and political factors, but also of religious prejudices. Here let us merely point out that forces minimizing women's role in Western European society were plentiful in the wake of Augustine's influence in the Middle Ages.

Turning to factors which re-establish the equality of women's role in the churches, we begin with an essentially Orthodox factor – the role of the wives of priests.

Not only are Orthodox secular priests married, but before being ordained a priest must have his wife's consent. No doubt this has prevented a good many difficulties for the church. During the priestly couple's life together, it is in fact the role of the wife to ensure that the church's rules regarding the private life of the men in its service are observed. Since the wives of priests have themselves sometimes come from priestly families, they have generally been better educated than the parishioners. Thus they became, by right or in fact, Christian educators, well-informed about the practice of the faith, and this reinforced their social and religious influence.

Among the factors favouring the development of the role of women, we should mention the example of the growing participation of women in teaching at various levels, as well as in a number of scientific disciplines, in the midst of the complex modern relation between theological knowledge and that of the other sciences. A recent symposium in Oxford provided striking examples of the potential links between Orthodox evangelization and mission activities, in far eastern Russia and Alaska, and the development of ecological approaches to the largely unexplored natural environment of these regions. The example of a missionary couple named Veniaminov working in the Aleutian Archipelago is particularly striking. Their ecological research has been widely acknowledged in scientific circles. Action by a woman to protect the environment in close connection with Orthodoxy is a particularly modern theme.

Among the exemplary areas as far as women's participation in the life of the Orthodox church is concerned is the perfect equality which can exist between the theological commitments of men and women. Today, committed Orthodox women can be found in the ecumenical movement at the worldwide level. No doubt it is the character of theology, which is somehow prophetic and completely free, which has allowed this rapid development. Change has been slower in other, more institutional areas, particularly in the restoration of the diaconate for women or the creation of new responsibilities. This is a consequence of the complex features of conciliarity in the Orthodox church.

Ecumenically, such discrepancies create difficulties in dialogues regarding the role of women. Certainly the surpassing importance accorded to confessional language in the West during the second millennium, at the expense of the affirmation of the common faith, has produced complex theological developments which have sometimes even justified the discriminations. These issues, which have generally been excluded from ecumenical discussion over the past seventy years, can be approached more easily today thanks to the growing importance of the theme of *koinonia* or communion in the various dialogues.

The role of women in the transmission of the faith is beginning to be re-evaluated. Its paramount importance during the recent period of persecution in Russia, for example, needs to attract the attention of more historians, theologians and poets. Hymn-writers must be found to give expression to this historical witness down into modern times, taking account of both the historical period and the Christian witness given within it. This is not a matter of copying ancient prayers, but of creating new texts which truly read the signs of the times in the light of Easter. For it is only when the people of the church are gathered that there can be effective inculturation and the creation of liturgies of praise which open the church to the world.

As for the service of women in the church, it is appearing today in all its diversity. The needs of the world create new situations. The possibilities are limitless, infinitely varied. Still there is sometimes a lack of aptitude in discerning these possibilities and in opening up the range of Christian activity.

Perspectives in building a united Europe

A certain aptitude for effectively organizing the equality of activities of men and women seems apparent in the contemporary example of building a united Europe.

In this context, the approach to the role of women in this or that area of parish work should also be brought up to date and made more systematic, leading to reflection on the working conditions of women in the church. A useful meeting on "Orthodox Women in a United Europe" (Levadia, Greece, November 1994) stimulated some profound reflection as well as information-sharing. If it is urgent to take up this matter of adapting our point of view to the modern world, then it is also appropriate not to reduce the role of women to one of serving only. A variety of recent studies, particularly in the context of the Ecumenical Decade – Churches in Solidarity with Women, have made explicit the imbalances between the confessions.

As moderator of an inter-religious round table on the role of women in the three monotheistic religions, organized by the Forward Studies Unit of the European Commission in Toledo in November 1995, I was struck by a theme which came up several times in the presentation and discussion of "Mediterranean Society: A Challenge for Three Civilizations?":

> Historians are beginning to recognize a disturbing fact: while women made rich, profound and specific contributions to the development of European culture during the first millennium, their contributions were absent from the cultural scene during the centuries which followed. Women suddenly became culturally invisible in the West, from the beginning of the second millennium.

Subsequently, during a seminar on "The Cultural and Religious Dimensions of Euro-Mediterranean Dialogue", organized in Brussels by the European Commission, we demonstrated the new perspectives on this issue which Orthodoxy could open for Western Europe.

Orthodox theology in fact escaped the deviations of mediaeval Western scholasticism – and thus also the consequences of these for various areas in church and society, particularly concerning the place of women in the church. The resulting openness is now being made more explicit, within Orthodox communities themselves as well as through Orthodox activity in the ecumenical and indeed inter-religious contexts. This is a vision which has a great future for the social and economic reality of Europe as a whole.

Nevertheless, despite the success of modern advances, theological vigilance is called for in order to prevent a one-sided interpretation of purely symbolic factors. Paradoxically, the wealth of Orthodox symbolism could be at risk of exploitation in superfluous developments with regard to femininity and masculinity. Extremist arguments could lead to theological formulations harmful to the cause of unity. Orthodox dogma is beginning to examine this area, and it is hoped that this will contribute to making the sometimes intricate complementarity of these symbols better understood. This would be an enriching contribution to ecumenical thought. Despite the wide diversity of points of view, it is important to develop the process of dialogue and exchange of ideas, so that questions which have gone unanswered in the past can be discussed.

Let me conclude by mentioning one of the most spectacular ecumenical advances of recent years: the growing use of icons in shared worship services. When the icon of the Mother of God known as the Icon of the Sign or the Icon of the Life-Giving Source is before the eyes of everyone, it begins to direct the prayers towards Christ and his mother. In seeking a harmonious solution to our outstanding questions about the role of women in the church, we turn to the Mother of God in prayer. We realize that even if theological consciousness is not always completely clear, the visions offered by Orthodox icons open up new approaches for all of Christianity.

Varieties of Gifts

Women's Ministries in the Contemporary Church

DESPINA D. PRASSAS

> There are varieties of gifts, but the same Spirit; and there are varieties of service, but the same Lord; and there are varieties of activities, but it is the same God who activates all of them in everyone (1 Cor. 12:4-6).

A community of monastics growing and manufacturing medicinal herbs in Guatemala; a young Romanian woman who is among 300 studying at a theological school dedicated to training women theologians; a group of Orthodox women in France discussing the ordination of women to the priesthood; a deaf woman who has converted from the Baptist faith to Orthodoxy, working with deaf children at an ecumenical school in Costa Rica; a woman from Uganda who, along with other Orthodox women, is running a poultry farm; a monastic who has travelled to Korea to set up a convent; a missionary from the United States who has dedicated five years of her life to the church in Tirana, Albania; the sole woman on the faculty of a major Orthodox seminary; a Finnish woman working in the youth office at the World Council of Churches; the wife of a priest leading a Bible study group in the local parish; a group of widows who minister to the elderly at a hospital which has no funds to provide a full-time staff; a deaconess teaching religion at a private school in Damascus.

All of these women have names and ministries to which they have been called. This is a small sample of the ministries in which contemporary Orthodox women are sharing. The list continues to grow every day. Our church is a body of believers which "does not consist of one member but of many" (1 Cor. 12:14). St Paul tells us: "Now you are the body of Christ and individually members of it" (1 Cor. 12:27); and it seems as if this body is growing – not growing extra limbs, but strengthening those which exist. After almost 2000 years, our church is reaching out in ways which in one sense are not new (since it has a long history of philanthopic and diaconal work) but which fully engage the challenges of contemporary society.

Orthodox tradition supports an understanding of ministry which asserts the dignity and equality of all. It speaks out against superior/inferior models of ministry in which some are the elect and others are the followers. All are called to be participants in the holy life. The sacred tradition of our church emphasizes the contribution of all, including women.

The tradition of the church

Three fundamental Orthodox teachings support this tradition:

1. We believe that the divine image and likeness (Gen. 1:26) exists within every person, both male and female. The Bible tells us "God created humankind in his image, in the image of God he created them; male and female he created them" (Gen. 1:27). While certain fathers of the church have distinguished "image" *(eikōn)*, as the potential for life in God, from "likeness" *(homoiōsis)* as the realization of life in God, for others no distinction exists.[1] With the human being as image of God, God becomes the innermost centre of the human being.[2] St Gregory the Theologian states that men and women share a single nature and destiny:

> There is only one Creator of man and of woman, one dust from which both have come, one image [of God], one law, one death, one resurrection... The serpent deceived them both, and one was not found to be the stronger and the other the weaker... Christ saves both by his sufferings. Was he made flesh for the man? This also for the woman. Did he die for the man? The woman is also saved by his death.[3]

St Basil the Great agrees with St Gregory that the image of God exists in women. In an encomium to St Julitta the Martyr, he puts the following words in her mouth: "We women are taken from the same matter as men, we were created in the image of God like them. Like the masculine sex, the feminine sex is capable of virtue, and this is by the will of the Creator."[4]

2. Our church also believes that all Christians are called to theosis or union with God – to be "participants of the divine nature" (2 Pet. 1:4). For the Orthodox, the salvation and redemption of the human being is theosis.[5] This is not an instantaneous event but a life-long endeavour, a relationship with God which takes one's entire life to perfect. All receive the calling from God to be in union with him and to achieve holiness.

3. Since Pentecost, it is the Holy Spirit who has made and continues to make Christ present in the world through his body, the church. Each person must discover, regardless of his or her station in life, the work to which he or she is called by God and through this work make Christ present to the whole world, by the power of the Holy Spirit working within.

The image and likeness of God in the human being, the call for all to union with God (*theosis*) and the commission to make Christ present to the world allow for the full participation of all members, both men and women, in the life of the church. It is not just that all Christians who have been baptized and chrismated are allowed to be members of "a chosen race, a royal priesthood, a holy nation" (1 Pet. 2:9), in other words, members of the body of Christ, but it is their responsibility and the means for their salvation. At the time of chrismation, believers take their place in the order of the laity. The presence of and our response to the Holy Spirit in our lives enable us to take part in the various Spirit-bearing ministries of the church. Ministries are the responsibilities to which God calls his people. Through these ministries we come face to face with the risen Christ through the lives of others. This encounter is a type of union with God.

Therefore, through the ministries to which we have been called, we engage in *theosis* or union with God. And it is through this *theosis*, this very unique and specific ministry, that we take part in our personal salvation. Since the personal salvation as ministry includes those with whom we work, the ministry becomes the salvation not only of the individual but of all involved. The working of the ministries of the church – in reality, the Holy Spirit working in the body of believers – is in a way the working of the salvation of the world.

We see today a development of many of the women's ministries which have been documented from the past. These older ministries include those of disciples, apostles, evangelists, deaconesses, miracle workers, missionaries, prophets, teachers, healers, founders of churches, monasteries and philanthropic institutions, conveners of councils, defenders of the faith, saints, martyrs, spiritual mothers, and monastics.[6] Many of these ministries have developed with the changing times; others have fallen away or, should I say, are awaiting recognition. In fact, we have many women "doing the work", engaging in many of these older ministries, yet both these women and their ministries have not been recognized by the church on earth.

Contemporary ministries in the church

What are these "new ministries"? How have the older ministries developed? How are women ministering to the needs of our church and world? The list of current ministries among women in our church is a long one.

More and more often women are playing administrative roles within local parishes, dioceses and archdioceses. Women serve as members and presidents of local parish councils. Organized groups of women are engaging in desperately needed philanthropic work. For example, the Philoptochos Society in North America has contributed a great deal to the Orthodox church by providing funding for medical and other non-profit organizations.

In local parishes more and more women are taking part in activities which historically have involved only men. While the majority of positions as Sunday school teachers and choir members continue to be filled by women, we now also find women who have been blessed as readers, chanters and youth directors. Moreover, a re-evaluation of the minor order of acolyte has been called for.[7] While some believe a woman is not allowed to enter the altar area, the deaconesses within our tradition were in fact allowed to enter the sanctuary to perform their work. On the basis of this, those who advocate the tonsuring of young girls to the minor order of acolyte consider that this is in keeping with the theology of our church.

In some US parishes young girls are participating in the procession during the Great Entrance; in others they are assisting the priest during the dispensing of the eucharist. They may stand holding the cloth used by communicants to dry their lips, or carry the container holding the bread offered to the communicant after partaking of the eucharist.

Of the women who have pursued theological degrees at Orthodox seminaries, a few are working as members of seminary faculties. Some are serving as religious education directors at the parish, diocesan or archdiocesan level; some are theologians dedicated to research and writing; some are taking part in ecumenical or interdisciplinary theological consultations and dialogues at the national or international level; some are pastoral assistants in charge of programmes at local parishes which include Bible study, youth work, providing food and clothing for the poor in the community, adult education, prison and hospital ministries, ecumenical and inter-religious activities; some are teachers in religious and ecumenical organizations.

There are women health-care professionals who are offering care to parish members; women missionaries, both short-term and long-term, working in domestic and overseas settings; lay groups of women who come together for Orthodox fellowship. The work of women who serve as pastoral counsellors is extremely valuable and important, for they can provide or organize support groups to deal with many issues which are not adequately addressed in the local churches, such as divorce, rape, incest, physical and emotional abuse, euthanasia, abortion and suicide.

We are also seeing a slow but steady resurgence of women entering monastic orders. Along with this, we are seeing a re-emergence of the order of the deaconess. Though their numbers remain few, they are serving churches in Greece, Syria and Egypt. Their responsibilities are culturally dictated and there are also some differences in liturgical practice – deaconesses are blessed in certain Orthodox churches and ordained in others. It is interesting that in the Orthodox churches of Western Europe and North America, there has been a greater focus on the theological implications of the re-emergence of the order of the diaconate, while in the Oriental Orthodox churches the emphasis has been on the practical implications.

A discussion is taking place in North America and Western Europe on the ordination of women to the priesthood. While this issue may have come to Orthodoxy from "the outside" – from contact with Protestant churches – it has generated some interest among Orthodox women and men. The theologians of our church are delving more deeply into the topic, searching the writings of the fathers of the church for an Orthodox understanding of this issue. But the discussion is not simply a theoretical one. I have been told of three women in the United States who have left the Armenian Apostolic Church and joined the Episcopal Church (Anglican) because they felt they were being called to serve God as a priest/minister.

The ministry of women which is perhaps least known in our church is that of spiritual director. Simply through the way in which women communicate many women are providing spiritual direction to one another every day. I know of one woman whose bishop has granted her the blessing of hearing confessions and providing spiritual direction, though she does not recite the prayer from the sacramental rite. This ministry of the church needs to be explored more thoroughly; I mention it here simply to acknowledge those women, whether they be monastics, the wives of priests or wiser and more experienced members of our communities.

Last, but certainly not least, is the ministry of the wife of the priest. This extremely valuable ministry is sometimes thrust upon women without anyone having informed them of exactly what is involved in fulfilling it. Unlike the priesthood and other vocations in the church, there seems to be no "school" which one can attend to prepare for the ministry of the wife of the priest. As a woman whose mother is the wife of a priest, I can personally attest to how difficult, emotionally and physically, this job can be. The expectations put upon the priest's wife are great. More and more we do find that the wives of priests are organizing to provide support for one another, enabling the younger wives to learn from the experience of the older ones. In the United States priests' wives have organized on a wider scale to assist the families of priests who are in crisis. When an unexpected tragedy strikes a priest and his family, this national organization does what it can to assist with financial support to the family.

Building on earlier work

I would like to conclude by recalling some of the recommendations of the Inter-Orthodox Consultation on Women and the Question of Ordination which took place in October-November 1988 in Rhodes.

1. Are women receiving the support and encouragement from the leadership of the church in ministries which work in harmony with the specific sacerdotal ministry of the clergy? Among these the report mentions the pursuit of education; access to pastoral counselling; participation in decision-making bodies at the level of the parish, diocesan and national church; social work; involvement as choir directors, readers and singers; as iconographers; in ecumenical work; as youth leaders; and in publications and communications work.[8]
2. Has the apostolic order of deaconess been restored in all places, in all churches? According to the report (sec. 32), revival of this order "would represent a positive response to many of the needs and demands of the contemporary world in many spheres".
3. Are women entering the lower orders of the church (for example, sub-deacon, reader, cantor, teacher) through a blessing (*cheirothesia*) (sec. 36)?
4. Are we addressing such issues raised by feminist theologians as the use of inclusive language, the necessary analysis of certain biblical texts, specifically those of St Paul, and the submission of women as it relates to bodily uncleanliness (reintroduced into our ethos from the Jewish tradition)? We have a responsibility to discuss these issues, if only to provide an Orthodox answer to these questions for our non-Orthodox fellow Christians (cf. sec. 39).

These are some of the more difficult issues which we as Orthodox women must address.

To close, I would like to recall the words of a prayer from the Orthodox ordination service of the deaconess:

> O God, the Holy and Almighty, you have blessed woman through the birth in the flesh of your only-begotten son and our God from the Virgin, and you have given the grace and visitation of the Holy Spirit not to men only, but to women as well. Lord, look now upon these your servants and call them to the work of your ministry. Send down upon us the rich gift of your Holy Spirit. Preserve us in the Orthodox faith, that we may fulfill our ministry in blameless conduct according to what is pleasing to you. For to you are due all honour, glory and worship, Father, Son and Holy Spirit, now and forever, and unto ages of ages. Amen.[9]

NOTES

[1] Among the latter are Athanasius, Gregory the Theologian and, though debated, Gregory of Nyssa; for a discussion of Nyssa's position see Thunberg, *Microcosm and Mediator: The Theological Anthropology of Maximus the Confessor*, 2d ed., Chicago, Open Court, 1995, pp. 122f. Those who distinguished "image" and "likeness" included Irenaeus (*Adv. Haer.*, V,6,1), Clement of Alexandria (*Stromata*, II,22), Origen (*De principiis*, III,6,1) and Basil (*Homil. in Ps.* 48, 8; *De Spiritu Sancto*, I,2). G.B. Ladner believes the distinction is of Gnostic (Valentinian) origin; cf. "The Philosophical Anthropology of St Gregory of Nyssa", *DOP*, Vol. 12, 1958, p.63n11. Regarding the distinction in the Fathers, see Thunberg, *op. cit.*, pp. 120-29.

[2] Kallistos Ware, *The Orthodox Way*, Crestwood NY, St Vladimir's Seminary Press, 1979, p.67.

[3] *Oratio XXXVII in Matt. 10:10*, 1-12.

[4] Cited by E. Behr-Sigel, *The Ministry of Women in the Church*, tr. S. Bingham, Redondo Beach CA, Oakwood Publications, 1991, p.90.

[5] Kallistos Ware, *The Orthodox Church*, New York, Penguin, 1964, p.236.

[6] On these ministries see Eva Topping, *Holy Mothers of Orthodoxy: Women and the Church*, Minneapolis, Life and Light, 1987; and *Saints and Sisterhood: The Lives of 48 Holy Women*, Minneapolis, Life and Light, 1990. Two of the most notable disciples were the sisters Mary and Martha (Luke 10:38); Joanna and Susanna (Luke 8:1) may also have accepted the call to discipleship after being healed of evil spirits and infirmities. Among the first women apostles were Mary Magdalene, Junia, Prisca, Apphia, Nyumpha, Mariamne, Fotini and Thekla; there is also St Horiaioele, who was commissioned by St Andrew, the first ecumenical patriarch of Constantinople, to continue his work. Phoebe (Rom. 16:1-2) was the first deaconess, but we have a clearer understanding of the ministry of the deaconess from the account of St Olympias by St John Chrysostom (*PG*, Vol. 52, pp.549-623; cf. Kyriaki FitzGerald, "The Characteristics and Nature of the Order of the Deaconess", in T. Hopko, ed., *Women and the Priesthood*, Crestwood NY, St Vladimir's Seminary Press, 1981, pp.75-95). Among women missionaries are St Nina, who evangelized Georgia, and St Verena, who evangelized Switzerland and Germany. Women prophets mentioned in the New Testament include Anna (Luke 2:36) and the four daughters of the evangelist Philip (Acts 21:8f.). The most notable example of a woman convener of a council was the Empress Irene (Nicea 787); Eudoxia and Pulcheria had leading roles in the events which led up to Ephesus (431) and Chalcedon (451) respectively. A noted woman defender of the faith was the Empress Theodora, who played a crucial role in the restoration of icons in 843. Two "ammas" or spiritual mothers — Sarah and Synkletika — are included along with the spiritual fathers in the Apophthegmata Patrum or Gerontikon (*PG*, Vol. 65, pp.420b-428a). Benedicta Ward includes in this category Amma Theodora, a woman who was said to be consulted by many monks; *The Sayings of the Desert Fathers*, Kalamazoo MI, Cistercian Publications, 1984, pp.82-84.

[7] Emilianos Timiadis, "The Concern for Women in the Orthodox Tradition", *Diakonia*, Vol. 12, no.1, 1977, p.19.

[8] Sec. 28; for the complete text see *Ecumenical Trends*, Vol. 18, no.3, March 1989, pp.36-42.

[9] Cited by Kyriaki FitzGerald, "Orthodox Women and Pastoral Praxis: Observations and Concerns for the Church in America", in T. Stylianopoulos, ed., *Orthodox Perspectives on Pastoral Praxis*, Brookline MA, Holy Cross Orthodox Press, 1988, p.111.

Women in Jesus' Earthly Life

ELISABETH BEHR-SIGEL

From the beginning to the end – from the stable of Bethlehem, to Golgotha, to the garden on Easter morning – women are present in Jesus' earthly life. This is the witness of the gospels. Uncommon in terms of Jewish customs of the day, the presence of women, including some of dubious morals, among those closest to the Galilean rabbi was striking for his contemporaries. Jesus' adversaries, the Pharisees, criticized him for it, as is seen in the story of the woman caught in adultery who was brought to him (John 8:2-12). It discredited him in their eyes. His disciples as well were astonished when they found him in conversation with a woman, who was also a Samaritan and thus considered a heretic (John 4:27).

Jesus allowed himself to be touched by women: by the woman with a haemorrhage, who was considered impure (Matt. 9:18-22); by the woman who had sinned, who covered his feet with her tears and kisses (Luke 7:36-50). He gave in to the moving pleas of the Canaanite woman (Matt. 15:21-28; Mark 7:24-30). From Galilee, a group of women accompanied him who "had been cured of evil spirits and infirmities" (Luke 8:2). Among these women, one is always named, while the names of the others differ in the different gospels: Mary called Magdalene, "from whom seven demons had gone out", an intimate friend of Jesus, who would be the first to see the Resurrected One.

The gospel texts which recall the Lord's numerous relationships with women created a problem for later Christian commentators. They thought to resolve it by covering what would normally be disreputable with pious intentions, thus justifying these dubious associations. The miseries of women – illness, impurity, ignorance, sin – are supposed to have called forth the Saviour's infinite mercy. These women represented humanity, totally lost without him. Male human beings, on the other hand, were chosen to be his apostles, to represent him and to proclaim his message of grace.

Does such an interpretation, which bears the marks of plain old androcentrism, stand up to an honest and rigorous examination of the New Testament texts? Does it correspond to Jesus' intentions as they are revealed there?

* * *

The first thing to note is that although Jesus relates to quite a few women, he never speaks to them as a separate group, characterized by vice and perhaps also by certain specific virtues. He never denounces the faults usually ascribed to women: weakness, frivolity, coquetry, sensuality, excessive emotionality. Nor does he exalt feminine virtues. Jesus does not exhort women to be obedient and submissive, as is proper for them. He does not speak of feminine tenderness as opposed to masculine toughness. Dare I say that Jesus is not interested in *Woman*, but rather in *women*, in each of them as he meets her personally. He enters directly into dialogue with each, deducing her needs and endeavouring to respond to them. To women just as to men, to each one personally, he addresses the message of grace, the invitation to enter the kingdom of heaven, which is brought near to them in him. He does not see women as a "breed", a category of dangerous and despicable beings. In the words of the Protestant woman theologian France Quéré: through his behaviour towards women, "Jesus broke with the myth of Eve as having brought sin into the world, as a woman, and having passed on her evil spells and her guilt to all female posterity."[1]

The Son of God made man is fully human. The one who inaugurated his ministry by attending the wedding at which he changed the water of human joy into the wine of the kingdom of heaven does not despise sexuality. Jesus is not unaware of the reality of differences between the sexes, but for him women are not limited to their sexual role. As humans they are, like their male partners, beings endowed with speech: *persons*. God speaks to them. According to the Orthodox theologian Olivier Clément, at the anthropological level, the revolution brought about by the gospel "is the advent of the person, as opposed to the species simply as a whole, and as opposed to the ecstasies of union".[2]

* * *

The gospels evoke the relationships of Jesus with various women: brief, dazzling encounters, or long, peaceful friendships where the decisive word suddenly breaks in, such as Martha of Bethany's confession of faith (John 11:27). Jesus touches the bent-over woman, and she stands up straight (Luke 13:10-17). To the widow of Nain he gives back her only son (Luke 7:11-17). A force, an "energy" goes out of him and he cures the woman with a haemorrhage who has dared to touch his cloak

(Matt. 9:20-22). Jesus takes the woman caught in the act of adultery away from the Pharisees who claimed the right to judge her (John 8:1-11). Each time, the miracle – healing, liberation, forgiveness – is accompanied by a saying of Jesus which reveals its deep meaning. These sayings proclaim the restored dignity of these women as daughters of Abraham the faithful, and direct them towards a new life: "Take heart, daughter; your faith has made you well" (Matt. 9:23); "Neither do I condemn you. Go your way, and from now on do not sin again" (John 8:11). "Go in peace" – or, to translate it more exactly, "Go *towards* peace", peace in the sense of the fullness of life in the kingdom of God (Luke 7:50).

Between Jesus and the women who have accompanied him from Galilee a truly intimate relationship is established. Mary Magdalene bears witness to this. She recognizes the risen Christ – the master and friend who now looks *different* – simply by the tone of his voice when he calls her by her name, "Mary". From this supremely personal encounter, as the "monk of the Eastern Church" has written, "an emotion shines into the world, which still gives us life".[3]

Several of the women who followed Jesus from the beginning of his ministry obviously came from well-to-do circumstances. They were economically and morally independent. Jesus does not send them back to their husbands. We can guess that they provided for the Master's material needs. Thanks to them, the Son of Man had shelter and food, and did not need to envy the birds of the air. However, as illustrated by the case of Mary Magdalene in particular, the role of these women was not limited to that of patrons or housekeepers. They were Jesus' disciples and friends. When he was arrested and condemned to death, they remained faithful to him. Not one of them betrayed him. When the disciples scattered and ran away, except for the one "whom Jesus loved", the women remained with Jesus and his mother, "near the cross", communing with the Crucified One in his suffering (John 19:25). Though trembling with shock on seeing the empty tomb, they obeyed the angel's command to go and tell the news. "Apostles of the apostles", they are called in the Byzantine liturgy – the first messengers of the resurrection.

Though capable of courageously taking the initiative, these women believers normally behaved in accordance with the Jewish-Hellenistic social customs of their time. Martha and Mary of Bethany, in whose home Jesus was a familiar guest, served him according to the rules of hospitality of their society. For them, this service was not at all humiliating. Did not their master call himself the servant of all? While accepting their service, Jesus nevertheless did not confine women to housekeeping, cooking and serving at table. He praised Mary when she left these duties to her sister and sat at his feet like a pupil – a student of the

Torah – being taught by a rabbi. Can we not see Mary of Bethany as the patron of modern women students of theology? Even so, however, Martha the housekeeper is not disdained. It is with Martha that Jesus has the conversation which culminates in her confession of faith, a confession in every way comparable with that of Peter, chief of the apostles. When Jesus proclaimed his Messiahship, Martha replied: "Yes, Lord, I believe that you are the Messiah, the Son of God, the one coming into the world" (John 11:27).

Other women also have profound dialogues with Jesus. Far from being passive receivers of grace, they are awakened by their encounters with him to their own thinking and faith, and are called to be among Jesus' witnesses in the world. Upon the revelation of "Jesus' mysteries", they become important and active agents. It was to a woman, the Samaritan whom Jesus met at the ancient well of Jacob, that he entrusted the revolutionary secret of the "worshippers... in spirit and in truth". She then brought this message to the inhabitants of the city of Sychar (John 4:1-42).

The irony-laden dialogue between Jesus and the foreign, "pagan" Canaanite woman, who answers him tit for tat, leads to the revelation of Christian universalism, beyond the borders of Israel. Admiring the magnitude of her faith, Jesus exclaims, "Woman, great is your faith! Let it be done for you as you wish" (Matt. 15:28).

A woman is at the centre of the slightly differing accounts in Mark, Matthew and John of the anointing at Bethany. Who is she? Mary of Bethany, or Mary Magdalene, as some scholars suggest? Or another unknown, anonymous woman? In fact, the historical identity of this woman is not important. What is essential is the meaning of her gesture.

On the eve of Passover, on his way to celebrate it in Jerusalem, where he will, as he knows, meet his death, Jesus is at table. The ceremony of the meal is disturbed as he receives from a woman the priestly anointing which, particularly in the context of Matthew's gospel, serves to consecrate him as king of Israel and at the same time foretells his death (Matt. 26:6-13; Mark 14:3-9; John 12:1-8). The unknown woman (or, in John's account, Mary of Bethany) breaks open an alabaster jar and pours upon Jesus a "perfume", a very costly "ointment of nard". This extraordinary gesture is not understood by the male disciples. On their petty calculations, this is nothing but a waste, to no purpose. They rebuke the woman: the money she has spent could have been given to the poor. Jesus alone understands her. They are united in a deep communion, the woman and the suffering, victorious God. "Truly I tell you, wherever the good news is proclaimed in the whole world, what she has done will be told in remembrance of her" (Mark 14:9). In these words we can discern a sort of mysterious correspondence with the "in remembrance of me" of the institution of the eucharist.

Have the churches preserved this exhortation and meditated on it sufficiently? Has the perfume of this gesture filled our entire house, as the gospel of John says it did in the house of Martha, Mary and Lazarus?[4]

NOTES

[1] France Quéré, *Les Femmes de l'Evangile*, p.13.

[2] Olivier Clément, *L'Œil de Feu*, p.18.

[3] Archimandrite Lev Gillet, "Jésus lui dit Marie'", *Contacts*, no. 100, 1977, p.4.

[4] A full account of Jesus' relationships with women would of course also have to include his mother Mary. To exalt the Mother of God by pushing her poor sisters back in the direction of Eve the temptress, by whom came sin and death, is to falsify the meaning of the scriptures and ignore the words of Jesus, who saw his mother as the image of the true disciple, the prototype of those "who hear the word of God and do it" (Luke 8:21; 11:27-28; cf. 1:45; 2:19). But to speak of Mary together with the other women would require another exposition. Cf. E. Behr-Sigel, *Marie et les autres femmes* (in preparation, Catholic Theological Faculty, University of Lyons).

Love and Transformation

Women Who Met Jesus

DEBORAH MALACKY BELONICK

Jesus' relationship with women brings to mind the Old Testament Song of Solomon, a collection of lyric poems of love and courtship which express intense yearning, jealous possession, extreme admiration and deep contentment between a bridegroom and his bride. The poems declare a singular commitment and an unbreakable bond between two lovers.

This sensuous poetry was included in the Old Testament as an allegory. The Lord of the Hebrews was perceived as the "husband" of his people (Hos. 2:16-19). Christian tradition has recast the allegory to point to the love of Christ and his bride, the church (Rev. 21:2,9).[1] Saints have viewed it as the intimate experience of Divine Love embracing the individual soul.[2]

This passionate poetry foreshadowed Jesus' attitudes and actions towards women. Jesus did not romantically court women, and of course he did not marry. But he did court souls, and the souls of women he engaged became loyally and unremittingly wed to him. All of Jesus' personal encounters with women bore the common experience of being wooed by love, falling in love, surrendering to love and being transfigured by love. This love was not a shallow physical attraction, but a burning fire that transformed the person and made her a daughter of the Most High God.

Essentially, Jesus' encounters with women resulted not in social programmes or political philosophies but in the purification of souls and the integration of personalities. Essentially, these encounters were dramas about ordinary women who became extraordinary women, about women being united to Jesus who is Love (1 John 4:8) and what that love cultivated in their souls. I want to speak of the transfigurations wrought in three women by the Lover of humanity.

The Samaritan woman (John 4:1-42)

Tell me, you whom my soul loves,
where you pasture your flock,
where you make it lie down at noon;

> for why should I be like one who is veiled
> beside the flocks of your companions? (S. of S. 1:7).

Once, on his way from Judaea to Galilee, Jesus had to pass through Samaria. He came to the town of Sychar (Shechem) which was "near the field that Jacob had given to his son Joseph" (cf. Gen. 33:19; 48:22; Josh. 24:32). Weary from his journey, he stopped about noon at a well and sat on the ground beside it. A woman from Samaria came to draw water, bringing the usual equipment – a pitcher and a hard leather bucket with a rope.[3] Jesus had no such equipment with him, and being thirsty he asked the woman for a drink. Here their intriguing conversation began.

The woman at first appeared startled by Jesus' overture since it was unheard of not only for a rabbi to speak familiarly with a woman in public but also for Jews to have any dealings with Samaritans. Jews also considered the eating and drinking utensils of Samaritans to be unclean.[4] When the woman questioned Jesus about this, she received an even more startling response. Jesus claimed he could give her "living water" (v.10). She mistook this to mean "running water", as opposed to water from a well or cistern, but Jesus explained that he was talking about the "water of life" referred to by the Old Testament prophets (Jer. 2:13; Zech. 14:8; Ezek. 47:9; Prov. 13:14).[5] He then went on to reveal the intimate details of the woman's life: she had had five husbands and was now living with a man without the benefit of marriage.

Impressed by his prophetic abilities, or perhaps wanting to shift the conversation away from her own embarrassing personal affairs, she posed a theological question. She wanted this prophet to solve a long-standing controversy between the Samaritans and Jews: where was the proper place to worship, on Mount Gerizim or in Jerusalem? Jesus assured her that this question very soon would be superfluous; those who worshipped God within the new covenant through the Messiah would worship in spirit and truth. He also revealed himself as that Messiah, the one whom the Samaritans called *Tā' eb*, "He who returns", or "He who restores".[6] At this revelation, the woman left her water jar at the well, summoned the people of Sychar, and directed them to Jesus.

Jesus appears in this account as the divine Shepherd seeking a lost lamb (Luke 15:6). The writer of the fourth gospel used this pastoral imagery extensively. Jesus stopped by the well at noon, the usual time for watering sheep in Palestine. When the patriarch Jacob himself met shepherds at a well in Haran, he said, "Look, it is still broad daylight... Water the sheep and go pasture them" (Gen. 29:7). Usually sheep were stationed near streams of flowing (or "living") water; but when such watering places were dried up by the heat of summer, wells were used.[7]

Jesus stationed himself at Jacob's well and prepared to give his lamb, the Samaritan woman, living water.

Shepherds also knew each sheep so intimately that they were able to feel the absence of even one sheep, for the appearance of the entire flock seemed changed. Stories about this familiarity are legendary; for example, a contemporary witness stated that shortly after nightfall, an Arab shepherd was able to call out, one by one, the names of the mother ewes and to pick out each one's lamb and restore it to its mother to suckle.

Such a shepherd was Jesus when he revealed to the Samaritan woman all her secret actions and desires. He felt her absence from his flock; he felt her desolation and despondency. She had tried so hard, through relationships with five men, to feel fulfilled. She had failed. Now came a man who offered her something new and eternal. Now came a man who offered her the water of wisdom, so that she would never feel thirsty or dry in her soul again (v.14).

The woman thought Jesus wanted something *from her*, yet he appeared as the Good Shepherd taking an opportunity to offer something *to her*. St Romanos the Melodist expresses this beautifully in his poem about this woman:

> Woman..., pay attention and open your heart to me,
> So that I may enter in and dwell in it; for this I wish.
> For the one who drinks this water will again
> on each occasion be thirsty;
> But the water which I give to those who are on fire with faith
> will be refreshing after the thirst;
> For within those who drink it, there will be a stream,
> A spring of immortality which bursts forth
> and swells with eternal life.[8]

Perhaps this woman went to the well that day looking for another lover. She obviously had experienced great dissatisfaction with the men she had married, and she knew that shepherds would be coming to the well at noon. Instead she found the Lover and Shepherd of humanity who placed God in her soul. Her transformation was begun. Remembered in Orthodox Christian tradition as St Photini, she became a light to the people of her home town, as well as a great evangelist abroad. She sowed seeds of Christianity in Samaria, and the disciples eventually reaped a great harvest there (Acts 8:4-25). In addition, she taught her five daughters and two sons to follow Jesus, and they accompanied her on her missionary journeys.[9]

Her quest at the well recalls the words of the bride in the Song of Solomon quoted at the beginning of this section. Jesus' response to her was like that of the bridegroom: "Follow the tracks of the flock, and pasture your kids beside the shepherds' tents" (S. of S. 1:8). If we women seek fulfillment and are thirsty for joy in our lives, we can follow the example of St Photini. We can ask Jesus Christ to fill us with wisdom, renew our souls and send us on our proper missions.

The woman with an issue of blood (Luke 8:43-48)

> I will rise now and go about the city,
> in the streets and in the squares;
> I will seek him whom my soul loves (S. of S. 3:2).

Jesus sought to deliver diseased people from their illnesses and restore them to health. And so, sick people sought out Jesus. Many times whole cities gathered at the door of the place where he was staying (cf. Mark 1:32-34). People believed Jesus to be a prophet or a rabbi, and in ancient times the sick looked to pious people, holy people, for remedies.

People of that day also thought sickness was brought on by demons or disobedience to God's law. The Hebrews believed in God's promise:

> If you will listen carefully to the voice of the Lord your God, and do that which is right in his sight, and give heed to his commandments and keep all his statutes, I will not bring upon you any of the diseases that I brought upon the Egyptians; for I am the Lord who heals you (Ex. 15:26).

Moses (Num. 21:7), David (Ps. 107:17-21), Solomon (2 Chron. 6:28-30), and Hezekiah (2 Kings 20) all had prayed to God for the healing of illnesses among their people. The crowds thought Jesus could pray for their healing, and they rushed to him for this purpose.

The woman who had been haemorrhaging for twelve years was no exception. She pushed into a crowd to find Jesus. According to the account in Mark, she had spent all her money on doctors, but suffered from their treatments and only grew more ill (Mark 5:25-34). Rabbis of that time sometimes posed as physicians and prescribed eccentric remedies for her type of malady:

> Dig seven pits, and burn in them some vine branches not yet four years old. Then let the woman, carrying a cup of wine in her hand, come up to each pit in succession, and sit down by the side of it, and each time let the words be repeated: "Be free from thy sickness."[10]

We can imagine the despair of this woman. According to the law of Moses, her discharge of blood made her "unclean", separating her from the worshipping community (Lev. 15:25-27). Moreover, some thought her illness was caused by sin, so they ostracized her. Perhaps she *had* sinned, for there is no one who does not sin (Rom. 3:23), and this added to her depression. Twelve years of suffering had certainly depleted her mental and physical stamina; in addition, she suffered from degrading and harmful treatments prescribed by physicians. Finally, her money was gone. We can imagine how many times she has been rejected, embarrassed and mistreated. All of humanity had shamed her.

Yet, this spurned women still had the faith to approach Jesus with hope. She risked recognition from the crowd and possible rejection from Jesus. She was so fearful that she trembled (Mark 5:33). She did not want to ask Jesus for help, but believed that if she touched the tassel of his cloak,[11] she would receive healing power. Her determination had not been extinguished, and with this determination she touched his cloak and was healed.

St Romanos depicted her as a resolute "robber" in his hymn, *On the Woman with the Issue of Blood*:

> Secretly she touched the hem of his garment;
> She tried to rob him as though he were a man,
> He who in his divinity knows no sleep.
> However, Christ bore being robbed
> He who of old stole the side of Adam in Eden,
> He who formed the woman now crying out to him,
> "Saviour, save me."[12]

Jesus saw in this woman his beautiful creation which had been deformed by disease. He over-ruled the law of Moses by allowing her to touch him.[13] He freely allowed divine healing to flow from him. He rejoiced in her restoration. Jesus told her she had been healed, *sesōken* – meaning she had been snatched from peril and preserved, and was now within his saving grace. He also told her she had been made whole, *hygiēs* – meaning she was safe and sound. These words connoted healing beyond the physical realm. Whenever the gospel writers used the word *sōzein*, they intended a spiritual healing of the whole person, indicated by Jesus' words, "Your faith has saved you."[14]

The quest of this woman recalls the search of the bride in the Song of Solomon – the words quoted at the beginning of this section and then the words a couple verses later: "when I found him I held him, and would not let him go" (S. of S. 3:4). And Jesus reminds us of the bridegroom assuring his bride, "Arise, my love, my fair one, and come away; for now the winter is past, the rain is over and gone..., the time of singing has come" (S. of S. 2:10-12).

Jesus' divine compassion and healing overcame taboo, shame, spiritual sin and disease. For the first time in a long time, the woman belonged to a new community where she was whole, forgiven and safe. Likewise, when we women need a safe place, when we need a spiritual haven, we need to come to Jesus.

Implications of Jesus' relationship with women

In his encounters with both the Samaritan woman and the woman with the issue of blood, Jesus broke many Jewish rabbinic prohibitions. As a rabbi, he spoke with a woman, a foreigner, a prostitute and a person considered to be "unclean" according to the Levitical law. There are many other instances in which Jesus rebuffed rabbinic taboos and returned to authentic Mosaic tradition. He touched dead bodies, in the case of Jairus' daughter (Luke 8:54) and in healing the son of the widow from Nain (Luke 7:11-17). He extolled the sinful woman who anointed him prior to his burial (Luke 7:37-50). He forgave the woman caught in the act of adultery and convicted her accusers (John 8:1-12).

Jesus' example elevated woman to her proper place in creation. Woman regained her status as co-equal with man in regard to her union and relationship with the Creator. Several implications were drawn by the early Christian community as a result of Jesus' encounters with women.

First, husband and wife, equally submissive to Christ and each other, were yoked in a marital union which expressed the love and yielding between Christ and his church (Eph. 5:21-33).[15] Second, some in the early church dispensed with the Levitical codes regarding women's menstrual cycles. Third, husband and wife were equally bound in marriage; the husband could no longer issue a divorce decree for minor irritations or out of displeasure with his wife (Matt. 19:9). Husband and wife also became responsible for the care of each other's body and sexual pleasure (1 Cor. 7:2-5). Celibacy, in addition to marriage, became prized within the Christian community (1 Cor. 7:6-7); virgins and widows in the early church had their own particular ministries.[16] Through Jesus' actions, women were emancipated from rabbinic rigidity.

At the same time, gender distinction within the Christian community remained, even in the eschatological sense, though women and men enjoyed the fullness of union with God by the indwelling of the Holy Spirit. Jesus did not come to deliver humanity from the *distinction* of being female and male, but came to *restore* the primeval beauty of both forms.

A range of anthropological theories and philosophies influence current theological discussions. How we view gender, male and female, greatly influences how we view issues of the household of God and the spiritual and functional roles of women. If we view gender distinctions as relatively insignificant, pertinent only to earthly life and function and necessary only for procreation, we will feel comfortable blending and crossing roles of women and men in the church. If on the other hand we view gender distinctions as psychologically and biologically significant, continuing in the *eschaton*, and necessary to reflect the wholeness of humanity and even perhaps the Image of God, we will question such homogenizing.

Our anthropological stance is crucial to debating issues surrounding the royal and sacramental priesthoods in regard to women. In the Orthodox family today, there is a wide range of thought. Some would distinguish male and female roles within the royal priesthood. Others would blend roles within the royal priesthood without hesitation but would stop short of ordination of women to the sacramental priesthood. Still others would freely admit women to the sacramental priesthood in light of woman's equality within the royal priesthood.

It is exciting, exhilarating, to be in the midst of this contemporary anthropological and theological debate, and there are many distinguished theologians within the range of thoughts. Personally I fall into the middle category above, because ordination to the sacramental priesthood is not one of the charisms automatically granted to royal priests. We are not entitled to it by virtue of our baptism and chrismation. The sacramental priesthood requires a separate grace of ordination. However, I am open to wisdom from others on these issues, provided they are approaching the topics from Orthodox Tradition.

To this dialectic I should like to offer the example of the *Theotokos*, concentrating on her royal priesthood and her motherhood. By studying the *Theotokos* I believe we may best understand what St Paul meant when he said, "There is no longer Jew or Greek, there is no longer slave or free, there is no longer male and female; for all of you are one in Christ Jesus" (Gal. 3:28). I shall focus my remarks on Jesus' relationship with her within the context of two stories from the gospel of John.

The Theotokos, the Mother of God (John 2:1-11)

> For your love is better than wine,
> your anointing oils are fragrant,
> your name is perfume poured out;
> therefore the maidens love you (S. of S. 1:2-3).

We hear the gospel reading of the story of Jesus and his mother at the wedding in Cana of Galilee at every Orthodox Christian wedding. Often we think of it simply as a story about wine running short at a wedding feast and Jesus sparing the poor host embarrassment. Often we think that

Mary nags Jesus until he performs the miracle of changing water into wine, and that he is even a little annoyed with her request. However, the Greek text taken verse by verse reveals the depth and true meaning what John the Evangelist is trying to convey.

The first verse of John 2 begins: "On the third day". Since the previous chapter says nothing about a first or second day, we must discern what St John means by this verse. The only other biblical use of this exact phrase is in the account of Moses giving the Law on Mt Sinai. "On the third day" of the third month after the Hebrews escaped from the Pharaoh of Egypt and fled into the wilderness, they received the Ten Commandments from God (Exod. 19:16). Thus, a Jew reading this story which St John begins with "On the third day" would at once wonder: "On the third day in the wilderness, the children of Israel received the Law from Mt Sinai. What will happen on *this* third day? Will it bring a new covenant, a new law?"

The Jews were anticipating the coming of the Messiah who would write the law on their hearts. They were anticipating the time when God would pour out his spirit on all flesh, causing his sons and daughters to prophesy (Joel 2:28-32). They were anticipating the Messianic age when "the mountains shall drip with sweet wine" (Joel 3:18). All this is symbolized by the gospel writer throughout this apparently simple story of the marriage in Cana.

Mary, concerned with hospitality, points out to Jesus that the wine is gone. She is noting not only the absence of physical wine, but also an absence of "spiritual wine". In the Bible, wine is a symbol of the joy of being in God's presence. Wine is also often a symbol for God's Spirit. Thus when Mary says, "They have no wine" (John 2:3), she really is saying, "They have no joy in their spirits, no joy of the Spirit. Their souls are dry." She looks around at the drunken crowd (for the wine is gone!) and notices their spiritual desolation.

Jesus replies, "Woman, what concern is that to you and to me?" (v.4). He is saying to his mother, "Why should we who know the joy of the Holy Spirit be concerned with drinking wine? Anyway, I cannot do anything about it now, because I have not fulfilled my ministry. My hour has not yet come. I cannot yet send the Spirit, the new wine, the real joy, into their hearts, because I have not yet been crucified. I cannot yet form my church filled with Spirit (Acts 2:14-18). But I can give them a foretaste of this joy. I will give them sweet wine, fulfilling the prophecy of Joel, and they will know that I am the Messiah" (v.11).

Mary's response to the stewards of the wedding feast is interesting: "Do whatever he tells you" (v.5). In the Exodus story, the people replied to Moses, "Everything that the Lord has spoken we will do" (Exod.

19:8). Mary appears here as the Daughter of Zion, the personification of the people of God, their fulfillment. She becomes the faithful "Yes" to God and replaces the fickle Israel.[17] In St John's masterly comparison of the wedding at Cana with the Exodus story, Jesus, the Holy Spirit and Mary fulfill and replace the event which involved Moses, the Law and the people of Israel.

Mary is the quintessence of humanity in union with God. God dwelt in her womb, and she was overshadowed twice by the Spirit of God, once at the Annunciation and once at Pentecost (Luke 1:35; Acts 1:24; 2:14). She was joined to God in a personal way and allowed God's power to work within her. Notice the dialogue between the angel Gabriel and Mary at the Annunciation. Gabriel came to her and said, "Greetings, favoured one! The Lord is with you... You have found favour with God. You will conceive in your womb and bear a son, and you will name him Jesus" (Luke 1:28-31). The gospel tells us she was greatly troubled and asked how such a thing could be. Gabriel replied, "The Holy Spirit will come upon you, and the power of the Most High will overshadow you; therefore the child to be born will be holy; he will be called Son of God" (v.35). Mary replied, "Here am I, the servant of the Lord; let it be with me according to your word" (v.37).

Notice that Mary did two things. She invited the Word of God *in*, to live and grow inside of her, and she called him Jesus, which means "Saviour". She also assented to the power of the Holy Spirit coming upon her. She joyously prophesied, "Surely, from now on all generations will call me blessed" (v.48).

God asks women – and men – to do the same. Of course, we will never bear the Christ child. However, Scripture tells us Jesus stands at the door of our hearts and knocks (Rev. 3:20). Jesus wants to dwell in our hearts, as he did in Mary's. Scripture likewise says, "If you then, who are evil, know how to give good gifts to your children, how much more will the heavenly Father give the Holy Spirit to those who ask him!" (Luke 11:13). God offers to us, as he offered to Mary, the indwelling of the Holy Trinity for our holiness and the gifts of the Spirit for the building up of the church (1 Cor. 12).

When we are baptized and chrismated, we are called to be a holy nation, a royal priesthood (1 Pet. 3:9-10), anointed ones, little "Christs". St Cyril of Jerusalem says of the chrism given to us after baptism that "this holy ointment is no longer plain ointment... It is the gracious gift of Christ... While your body is anointed with the visible ointment, your soul is sanctified by the Holy and life-creating Spirit" (*Mystagogic*, 3,3). The priest marks us with the oil on our forehead, lips, eyes, ears, nose, chest, hands and feet. We are sealed with the Holy Spirit (1 John 2:20). Revelation 7:4 speaks of those servants of God who are *sealed* on their foreheads. The Greek word *sphragis* referred to the mark on a person who was to be a slave or a soldier, or an animal destined for sacrifice. After chrismation, we are to dedicate our senses to God and to seal them off from evil influences. We are invited to a charismatic life, to a holy use of our senses. The parts of our bodies anointed in chrismation correspond to the charismatic gifts listed in 1 Corinthians 12:4-11: utterance of wisdom, utterance of knowledge, faith, healing, working of miracles, prophecy, discernment of spirits, tongues and the interpretation of tongues.

We like Mary must allow the gifts of baptism and chrismation to work in us. We like Mary must accept the invitation of God. All the saints of the church emphasize this cooperation. St Theophan the Recluse said:

> We see in the lives of all who have preserved the grace of baptism that there was in these lives a moment when they decisively dedicated themselves to God; this is indicated by such words as "he became inflamed in spirit" or "he was ignited by the divine desire"... But let no one think that he himself can give birth to such a power of life; one must pray for this and be ready to receive it. The fire of zeal with power – this is the grace of the Lord. The Spirit of God, descending into the heart, begins to act in it with a zeal that is both devouring and all-active.[18]

St Simeon the New Theologian (949-1022) said of this indwelling of Christ and outpouring of the Spirit:

> He that lacks awareness of his baptism and was baptized in infancy, accepting it only by faith and having effaced it by sins, but refuses the second one – I mean baptism of the Spirit, given by God in His love to those who seek it in repentance – how can he ever be saved? Not in the least... It is the worst of all heresies to believe it is not possible for Christians in latter days to experience charismatic gifts. It is entirely possible when one desires it [Hymn 27:125-32]. Whenever a miracle takes place by the power of the Holy Spirit, or when one observes a divine charisma in one of his brothers..., [if] he contends that such a thing is of the devil's deception...., he blasphemes against the Holy Spirit (*Catechesis 29*).

Mary responded to God's invitation and gifts, and she became the model of a human being on fire with God. She became the model of the royal priesthood, full of the Holy Spirit. When the angel Gabriel called Mary "highly favoured", the Greek word used is *kecharitōmenē*, which means, "full of grace", "full of the charisms". St John Damascene says of Mary, "She is ointment poured out" *(Homily II on the Birth of Mary)*. Mary might say to Jesus, like the bride in the Song of Solomon, "your love is better than wine, your anointing oils are fragrant, your name is perfume poured out; therefore the maidens love you" (S. of S. 1:2-3). Jesus might reply, "You are altogether beautiful, my love; there is no flaw in you" (S. of S. 4:7).

At the foot of the cross

Though full of grace and anointed with the power of the Holy Spirit, Mary retained her femininity. Jesus honoured his creation, male and female, and the relationships of brotherhood, sisterhood, fatherhood and motherhood (Matt. 12:50; 15:6). The gospel of John illustrates the importance of these vocations during the scene at the foot of the cross (John 19).

In this drama, the Virgin Mary and the beloved disciple John stand and mourn Jesus' death on Golgotha. Jesus says to Mary, "Woman, here is your son!" To John he says, "Here is your mother!" (John 19:26-27). Some view Jesus' "giving" of Mary to John merely as a way of providing for her protection. However, the sentence structure used in this particular passage indicates that Mary is really being given to the community of the church which shortly will be formed. John 19:27 states that "from that hour the disciple took her into his own home". The Greek phrase translated "into his own home" – *eis ta idia* – is the same as is used in John 1:11: "He came *to what was his own*, and his own people did not accept him."

This parallel hardly can be accidental. John took Mary not just into his home, but to *his own*, meaning the community of the New Covenant. She was to be their mother as well as his. After completing this act, Jesus gave up his spirit. He was pierced in the side with a spear, and blood and water spilled forth. These were the signs of the New Covenant, baptism and the eucharist, sacraments which would nourish the infant church. However, before his death, Jesus also gave the church a mother, his own mother, to protect and succour it.[19]

According to church tradition, the Virgin Mary remains our mother in heaven. Gender distinctions and gendered relationships remain even in the heavenly realms. Even there we will relate to one another as brothers and sisters, mothers and fathers, male and female. The Spirit's indwelling does not annihilate gender distinction on earth, nor will it be annihilated after our resurrection from the dead, even in our spiritual bodies.[20] The woman and man of creation are to be equally renewed and restored, not blended or eradicated. Gender distinction within the charismatic life remains, although there is equal opportunity between women and men for the obtaining and expression of charisms.

Some conclusions

People use examples of Jesus' relationship with women to support various political, sociological and theological positions. But in order to draw conclusions today from these ancient stories we must remember what was Jesus' main concern. His main concern for women mirrored his main concern for all humans. He wished for and required a *metanoia*, a change, a transfiguration of their hearts.

A woman did not meet Jesus and remain the same person. She experienced change. The change may have been repentance from sin, a desire to support his ministry, theological insight and clarification. The change may have been in her life-style, her goals, her dreams or her direction.

Meeting Jesus is meeting the God who brings integration, direction and purpose to our lives. Meeting Jesus is falling in love with the man who can tell us everything we have ever done, like the Samaritan woman, and yet forgive us. Meeting Jesus is being healed and restored like the woman with the issue of blood. Meeting Jesus is having the opportunity to be filled with the Spirit of God, like Mary, so that we may be holy daughters, sisters and mothers.

When we meet Jesus, when Jesus dwells within us, we will have our minds renewed to answer the pressing questions regarding church life and society. First, however, we must meet Jesus in the way he desires. We must open the door of our hearts to him when he knocks. We must be filled with the Spirit of God through the oil of chrismation. We must gain the mind of Christ (1 Cor. 2:16) and become royal priests. Then, like the bride in the Song of Solomon, we may exclaim, "My beloved put his hand to the latch, and my heart was thrilled within me... I arose to open to my beloved, and my hands dripped with myrrh" (S. of S. 5:4).

NOTES

1 Cf. H May and B.M. Metzger, eds, *The New Oxford Annotated Bible*, Oxford, Oxford U.P., 1973, p.815.
2 Cf. Jean Daniélou, ed., *From Glory to Glory: Texts from Gregory of Nyssa's Mystical Writings*, Crestwood NY, St Vladimir's Seminary Press, 1979.
3 Fred H. Wight, *Manners and Customs of Bible Lands*, Chicago, Moody, 1953, p.281.
4 On the Jews' attitudes towards the Samaritans see R.E. Brown, J.A. Fitzmyer and R.E. Murphy, eds, *The Jerome Bible Commentary*, Englewood Cliffs NJ, Prentice-Hall, 1968, p.431.
5 *Ibid.*
6 *Ibid.*, p.432.
7 On shepherds in biblical times, cf. Wight, *op. cit.*, pp.153ff.
8 Cited in *Kontakio of Romanos, Byzantine Melodist, Vol. 1: On the Person of Christ*, tr. Marjorie Carpenter, Columbia, Univ. of Missouri Press, 1970, p.90.
9 Alan Wallerstedt, ed., *The Orthodox Study Bible*, Nashville, Thomas Nelson, 1993, p.222.
10 Wight, *op. cit.*, p.140; cf. J.M. Freeman, *Handbook of Bible Manners and Customs*, New York, Nelson & Philips, 1874, p.21.

[11] *The Jerome Biblical Commentary*, p.140; cf. Num. 15:37-41; Deut. 22:12.

[12] *Kontakio of Romanos*, p.124.

[13] Here we should mention an ancient non-conciliar canon of the Orthodox church – Canon II of *The Letter of the Blessed Dionysius*. It reads: "Menstruous women ought not to come to the holy table or touch the holy of holies (Greek: 'the body and blood of Christ'), nor to churches, but to pray elsewhere." Balsamon's note on this canon adduces the example of the woman with the issue of blood who dared to touch only the hem of Jesus' garment. Cf. Philip Schaff and Henry Wace, eds, *The Nicene and Post-Nicene Fathers*, 2d series, Vol. 16, repr. Grand Rapids, Eerdmans, 1974, p.600. This canon contradicts the views of the 3rd-century *Didascalia Apostolorum*, which objects to the view that Jewish ceremonial law is binding on Christians after baptism: "If you think, O woman, that in the seven days of your menstrual flow you are void of the Holy Spirit; if you die in those days, you will depart empty and without hope. But if the Holy Spirit is always in you..., why do you keep yourself from approaching the works of the Holy Spirit...? Wherefore, beloved..., do not observe these things, nor think them uncleanness; and do not refrain yourselves on their account, nor seek after sprinklings or baptisms or purification for these things."

[14] On *hygiēs*, cf. *The Analytical Greek Lexicon*, London, Samuel Bagster, 1973, pp.395, 412; on *sōzein*, G. Kittel and G. Friedrich, eds, *Theological Dictionary of the New Testament*, Vol. 7, Grand Rapids, Eerdmans, 1971, p.990.

[15] See Nancy Forest-Flier, "Headship in Marriage: A Closer Look at Ephesians 5", *The Handmaiden*, Vol. 1, 2, 1996, p.25.

[16] Cf. Roger Gryson, *The Ministry of Women in the Early Church*, Collegeville MN, Liturgical Press, 1976, pp.8, 55-61.

[17] Cf. René Laurentin, "Mary: Model of the Charismatic as Seen in Acts 1-2, Luke 1-2 and John", in Vincent P. Branick, ed., *Mary, the Spirit and the Church*, Ramsey NJ, Paulist Press, 1980, pp.39-41.

[18] Cf. Peter E. Gillquist, ed., *Raising Them Right: A Saint's Advice on Raising Children, by Theophan the Recluse*, Mt Hermon CA, Conciliar Press, 1989, pp.48, 15, 10ff.

[19] Cf. Andre Feuillet, *Jesus and His Mother*, Still River MA, St Bede's Publications, 1974, p.209.

[20] This is a topic of heated debate among Christians today, including Orthodox Christians. Patristic sources did not agree and indeed sometimes individual authors were inconsistent; for example, St Jerome said in one place that "if woman shall not rise again as woman, nor the man as man, there will be no resurrection of the dead" (*Letter 108 to the Virgin Eustochia*, 23), but at another point argued with Rufinus that in the resurrection women will be turned into men. To this Rufinus responds: "If it is man alone who is to receive at the resurrection the form of clay which was originally given in Paradise, what becomes of that which is written, 'He made them male and female, and blessed them'?"; *Apology*, I, 24, in *Nicene and Post-Nicene Fathers*, Vol. 3, p.447.

Women in the Early Christian Church

DIMITRA KOUKOURA

A study of the rich bibliography related to the position of women at different points in the historical course of Christianity leads directly to the conclusion that women and men are equal citizens of the kingdom of heaven, but that, compared to men, women are unequal and degraded members of the social expression of the church. The first reality is attributed to the grace, the mercy and the love of God, which has been manifested through the mystery of divine economy; the second is attributed to fallen human nature.

The kingdom of heaven is not only an eschatological reality. Within the eucharistic community, the faithful experience the sanctifying grace of God which transforms the holy gifts into the flesh and blood of Christ and the faithful into participants in the glory of the Lord; and created time is shifted from the seventh day of the perishable creation into the eighth day of the new creation, which is restored by Christ.

The fourth ecumenical council (Chalcedon 451) defined the divine and human nature of Jesus Christ and the salvation of the faithful by him and set forth succinctly the basic principle of the salvation of all humankind: what is not assumed is not healed.

This means that the Son and Word of God possessed all of human nature, both male and female, and gave it the possibility of being saved from the determinism of corruption and death. This possibility is given to everyone; and it depends upon the free cooperation of men and women whether they will become members of Christ's body and participants in his imperishable glory.

This unprecedented spiritual experience of the faithful, both men and women, has borne rich fruit throughout the history of the church from the earliest centuries until today. Men and women have testified to the truth of the gospel with their words, their behaviour and their lives, and have supported the faith of other Christians. A chorus of martyrs, men and women, were thrown to the lions because they did not worship the emperor as their god.

The redemptive grace of God does not make any exceptions. The generous gifts of the Holy Spirit are bestowed equally on men, women and children. In an Orthodox church this truth is depicted on the walls and on the iconostasis, where men and women saints are equally honoured. It is especially visible at the moment when all the faithful are invited, without discrimination, to participate in the life-giving holy banquet. In this holy communion for redemption and eternal life there are no exceptions.

However, the characteristics of this kingdom of God are quite different from those of this world of decay and corruption. That is why many propositions about life which would liberate people from self-centred behaviours gain acceptance only very slowly and with great effort.

Undoubtedly, the civilization that was dominant in the Mediterranean basin for about two thousand years before the birth of Christ was governed by men. Women were considered more or less as instruments of propagation and pleasure, inferior in intellectual ability and unsuitable for any form of creative social presence. The callous view of women and their position which prevailed in the Graeco-Roman world was reinforced by the curse of the Mosaic law, in which sin, evil and woman acquired the same negative connotations, making it impossible for women to play a creative role in social life. Woman's position was determined by reference to the man, who ruled over her, oppressed her, used her and approached or rejected her according to her menstrual cycle.

It was in this mosaic of cultures – in which the ancient classical spirit encountered the Orient and Rome, the rabbinic traditions in Palestine vigorously resisted outside influences and the culture of the Egyptians created strong tendencies to mingle ideas and values – that the first Christian communities were founded, consisting of men, women and children.

Clement, the bishop of Rome towards the end of the first century after the birth of Christ, offers in his letter to the church in Corinth a clear image of the moral standards and social behaviour of the Christian woman. She should have an unblemished, modest and clear conscience. She should submit to her husband, attend to her duties to the family and be prudent and self-controlled as to her impulses. In her communication with others gentleness and self-restraint should characterize everything she says, and she should prefer to remain silent. This obviously corresponds to the portrait of an exemplary woman according to the social standards of that time, when the culture did not permit a woman any role other than that of the faithful wife, the affectionate mother, the silent housekeeper, characterized by moderation in her actions and wishes. We could say that this model of the woman in society is not very different from the Penelope of the Homeric epic. However, there is one basic difference: the prospect of salvation. In this letter, however, Clement of Rome does not mention any other role for the women in the eucharistic community apart from the basic information that she participates in it.

A few years later, in his letters to the church of Smyrna and his student Polycarp, Ignatius of Antioch mentions the categories of virgins and widows in the church and the care that the church owes them. About the same time Polycarp, in his letter to the Philippians, also mentions the special class of widows, whose duty is to be virtuous, irreproachable and modest. Widows either receive the care of the community or devote themselves to acts of charity.

The works of the apostolic fathers in the middle of the second century underscore the differences between the pagan women and Christian women. The liberal morality of pagan women is not acceptable for the Christian woman, who is characterized by modesty and virtue.

The writings of the third-century Alexandrian fathers Clement and Origen offer a number of philosophical views about women but no significant information about their contribution to the life of the church. During this period the church had to face two conflicting movements of Gnostics. One, led by Epiphanius the son of Carpocrates, supported free love, while the other, with Tatian as its leader, showed contempt towards marriage and praised a life of extreme asceticism.

Clement of Alexandria responded to the heretical views of contemporary Gnostics by saying that men and women have the same substance and are spiritually equal and that their only difference lies in their biological functions; but he offers no further information about the position of women in the life of the church.

Origen, who was the successor of Clement in the catechetical school of Alexandria (185-254), demonstrated extreme ascetic tendencies in his own life, strictly following the passage in the gospel of Matthew which speaks of those "who have made themselves eunuchs for the sake of the kingdom of heaven" (Matt. 19:12). He praises chastity as a supreme quality, while allowing marriage only as a concession to human weakness.

It is obvious that the extreme ascetic tendencies of the Gnostics which influenced Origen were easily supported by the misogyny of the Old Testament. A similar attitude towards women was adopted by Tertullian (160-225), who identified Eve – and therefore all women – with sin. In this understanding, the sexual instinct is considered to be the source of sin. Rather than trying to transform it – as with any other human urge, wish or decision – in the new reality in Christ, the person chooses abstinence instead.

The general acceptance of abstinence nurtured asceticism, both male and female. Of course, not all of those flowers which bloomed and bore fruit in the desert were rooted in an heretical contempt for the human body which the Lord assumed and made incorruptible. The anchorite tendency started from a different perspective on the kingdom of heaven, which emphasized the possibility for the believer to experience the kingdom of heaven immediately. This would demand the renunciation of anything standing in the way of salvation, such as attachment to physical needs, earthly possessions, fame. It seems that the heretical challenges for abstinence and spirituality were intense at that time; and the church responded in its own spiritual way.

The sources indicate that female monasticism emerged towards the end of the third century. The reason it prospered was the desire on the part of gifted women to achieve spiritual perfection and to escape from the oppression of a society ruled by men, with its unwanted arranged marriages and restrictive social conventions. Women's monasticism was revolutionary by the standards of that time, not only because it overcame social prejudices, but also because women's monasteries were threatened by many dangers from the outside, such as raids by barbarians and bandits. Not surprisingly, some of their contemporaries conceded with admiration that the nuns had acquired a "male ethos".

Irenaeus, bishop of Lyons, and Epiphanius, bishop of Salamine in Cyprus, specifically mention in their writings the roles that women cannot play in the eucharistic community. The church's response to the challenge of Gnosticism for the priesthood of women was clearly negative. At a time when the social role of women was confined either to silence and modesty at the margins of society or to vulgarity, immorality and intrigues, the Gnostics offered women the possibility of playing an important role in the community. Epiphanius rejects any such prospect for Christian women, while clearly delimiting the duties of deaconesses.

Basil of Ankara and Methodius of Olympus, who wrote at the beginning of the fourth century, emphasized the quality of chastity. Spiritual freedom can be experienced in this world. It is possible for a woman with a chaste life to avoid the social repression of marriage and select another way of life, which is blessed and protected by the church. Thus she enters the order of deaconesses, widows or virgins.

Deaconesses, widows and virgins

Besides the information provided by the New Testament about the role of *deaconesses* in the early church, their mission was depicted in subsequent Christian texts as providing guidance to women who had been converted to Christianity, so that they would live according to their new faith. The text of the *Apostolic Constitutions*, which is of Syrian origin and dates back to the fourth century, contains a very important piece of information bearing on the revival of the institution of deaconesses which has attracted great interest among Orthodox churches today. Its description of the service for the appointment of a deaconess sets out an order in which the prayer that is read and the laying on of hands prove that it is an ordination ceremony. The duties of the deaconess do not include priesthood, sermons or teaching but mostly support for women in suffering, especially in cases where it would be improper for male deacons to face or touch a woman's naked body.

It is obvious that the order of deaconesses derives from a sense of pastoral solicitude regarding the suffering of Christian woman and the spiritual guidance of newly converted women. At the same time, deaconesses had an auxiliary but active role during the sacrament of baptism, again probably in connection with the need to avoid scandal at the sight of a naked woman's body, especially before the baptism of infants was established, and in bringing the holy communion to sick women at home.

Widows were also a very active class in the New Testament and early Christian periods. A woman without a husband was excluded from any rights in the community. Even when the social environment chose the man she would marry, she still ran the risk of living in seclusion if she did not give birth to a son. Again, if she had given birth to a son and later lost her husband, she would have to face social rejection and actual poverty, for there was at this period of time no form of organized social welfare for widows and orphans. The solicitude of the church was thus substantial. Widows were unprotected women, who as a rule needed the charity of all Christians.

According to the historical sources, however, widows also played active roles in the Christian community. Not only did they accept the donations of others but they themselves participated efficiently in acts of charity and welfare. They visited the sick, gave advice to Christian women, prayed, fasted and participated in the sacramental life of the church. No form of the imposition of hands on widows is recorded anywhere; however, their duties do not seem to be different from those of deaconesses.

The particular emphasis given to chastity during the first two centuries, when the church was fighting against the heretics, led to the emergence of a recognized class of *virgins* within the life of the church.

At the end of the third century, Methodius of Olympus in his work *Symposium on Virgins, or Concerning Chastity* praises chastity as it is presented by women themselves and in the way they experience it. A virgin woman is full of glamour, radiance and magnificence since she is dedicated to the church, which according to the Apocalypse is "our mother", the "temple and tabernacle of God" (Rev. 12:1-6). Chastity is highly praised, whereas marriage is considered a need of the fallen human nature.

In fact, Christians in the Mediterranean basin at the end of the third century considered chastity as the supreme gift from heaven, an angelic quality on earth. Women who chose chastity belonged to the categories mentioned earlier – nuns, widows and virgins – and believed that the rejection of the sex instinct could contribute to spiritual perfection. Those who did not choose virginity are confined to the roles of mother and wife.

In the New Testament we see all the marginal and stigmatized groups of the society finding a place near Christ: prostitutes, tax-collectors, Gentiles, children, those possessed by demons, lepers, bandits. For the first time, women find their place. The idea of motherhood as a woman's sole mission was surpassed, and the reliability of women was recognized, as in the case of the Myrrh-Bearing Women who came to the empty tomb. These are signs pointing to the transformation of an ossified and callous society governed by men alone. But solidified mentalities change at a very slow pace, because the grace of God presupposes voluntary human cooperation. Hundreds of years later, after centuries of Christian life in Western societies, a different social situation seems possible for women, after the chain reaction in all aspects of life precipitated by the Industrial Revolution.

Women today are successfully assuming new and creative roles in society and are rightfully seeking a re-evaluation of their position in the life of the church. Certainly the service of contemporary women in the life of the parish and diocese varies according to the needs and the challenges that the local church accepts. This presence vindicates women and proves the spiritual equality concerning salvation and its expression in the society.

The Women in the Easter Narrative

Apostles of the Apostles

CONSTANTINA PEPPA

In his commentary on the Song of Solomon, St Hippolytus of Rome sets forth an allegorical interpretation of the biblical text, in which he also brings out his theological views.

Hippolytus interprets Song of Solomon 3:1ff. by means of the Easter narrative as found in the Matthean and Johannine gospel traditions. Here he introduces the symbolism of the old and the new Eve, who for Hippolytus are "types" (*typoi*) for the synagogue and the church respectively. According to the commentary (ch. 25), the transition from synagogue to church, from the old Eve to the new Eve, takes place by means of the Tree of Life, which is itself the Risen One and to which Eve clings passionately, "in order to be able to rise into the air". This begins at the moment in which the women encounter the Risen One and continues through their proclamation of the resurrection; as *typoi* of the new Eve, the women become "apostles of Christ".

In the woman who clings to the feet of Jesus (Johannine tradition) in order to ascend along with him, Hippolytus sees Eve, whom Christ brings with him as a "sacrifice" in the sense of an offering (*dōron*) to his Father. Eve is no longer a fallen woman, but rather one who has been redeemed; it is no longer the Tree of Knowledge which she is touching, but rather the Risen One, the Tree of Life. According to Hippolytus, the Eve who touches the Tree of Life, the tree which overcomes death, is the new Eve, the church.

In this same chapter of the commentary, Hippolytus speaks of the inner connection between the old Eve and the new Eve. As noted above, the women in the Easter narrative are *typoi* of the new Eve; and if the old Eve represents the synagogue, then the women witnesses to the resurrection, as *typoi* of the new Eve, represent the church. The women in the Easter narrative are sent by the Risen One to the disciples, to proclaim the resurrection to them. Thus they become "apostles to the apostles", or "apostles of the apostles".

That women too may become apostles is important for Hippolytus, because in this way they represent a counter-concept to the first Eve. For these witnesses to the resurrection are "good witnesses" who present a "good testimony".

The new Eve as *typos* of the church has been made new by Christ. The new Eve becomes the helper, the partner of the new Adam, because she does not lead him into wrongdoing as the old Eve did, but rather announces the good news and the truth of the resurrection.

The encounter of the Risen One with the women is the moment in which the new Eve, the church, takes the place of the old Eve, the synagogue. The women's proclamation of the resurrection brings about the end of the synagogue and the beginning of the church. The synagogue falls silent, the church declares itself.

In this commentary we do not find the comparison of Eve with Mary which is so often drawn in the patristic literature. Rather, the comparison is of Eve with the women of the Easter narrative. Since it was not Mary's task to make a proclamation, the comparison with the women in the Easter narrative is possible precisely because they became the ones who announced the news of the resurrection.

Conclusions

The mission given to women to proclaim the word of God at the very beginning of the church puts the service of women in this same church in a new light. In the new Eve, the church, women are called to proclaim "the resurrection as gospel". This is true even though the task of these "apostles of the apostles" was not to preach to the public, but rather to the disciples. The women in the Easter narrative are the first ones who not only heard the good news, but also brought it to the men, the disciples. These means that men have not only proclaimed the message to women, but also – and even, first of all – heard it from them. So the term "apostles of the apostles" is a correction of any image of the church in which women are only supposed to listen and preaching is to be done exclusively by men.

This is a translation from German of a portion of the author's dissertation (Bern, 1994) entitled Die Töchter der Kirche Christi und die frohe Botschaft des Sohnes Gottes *("The Daughters of Christ's Church and the Good News of the Son of God").*

Saints and Spirit-Bearers

Models for Orthodox Women

MOTHER MARIA (RULE)

Saints

The word "saints" was a term applied at an early date to all Christians. For example, it is used in the salutations at the beginning of Paul's letters to the Ephesians and the Philippians.

According to Luke, the name "Christians" was first used in Antioch (Acts 11:26). The next recorded use of it is in the account of Paul's trial in Jerusalem before Agrippa, who asks in response to Paul's proclamation of Christ in his defence: "Are you so quickly persuading me to become a Christian?" (Acts 26:28). Paul had spoken of his own upbringing, his persecution of Christ's followers, his conversion and his mission to preach repentance, forgiveness and Christ's rising from the dead to the Gentiles. St Peter writes of suffering as one of the fundamental marks of a Christian: "If any of you suffers as a Christian, do not consider it a disgrace" (1 Pet. 4:16). Christians are named for their Leader; the signs are witness and suffering, obedience, repentance and conversion.

I remember listening to an elderly archimandrite reminisce about events in western Serbia during the second world war, when he was in charge of a small monastery at Raća on the River Drina, just across from Bosnia. In the village marketplace one day he was complaining to an old peasant about the terrible burden of taxes imposed by the Nazis. The quota of cattle and grain was so crippling that he did not know how the monks could survive. The old man interrupted him: "But Father, what are you moaning about? We are Orthodox Christians and we must expect to suffer."

We have a calendar of saints, but only God knows the names of all the saints. This is wonderfully exemplified in C.S. Lewis's novel *The Great Divorce*. A young man – the writer in a dream – takes a bus trip from hell to heaven. His guide is a man he had always venerated, the 19th-century Scottish novelist and poet George Macdonald. The account of their journey, which develops the theme of transforming and redeeming love, includes this passage:

All down one long aisle of the forest the undersides of the leafy branches had begun to tremble with dancing light. Some kind of procession was approaching us, and the light came from the persons who composed it.

First came bright spirits, not the spirits of men, who danced and scattered flowers – soundlessly falling, lightly drifting flowers. Then, on the left and right, at each side of the forest avenue, came youthful shapes, boys upon one side and girls upon the other. If I could remember their singing and write down the notes, no man who read that score would ever grow sick or old. Between them went musicians; and after that a lady in whose honour all this was being done.

I cannot now remember whether she was naked or clothed. If she was naked, then it must have been the almost invisible penumbra of her courtesy and joy that produced in my memory the illusion of a great and shining train that followed her across the happy grass. If she was clothed, then the illusion of nakedness is doubtless due to the clarity with which her inmost spirit shone through the clothes. For clothes in that country are not a disguise: the spiritual body lives along each thread and turns them into living organs. A robe or crown is, there, as much one of the wearer's features as a lip or an eye.

But I have forgotten. And only partly do I remember the unbearable beauty of her face.

"Is it... is it?", I whispered to my guide.

"Not at all," said he, "It's someone you'll never have heard of. Her name on earth was Sarah Smith, and she lived in Golders Green."

"She seems to be... well, a person of particular importance."

"Aye, she is one of the great ones. You have heard that fame in this country and fame on earth are two quite different things."

"Who are all these young men and women on each side?"

"They are her sons and daughters."

"She must have had a very large family."

"Every young man or boy that met her became her son – even if it was only the boy who brought the meat to her back door. Every girl that met her was her daughter."

"Isn't that a bit hard on their own parents?"

"No. There are those who steal other people's children, but her motherhood was of a different kind. Those on whom it fell went back to their parents loving them more... Everything that came near her had a place in her love. In her they became themselves. And now the abundance of life that she has in Christ from the Father flows over into them. It is like when you throw a stone into a pool, and the concentric waves spread out further and further. Redeemed humanity is still young; it has hardly come to its full strength. But already there is joy enough in the little finger of a great saint such as yonder lady to waken all the dead things of the universe into life."

I have quoted this at some length, not only because it expresses the point that God alone knows in the end who is a saint, but also because it is a wonderful exposition of the compassion and sacrificial love which are the hallmarks of sanctity.

Spirit-bearers

The "Spirit" here is the Holy Spirit, promised by Christ. As he came nearer to the culmination of his earthly life – his suffering, death and resurrection – he spoke more and more of this. The fourth gospel spells out what he promised:

> I will ask the Father, and he will give you another advocate, to be with you forever. This is the Spirit of truth (John 14:16f.).
>
> But the Advocate, the Holy Spirit, whom the Father will send in my name, will teach you everything (14:26).
>
> When the Advocate comes, whom I will send to you from the Father, the Spirit of truth who comes from the Father, he will testify on my behalf (15:26).
>
> I still have many things to say to you, but you cannot bear them now. When the Spirit of truth comes, he will guide you into all the truth; for he will not speak on his own, but will speak whatever he hears (16:12f.).

These passages are then followed by Jesus' high priestly prayer (ch. 17), in which his relationship to the Father is expressed more clearly than anywhere else.

Surely the sending of the Spirit of truth is emphasized and reiterated because the disciples will soon be without the external physical presence of Christ, to whom they have become accustomed to turn at every moment for advice and help. Now they are to be the church, his body on earth, and to bring the good news to all creation. They will still need this support, this constant outpouring of wisdom; and Jesus reassures them that the wisdom of the triune Godhead will still be with them in the person of the Holy Spirit, sent by him from the Father.

All who have received chrismation have had their every orifice and member sealed by the gift of the Holy Spirit. We are all therefore Spirit-bearers. The saints are those who have lived out – and who live out today – this anointing with their whole hearts.

Models

Chapters 11 and 12 of the letter to the Hebrews give examples of the faith, trust in God and obedience of our forefathers in the faith. Whenever I read this, I add to the comments about Abraham's faith (vv.17-19) his trust and obedience when God told him to sacrifice his only son, through whom he had been promised so much. We know that God himself did this, and that the succession and inheritance were assured by it, but back in Abraham's day this seemed a total contradiction, as though God were playing with him. Yet Abraham was ready to obey God, even though it seemed that all his hopes would be dashed by this act.

I have recently lived with close friends through the tragedy of having their only child and her husband murdered in East Africa by persons who wanted only to steal their Land Rover. The parents are devout Christians, but this surpassed their understanding and almost overthrew their faith. Only some time after the burial was the mother able to say to me, "The greatest sacrifice was demanded of us and we have made it. God knows what is happening even if we do not. He has been through it."

The author of the letter to the Hebrews invites us to join this "cloud of witnesses" by "looking to Jesus" (12:2). Love is the source of this obedience, and its consequence. Recall Jesus' words: "I give you a new commandment, that you love one another. Just as I have loved you, you also should love one another" (John 13:34). "This is my commandment, that you love one another as I have loved you" (John 15:12). Jesus said these words shortly before his passion, when the cost of the love and obedience would be spelled out: the giving of his life. Each year we experience something new as we live through Holy Week. This year, perhaps because of the tragedy my friends were living through – and the way it deepened day by day as more information became available – I was intensely aware of the cumulative horror that Jesus' suffering must have caused those who were there at the time. We cannot go through the days of Holy Week as they did, and we know that it ended in resurrection; but we can catch a glimpse of the naked trust that was needed to live through the breathtakingly incredible horror of the situation as it developed hour by hour.

When I was a novice in an Anglican community in my early twenties, I was greatly confused by Jesus' image of the man planning to build a tower and sitting down to count the cost (Luke 14:28-30). Jesus' advice seemed so calculating. But as I wrestled with this story, I realized that for us as Christians there really is only one cost: everything, all that we have and are. As I said about the "Spirit-bearers", the saints are those who live this to the full, and those who live it to the full are saints.

All this is not of course confined to Orthodox women, as the title assigned to this article might suggest. The saints are models for all who are baptized in the name of the holy Trinity, women and men, Orthodox Christians and those of other Christian traditions.

Obedience, love and freedom

I have already touched on obedience, love and freedom as marks or attributes of sanctity. Here I shall look much more closely at the third of these.

The world often uses the word "freedom" to mean licence or choice. I am *free* to do this or that, good or evil. For Christians the meaning of the word is both more limited and infinitely wider. Freedom is not doing what we like but saying "yes" to God, keeping his commandments and doing his will. If we do this we are free; if we do not we are the slaves of sin and the devil. But why do we obey God and keep his commandments? It is because, however haltingly, we love him. This love transforms freedom, taking it from the seeming limitation of obedience to "the freedom of the glory of the children of God" (Rom. 8:21).

For several years I worked on an English translation of the lives of the saints by the Serbian bishop Nikolai Velimirovič, in his *Prologue from Ochrid*. Thinking about saints as models, I find that I turn most often to those saints who have demonstrated the love and true obedience to live this risky freedom and to recognize that superficial patterns of "correctness" are our servants, not our masters. Just as "the sabbath was made for humankind, and not humankind for the sabbath" (Mark 2:27), so rules, even canons, are subject to the royal law of love. Let me cite a few examples.

The first is *St Vitalis* (22 April). As Bishop Nikolai tells the story:

> In the time of Patriarch John the Merciful, a young monk appeared who, as soon as he arrived, compiled a list of all the prostitutes in Alexandria. His way of asceticism was exceptional and singular. During the day he hired himself out for the heaviest work, and at night he went into the brothels, gave the money he had earned to some prostitute and shut himself in her room with her for the whole night. As soon as he had shut the door, Vitalis begged the woman to lie down and sleep, while he spent the entire night in a corner of the room in prayer to God for that sinner.
>
> So he kept the sinner from sinning even for one night. The second night he would go to another, the third to another, and so on in order, till he had gone through them all; then he went back to the one with whom he had started. By his counsel, many of these sinners left their foul calling. Some married, some went into monasteries and others began some honest work for payment.
>
> All these women were forbidden by Vitalis to say why he came to them. As a result, he became a scandal to the whole of Alexandria. People reviled him in the streets, spat on him and buffeted him. But he bore it all patiently, revealing his good works to the Lord, but concealing them from men. When he died, all became known about him. There began to be many miraculous healings over his grave; people came from far and wide, bringing their sick to it. Spat upon by men, he was and is glorified by the all-seeing God (*Prologue*, II, p.87).

Saint Abraham (29 October; *Prologue*, IV, pp.125f.) would not rest until he had found his niece Maria. After growing up with a desire for virginity, she had fallen into fornication with a monk and, believing herself to be lost, became a prostitute. He found her and, pretending to be a customer, went to her room and revealed himself as her uncle, finally bringing her to repentance and the knowledge of forgiveness.

Another prostitute whose repentance we commemorate by giving her a special Sunday in Lent as well as a date in the calendar (1 April) is *St Mary of Egypt*, my own patron. I remember first hearing her life read 25 years ago in a tiny church in Walsingham, an ancient pilgrimage centre in England which for many years has had a strong Orthodox presence. The first hearing of the vivid account of her life by St Sophronius of Jerusalem is unforgettable: the completeness of her sudden *metanoia*, her turning round and looking to God; the drastic acuteness of her external asceticism, strengthening her to wrestle with the temptations that assailed her; the profound humility of her relationship with Abba Zossima, culminating in the moment when they were both lying on the ground asking the other's blessing – and in the end it was she who obeyed and blessed him.

In this century, *Mother Maria Skobtsova* is not formally in the calendar of saints, but bears the marks of sainthood. A Russian aristocrat and intellectual, she married twice and had three children. Then, in Paris in the early 1930s, she was called by her bishop, Metropolitan Evlogiy, to be a nun "in the world", to live for the succour and salvation of others. She worked with Russian women students, with the poor and needy who found a refuge in her house and then, during the war, with Jews in danger of arrest by the Nazis. For this last activity, she was denounced, arrested and sent to Ravensbrück, where she died. There is a strong probability that she took the place of another prisoner who had been condemned to the gas chamber; in any case, this would be consistent with – and the culmination of – a life spent in the loving, sacrificial service of others.

These are examples of saints who have dared to put the law of love above all others, to be unconventional for the love of God. Only God knows how far they were upheld by the prayers of those who, in withdrawal and silence, prayed for them and for those with whom they were engaged, and wrestled with the devil for the souls of those who had fallen away.

There is a lovely story about St Bridget of Kildare and one of her nuns. St Bridget was abbess of a large monastery in Ireland and one of her nuns was blind. St Bridget had the gift of healing, and she restored the sight of this nun. However, after a few days, the nun went to her and said, "Close my eyes again, dear Mother. When the world is clear to the eyes, God is less clear to the soul."

All of them – those who were in the world and those who withdrew from it – were free with the freedom of obedience to God. I believe that this is a message which we today dare not ignore. In a quarter of a century in the Orthodox church, I have lived both within an atmosphere of freedom in the Spirit, within the discipline of loving obedience, which Metropolitan Anthony of Sourozh has tried to teach me, and within an atmosphere of rigid canonical observance, in which a disciplined freedom in love has had to struggle not to be stifled and the holy Tradition has become more a set of rules to be adhered to than life with the Spirit in the discipline of the church. Let me offer just a few examples.

In Bishop Nikolai's *Prologue* there is a wonderful incident about fasting involving Jeladin Bey, who ruled Ochrid in the first half of the previous century, and Metropolitan Kalinik, who was head of the church at that time.

> Jeladin and Kalinik, although of different faiths, were very good friends and often visited each other. It happened that Jeladin Bey condemned 25 Christians to death by hanging, and the execution was to take place on Great Friday. The Metropolitan, deeply distressed by this event, went to Jeladin and besought him to mitigate the sentence. While they were talking the hour of the midday meal arrived, and the Bey invited the metropolitan to eat with him. A dish of lamb had been prepared for the meal. The metropolitan excused himself, as the fast prevented him from remaining to eat, and prepared to leave. The Bey was angry and said to him: "Choose: either you eat with me and free 25 people from hanging, or you refrain and they hang." The metropolitan crossed himself and sat down to lunch, and Jeladin freed the people from the death sentence.

Bishop Nikolai introduces this account with the words: "Fasting is a great thing, but love is greater."

As against this, I remember a friend Ljubinka coming to help us prepare for the Feast of the Holy Cross. Ljubinka's leukaemia, which had been in remission, had flared up again, and she knew she did not have much time left in this world. The Feast of the Holy Cross was a very special feast for the monastery and the village below it, and we asked blessing to fast and receive communion on the Feast. The rest of us were given the blessing, but Ljubinka was told that, as she had fasted and received communion the previous week, she was too ill to fast again, and so she could not receive communion.

Christ's teaching about fasting is unmistakably clear:

> And whenever you fast, do not look dismal, like the hypocrites, for they disfigure their faces so as to show others that they are fasting... But when you fast, put oil on your head and wash your face, so that your fasting may be seen not by others but by your Father who is in secret (Matt. 6:16f.).

We must not inflict our fasting on others. I have often heard the comment, "I am sorry, I cannot eat this; I am fasting." In those circumstances, we have already had a choice. If it is during the fasts, should we be there, in company, at all? If the call of love sends us there, surely it sends us to find some other way of fasting at that moment, and not to fly in the face of Christ's teaching, proclaiming our fasting to all around us. One of the monasteries in which I lived served as the parish church for a small hamlet, and we all knew each other. One small boy was a terror to his parents and his sisters. When he came to communion, I heard the priest ask him if he had fasted from this or that food, but I never heard him ask whether he had stopped hitting his sisters.

Many women suffer from a rigid interpretation of the rules about blood and participation in the life of the church. What woman knows herself able to approach rules about not receiving communion, not entering the sanctuary, not venerating icons when she is menstruating with the same inner freedom and joy with which we embrace the rule about fasting before communion? Whatever insights the church may have into this question, I hope with all my heart that it will be far from the mindless assumption of "uncleanness" which I have so often met both among the clergy and among other nuns. Christ's healing of the deformed woman in the synagogue on the Sabbath (Luke 13:10-17) gives us the priorities here: liberating from bondage and letting the woman walk tall!

On this matter of living in freedom within a framework and at times interpreting the rules with great flexibility in the name of love, I believe that women have a special contribution to make. It is an insensitive generalization to say that men make the rules and women bend them, but there is a great deal of truth in it. Women tend more easily to react with their hearts first and their heads afterwards, and to see the personal implications of a situation in which compassion and understanding are needed. We need to question the arbitrary decisions that are sometimes made by men in authority in the church, and I have learned by experience that the only way of being listened to is to be prepared to obey as wholeheartedly as possible, and in this way to have the inner authority to ask a hearing.

The Myrrh-Bearing Women, of all human creation, were the first to whom the Lord's resurrection was proclaimed. It is within the mystery of God's dispensation why this was so, but we are given the same joy and task of this proclamation as they were.

I believe that we in Orthodoxy are at a watershed on this issue of disciplined freedom in love on one side and narrow, rigorous observance on the other. We need great wisdom, but that is what we have been promised in the gift of the Holy Spirit. We are called to be saints and Spirit-Bearers.

In the Blachernae Church, across the Golden Horn, the Mother of God appeared to St Andrew the Fool for Christ in the year 911, as a sign of her protection of the city of Constantinople. The Feast of the Protecting Veil of the Mother of God is celebrated every year, in the knowledge of her protection and intercession. Chief among the saints, she is a creature as we are. She was for a short time physically the Christ-Bearer, the God-Bearer, and she was a Spirit-Bearer throughout her life. She will help us, if we ask her, to live in that glorious liberty that Christ has promised us: to know what it means to be a child of God our Father and a fellow-citizen with the saints in the heavenly kingdom.

The Witness of Women Saints

THAMAR DASNABEDIAN

In his novel *By the River Piedra I Sat Down and Wept*, Paulo Coelho tells the following story:

"Do you know the exercise of the Other? It's part of a story written a hundred years ago, whose author..."

"Forget the author, and tell me the story," I interrupted. We were once more walking along the only street in Saint-Savin.

"A man runs into an old friend who had somehow never been able to make it in life. 'I should give him some money,' he thinks. But instead he learns that his old friend has grown rich and is actually seeking him out to repay the old debts he had run up over the years.

"They go to a bar they used to frequent together, and the friend buys drinks for everyone there. When they ask him how he became so successful, he answers that until only a few days ago, he had been living the role of the 'Other'.

" 'What is the Other?', they ask.

"The 'Other is the one who taught me what I should be like, not what I am. The Other believes that it is our obligation to spend our entire life thinking about how to get our hands on as much money as possible so that we will not die of hunger when we are old. So we think so much about money and our plans for acquiring it that we discover we are alive only when our days on earth are practically done. And then it's too late.'

" 'And you? Who are you?'

" 'I am just like everyone else who listens to their heart: a person who is enchanted by the mystery of life. Who is open to miracles, who experiences joy and enthusiasm for what they do. It's just that the Other, afraid of disappointment, kept me from taking action.' "'But there is suffering in life,' one of the listeners said. "'And there are defeats. No one can avoid them. But it's better to lose some of the battles in the struggle for your dreams than to be defeated without ever even knowing what you're fighting for.'

"'That's it?', another listener asked.

"'Yes, that's it. When I learned this, I resolved to become the person I had always wanted to be. The Other stood there in the corner of my room, watching me, but I will never let the Other into myself again – even though it has already tried to frighten me, warning me that it's risky not to think about the future.

"'From the moment that I ousted the Other from my life, the Divine Energy began to perform its miracles.'"[1]

What sainthood does is to articulate the entire meaning of the reality of the Christ event for humankind.

A number of ways of doing this present themselves to us. But the dominant one within the churches is always the doctrinal approach. Orthodox believers are supposed to stick to the "articles of faith as revealed by God". In this way, however, Christ is often reduced to a sublime abstraction – always a positive abstraction, to be sure, but one that we can find we do not really know when we have to translate it into our experience in the communities where we live.

I suggest that there is another way of proceeding, which is simply to contemplate and experience Christ in relation to our own situation and our way of doing things. As indicated by the passage quoted above, the liberation Jesus brings is total liberation. It is not possible to speak of physical liberation separated or divorced from spiritual liberation. The physical is included in the spiritual. The truly spiritual embraces all the material, physical life of human beings and of our communities.

The veneration of the women saints for me is linked to the sort of religion my grandmothers had and I imagine will be a phase in our children's religion. The cult of Mary seems to me to be linked to that of the women saints.

There are women saints who were the incarnation of Christianity for their time, such as St Sanduxt at the time of the apostle Thaddaeus and St Rhipsimea in the midst of turmoil during the conversion of Armenia. But we must rediscover more recent saints. I cannot imagine offering the ancient ones as examples to people who come to confide their troubles to me. We should be aware that sainthood does not stop with the Middle Ages, that our age has its own women saints, who can enter into our private devotions. If they feel real to us, this will not be just folklore we have picked up.

I have often experienced a sort of intimacy or friendship with the Blessed Virgin Mary, as though I have entered into a personal relationship with her as a figure emerging from history at the impulse of the Spirit. I perceive her within an historical perspective that causes me to feel equally in solidarity with the religious society of past centuries, that is, with the entire society and not just a few representative individuals. This historical perspective is part (though only a part) of the total perspective of the church – one of the "points of contact" which when gathered together will reveal to us the universal Christ.

This nearness of the holy is not difficult to imagine, Paulo Coelho tells us:

> She is the feminine face of God. She has her own divinity... You should know that this woman – the Goddess, the Virgin Mary, the Shechinah, the Great Mother, Isis, Sofia, slave and mistress – is present in every religion on the face of the earth. She has been forgotten, prohibited and disguised, but Her cult has come down from millennium to millennium and continues to survive today.
>
> One of the faces of God is the face of a woman.

Sainthood is being like God, who is love. I have never met a man or a woman, however debased, in whom I could not finally recognize this germ of sainthood; but the sainthood which is canonized or at least recognized is that which has grown and blossomed and is conscious of its origin – "It is no longer I who live, but it is Christ who lives in me" (Gal. 2:20). This sainthood does not do away with our human limitations of character or intelligence, our various complexes, nor the repercussions all this can have for what is called a "moral" life. Sainthood for each person is to love God and other people as greatly as possible, just with that which he or she is.

There is no sainthood without the often painful detachment which the love of God and of others demands. In this sense, mortification is necessarily linked to the very mission and vocation of sainthood. In this mortification there is inevitably an ascetic element, which is no less inevitably disagreeable. But as the Armenian philosopher David the Invincible taught, one cannot die to oneself without giving oneself up.

This necessary mortification, according to David the Invincible, can be authentic only under three conditions. The first is relationship to Jesus Christ:

> If mortification is purely external, and does not take place in a spirit of poverty or in harmony with Christ or Mary as model, it does not amount to much. Mortification has meaning only in the course of an authentic spiritual life whose source is Jesus Christ, and which is bent on following him through all the gropings, the acquiescences, the joys, the sorrows, the choices of a human life, nourished by his word, the sacraments and the example of the saints.

The second condition is freeing oneself for prayer:

> There is, perhaps, one mortification, namely the regular insertion of times of prayer into one's life.

And the third is service to others:

> The privileged realm in which one experiences self-divestment is that of service to others, in any case for a layperson. There seems to be a deep link between really giving one's attention to others and becoming detached from oneself.

Indeed, a woman saint is a woman who has succeeded in the greatest of successes, in being the way God intended to make us. In dying on the cross, our Master succeeded in starting a movement which turned the world upside down and which is still going after two thousand years. Can we imagine, apart from him, any man or woman more successful than St Augustine, or the sainted women of the gospels, or St Theresa? Anyone who would have had more influence on history, or carried to a higher degree the highest human potentialities? And was it not their saintliness which enabled them to succeed? Where would they have been without it?

But are there saints among us today?

Saints can be recognized by a radiance which one suspects is the result of a secret success, for it conceals itself behind a profound modesty. These are persons whose depth is not written in their faces or gestures, nor heard in their voices or what they say, but which reveals itself gradually when we know them very well and have experienced it ourselves, most often by chance.

We may consider Mary to be the greatest example of sainthood, but it is unlikely that she appeared to be so to people of her own time. It is not by chance that the gospels are practically silent about her. The same has probably been true for the women saints of every age, and even more so for those of today. Our world is too involved in running after sports stars and entertainers for the woman saint not to be left completely in the shadows. It is in the very nature of a saint to be in the shadow. *But it is a shadow that shines.*

* * *

When I think about the reasons why I believe, my philosophy of course appears to me to be a fairly stable edifice. But what is most important is that I have encountered the living God in other people. I have guessed at, I have seen, I have recognized God's face in certain persons.

Mamie's witness

My maternal grandmother, Fendok Nouchik Avighian (Mamie), moulded my way of being and passed on to me the oral tradition of the Scriptures and theology in a lyrical, spontaneous, specifically feminine way which had nothing formal about it.

Fendok was the daughter of a couple who adored her from birth. They were heads of the village of Mouch in western Armenia, and could give her whatever she wanted. Fendok was a pretty girl, but did not become aware of her beauty even when she grew up. She was introverted and had no lack of imagination, but the massacres of the Armenians carried out by the Turks allowed her no chance to develop her gifts.

After the genocide, she found herself an orphan in Tigranagert, waiting to be married. She soon made the acquaintance of a rich woman of that region, who adopted her. Like many young women of that era she was happy when, on arriving at Aleppo, a marriage was arranged for her.

From the day she was married, Fendok concentrated actively on her husband and her housework. She brought a daughter into the world, soon after settling in Décines, in France. With the birth of her daughter, her happiness seemed complete, and she devoted all her energies to the comfort of her little family. She was also frequently employed as a factory worker, generously helping her husband. From time to time she received a call for help from a neighbour, but Fendok preferred to keep her time and energy for her own needs. Why should she get involved in other people's problems? Her innocence would be compromised.

As an Armenian and a woman, many no doubt considered her the lowest of the low. But I was struck by her confession of faith in Jesus the Messiah, and by the reason she gave for her faith: "Lord God, light of mercy," she called him. Compare this with Mary Magdalene's confession of Jesus after his resurrection.

What do we mean when we say we considered Mamie as a disciple – a saint – in our family?

Although she was illiterate, she read the Bible through her own experiences. This is the essential thing.

The life of faith gave her back her real humanity, the way God created her, so that she could go beyond her child-martyr experience. What was eternal life for her, if not abundance, both physical and spiritual? It is being thirsty which can make us understand that we need the water of eternal life. Hunger and thirst are dehumanizing experiences. Those who are hungry and thirsty lose their dignity entirely. It is sinful to separate the needs of the body from those of the spirit.

Jesus says: life is here. The kingdom is here, now; eternal life is life in all its fullness, love and justice here and now, in our earthly lives.

After the long illness and death of her husband, Fendok was condemned to doing the most menial and lowest-paid work. She had to wait on her landlord whenever he sent for her. Even at home in her miserable lodgings, there was no chance for her to rest.

The rest of Fendok's story is of little importance, but when she returned to Lebanon her family welcomed her most joyfully. What strikes me is that when this woman had discovered the truth she became a witness to those she loved. She must have been very convincing, because we believed what she told us. She realized that Jesus came especially for the poor and the oppressed.

When Fendok died, nobody said that a unique woman was gone from this earth. Who knows? Perhaps it was her "angel"-like quality which drew her to Jesus. For me, what is interesting about Mamie's witness is the way it shows how someone very humble *can* pass on the gospel. And that is just what the high and mighty would deny!

A kind of resurrection

Mamie's elder sister Margaret had spent her life taking care of and serving others and raising her family. She was happy with her family and her life was going well.

Late one night, young Mamie was awakened by a Kurd who told her that her sister had been in a quarrel with Turkish soldiers. She was taken to the bank of the Euphrates River. When she saw the group of police officers by the river, she realized that something terrible had happened. And there on the wet ground she saw the body of her sister, carefully laid on a mat on the bare earth.

Stunned by grief, Mamie felt her legs give way. She began to weep, and threw herself at the feet of a Kurdish officer, begging him to tell her what had happened. "Your sister committed suicide," they told her. "She threw herself in the river."

But Mamie could not believe it. She kept saying over and over, "My sister would never have committed suicide. She was murdered."

Mamie was informed that the suicide had been discovered by the servant of her father Sarkis, who had recently been killed, and that she must now wait patiently for justice to take its course. There was nothing else to do for the time being. "Don't worry," they told her, "justice will be done."

It did not take long for Mamie to understand that if she just waited, nothing would happen. She had to take charge of things herself. She decided that the criminal who had murdered her sister should be punished. A new woman was born in her.

With the help of some political groups, she had her story published in the newspapers. She joined in the struggle of those fighting against the deaths caused by the Genocide of 1915, and she rallied the courage of women who had lost daughters or sisters. She worked with the women in the shanty towns, teaching them to recognize their rights and their dignity. Mamie was once bent beneath her yoke, made timid by tradition, fear and resignation, but today she stands up straight. She dedicates her life to helping other women to stand up straight as well.

> Now he was teaching in one of the synagogues on the sabbath. And just then there appeared a woman with a spirit that had crippled her for eighteen years. She was bent over and was quite unable to stand up straight. When Jesus saw her, he called her over and said, "Woman, you are set free from your ailment."
>
> When he laid his hands on her, immediately she stood up straight and began praising God. But the leader of the synagogue, indignant because Jesus had cured on the sabbath, kept saying to the crowd, "There are six days on which work ought to be done; come on those days and be cured, and not on the sabbath day."
>
> But the Lord answered him and said, "You hypocrites! Does not each of you on the sabbath untie his ox and his donkey from the manger, and lead it away to give it water? And ought not this woman, a daughter of Abraham whom Satan bound for eighteen long years, be set free from this bondage on the sabbath day?"
>
> When he said this, all his opponents were put to shame; and the entire crowd was rejoicing at all the wonderful things that he was doing (Luke 13:10-18).

Jesus said to Mamie without hesitation: "Woman, you are set free from your infirmity!" *You are somebody*, he said to her. *You are a child of God. You are a human being, as marvellous and as wise as every other. You are as capable of dignity and fulfilment as anyone.*

Jesus made his way to Mamie, and he touched her. Human contact can make all the difference between an existence bowed with resignation and a life which goes forward, upright and confident. Her body, which was bowed, straightened up. That is what his kind hands could mean to someone.

"She is the daughter of Sarkis," Jesus says to us now. Sarkis's family can count descendants, men and women. *She* counts too.

NOTE

[1] Paulo Coelho, *By the River Piedra I Sat Down and Wept*, tr. Alan R. Clarke, New York, Harper Collins, 1966.

The Meaning of Ministry

ELISABETH BEHR-SIGEL

An introductory note by Fr Boris Bobrinskoy: For some years, the access of women to certain ordained ministries in the church has become more and more of an issue within Orthodoxy. This is due not only to the indirect influence of other churches, but also to the cumulative effect of the profound changes in the place of women in modern society and the consequent reflection by a number of Orthodox women. Among the most notable of these is Elisabeth Behr-Sigel. In this short essay she offers a remarkable synthesis of earlier discussions regarding the theological meaning of ministries in the church.

To be sure, on this complex topic on which no Orthodox position has yet been clearly defined (because it is a new issue), anyone can have intuitions, convictions and even prejudices – and the viewpoint set forth in what follows is one respectable position among others which are equally respectable. What is important is that reflection is taking place, even if we do not yet know the outcome. The church is constantly being confronted with challenges from the world, and if it is to show itself in its eternal youthfulness it must respond to the signs of the times. Of course this does not mean bending under pressure from the world, but rather, with the help of the Holy Spirit – thus, in the tradition of the church – having serious, profound and creative answers corresponding to the new realities of the human race on its way towards the kingdom of God.

* * *

Ministry, from the Latin *ministerium*, means, according to its etymology, "service". Ministry is the office of one who serves. A minister is a servant. In the ecclesiastical language of today, the semantic field of these terms has come to be limited to the clerical. We speak of the "ministry" of a bishop or a priest, or of a Protestant pastor, a rabbi or an imam. These are "ministers of religion". On the other hand, lay persons who fulfil offices within the church, even if they do so regularly, are not referred to as "ministers". Their service is not "ministry". The royal priesthood of lay believers is recognized by theologians, but they carefully distinguish it from the so-called "ministerial" priesthood, which belongs to the priest.

This semantic evolution has not been innocuous. It is a symptom of the separation which has been instituted and emphasized, especially since the Middle Ages, between those called the clergy, people set apart for divine service, and the laity. Yet, the laity are also members of the people of God: The English word "laity" comes from the Greek *laos tou Theou*, "people of God". The semantics seem to reveal a cleavage in the social reality of the church. Does this mean that Christianity, which began as a lay movement – a movement suspect in the eyes of the clergy of the time (the priests who pushed for Jesus to be condemned and put to death) – has turned into an institution ruled by the clergy? Is there no place for rethinking and clarifying in the light of the gospel the meaning of the royal priesthood to which all the baptized are called, and that of the specific ministry which has become the province of a few?

From its beginnings the church did distinguish between different offices or ministries. In the most ancient texts, such as Paul's letters, this appears in connection with the vision of the church as the body of Christ, whose members have different functions, or as a spiritual house being built by everyone and in everyone, with each person participating in the common task according to the charisms which he or she has received as the free and sovereign dispensation of the Lord, through the Spirit: "The gifts he gave were that some would be apostles, some prophets, some evangelists, some pastors and teachers, to equip the saints for the work of ministry, for building up the body of Christ, until all of us come to... maturity, to the measure of the full stature of Christ" (Eph. 4:11-13).

Diversity of ministries is thus part of our divine calling – but diversity in unity: "Now there are varieties of gifts, but the same Spirit; and there are varieties of services, but the same Lord; and there are varieties of activities, but it is the same God who activates all of them in everyone" (1 Cor. 12:4-5). Here the church is understood and experienced as a community, or better, as a communion of persons – in the image of the communion of the Trinity – who are working in a conciliar manner to build up the body of Christ, which is also the temple of the Holy Spirit.

However, over the centuries, through various influences and as consequence of human weakness and sin, this luminous vision was replaced by the image of the church as a pyramid of "powers" in which the distinction among charisms hardened into an instrument of separation and exclusion. In different ways, this overshadowing of the true "ecclesial being" took place in both East and West. A symptom of this can be seen in the evolution of the iconostasis in the Orthodox churches. What began as a slight and transparent barrier, a stand for the guiding images of Christ and of the Mother of God, has turned into a wall of images, behind which, in a sacred space apparently separate from the people, the clergy officiates.

But such separation of the clergy from the laity has never been a dogma of the Orthodox church and is foreign to Orthodox theology of the priesthood. The consciousness of the royal priesthood of all the baptized is conveyed by the gospel, by the Christian rites of initiation and by the eucharistic prayers, and it continues to exist in the depths of ecclesiastical consciousness – at times, alas, hidden like the talent buried in the earth or the treasure in a field of Jesus' parables. From time to time prophetic voices are raised to arouse the church and Christians from their numbness. A notable example was St Seraphim of Sarov in 19th-century Russia, who called upon everyone, clergy and laity, men and women, to "acquire the Holy Spirit" and was the mystical inspiration of those who afterwards became the confessors and martyrs of the faith under Communist persecution.

This sense of a common ministry and a responsibility shared by all was manifested in another way during the ordeal of the great Orthodox diaspora of the 20th century. Living in the diaspora has meant for millions of Orthodox a traumatic and at the same time stimulating encounter with the Western world – and for a handful of Western Christians it has meant encountering Eastern Christian theology and spirituality. This situation is producing today – not without resistance – a creative return to the sources of our ecclesiology and of the theology of ministry which is its corollary. From among the several Orthodox theological works which might be mentioned in this connection, I shall draw on only one small work, both synthetic and poetic, clear and profound, by a spiritual leader who was also a great theologian: Father Lev Gillet.[1]

The source of all ministry, Lev Gillet affirms, is found in Jesus Christ, who was both servant par excellence, having humbled himself and become a human being (Phil. 2:6-11; cf. John 13:3-16), and the only priest in the full sense of the word, as the letter to the Hebrews forcefully maintains. It is he who is "the Offerer and the Offered", in the words of the liturgy of St John Chrysostom. Offered to God "once for all" (Heb. 10:10), the sacrifice of Jesus made him "the one mediator between God and humankind" (1 Tim. 2:5). However, Jesus wanted people, human beings, to share in his work of redemption and sanctification. He entrusted tasks to his disciples, he sent out the apostles. This is the foundation of the common priesthood of all the baptized. The words of the apostle Peter are addressed to all Christians: "let yourselves... be a holy priesthood, to offer spiritual sacrifices acceptable to God through Jesus Christ... You are... a royal priesthood" (1 Pet. 2:5,9). What is meant, in a very real sense, is a universal priesthood, the realization of humanity's calling according to Genesis 1 – a calling overshadowed by sin, but never abolished, and brought to accomplishment in the God-Man; a calling in which, in communion with Jesus Christ through the Spirit, all the baptized participate in the church, the womb of the new humanity.

This is the meaning of the chrismation or confirmation of the newly baptized immediately following their baptism: unction – or signing with the mark of the Holy Spirit – of the arms and legs, and particularly of the sensory organs, through which the human person enters into relations with other humans and with the living and inanimate world; consecration of the entire person, called to offer himself or herself and to offer to the Creator all the creation which is entrusted to his or her care (Gen 1:28). "Thine own of Thine own we offer unto thee, on behalf of all and for all" – this is the prayer of the Orthodox faithful during the offertory in the eucharistic liturgy.

> In this moment, the divine work of creation reaches its goal and its climax. In this moment we pray for the whole creation, we dedicate to God all human beings and the entire world, we fulfil the office of priest, so that our priesthood may be the ministerial priesthood delegated by the church, or the royal priesthood which the Scriptures ascribe to all believers.[2]

This priesthood is expressed and given meaning by the prayers and liturgical rites, but all the baptized together are called to live it out in the world, in whatever form their service takes.

However, a few persons in the church are called to be the "ministers" of Christ's mysteries in a particular sense. The mission of bishops and presbyters in the apostolic succession is to be the witnesses of the apostolic faith, the pastors and guides of the local churches for which they are responsible and in which, as such, they preside over community worship. As those who dispense the Word and the sacraments, they are (again in the words of Fr Gillet) "those who speak for and are the external, visible instruments of that invisible priestly grace of which the whole church, laity and clergy, is the depository". Their priesthood, according to Orthodox teaching, is not ontologically different from the priesthood of all the faithful. It is not of "another essence" than theirs. But they are responsible for a particular office, for the fulfilment of which the church, confident in the Lord's promises, prays that they may receive the gifts of the Spirit.

This is the meaning of the blessings which we call "ordinations", conferred on those whom the church has called to the ministries of deacon, presbyter or bishop. Ordination does not mean promotion to a higher grade in a hierarchy of which the royal priesthood or the so-called "minor" orders are the lower degrees. Rather, it is the sign of the gifts of the Spirit granted by the Lord – on condition that one be open to his grace – to the servants to whom he gives the task of nourishing and strengthening, in those whom they serve in his name, the calling of all to a common priesthood.[3]

This theology of the priesthood and of ministries is the context in which the issue is being raised today in the Orthodox church – still very timidly – of the possibility of women's access to the ministerial priesthood. In the opinion of Bishop Kallistos Ware – one of the best contemporary Orthodox theologians – it remains an "open question".[4]

NOTES

[1] Most of Gillet's writings appear under the pseudonym "A Monk of the Eastern Church". The work used here is *L'Offrande liturgique*, Paris, Cerf, 1988, which consists of two studies first published in Beirut for the Orthodox youth movement of the Patriarchate of Antioch: "Notes sur la liturgie" and "Sois mon prêtre". Among other studies are Nicolas Afanasiev, *L'Eglise du Saint-Esprit*, Paris, Cerf, 1975, and John Zizioulas, *L'Etre Ecclesial*, Geneva, Labor et Fides, 1981.

[2] *L'Offrande liturgique*, p.46.

[3] Here I would refer especially to the insights of Alexander Boukharev (1822-71), a great Russian theologian who was not understood in his own time. Cf. E. Behr-Sigel, *Alexandre Boukharev*, Paris, Beauchesne, 1977.

[4] Cf. Kallistos Ware, "Man, Woman and the Priesthood of Christ", in Peter Moore, ed., *Man, Woman and Priesthood*, London, SPCK, 1979; a new revised edition is forthcoming from St Vladimir's Seminary Press. See also E. Behr-Sigel, *Le ministère de la femme dans l'Eglise*, Paris, Cerf, 1987; "La consultation de Rhodes sur la place de la femme dans l'Eglise", *Contacts*, no. 2, 1989; "Femmes et sacerdoce", *Contacts*, no. 2, 1990.

St Photini – The Woman at the Well

A Biblical Meditation

THOMAS FITZGERALD

The powerful story of the woman at the well (John 4:1-42) speaks to followers of Christ, women and men, in every place and every culture. This story about a particular Samaritan woman, whose name has come down to us in the tradition as Photini, reminds us of many of the fundamental themes of the teaching of our Lord – repentance, discernment, inspiration and discipleship.

In the Orthodox liturgical calendar, St Photini and her sister St Phota are remembered on 26 February. Additionally, this story is one of the five accounts from the gospel of John which are read during the eucharist on the five Sundays between Easter and Pentecost. One of the many hymns of the day which speak of her captures the spirit of the celebration:

> When the woman of everlasting memory came to the well,
> She found you, the water of wisdom.
> Because of her deep faith,
> You satisfied her completely, O Lord,
> And you bestowed on her
> The kingdom that lasts forever.

The initiative of the Lord

As with many accounts in the gospels, this story depicts Christ taking the initiative to heal and restore one of his precious children. At the well of Jacob, Jesus encounters a woman, a Samaritan woman, a woman who appears to be living in violation of the laws of Moses and whose life seems to be out of control. In initiating a dialogue with her – "Give me a drink" (v.7) – Jesus is going far beyond the letter of the Mosaic law to reach out to someone whom many would view as impure and immoral. A rabbi would be expected not to have any direct contact with such a person.

Photini knew this all too well. No doubt she had experienced her share of abuse and discrimination from "religious people", for it is all too easy to harm others in the name of religion and to misuse the Scriptures as a pretext for degrading someone else. And so she responds to the Lord's request with a question: "How is it that you, a Jew, ask a drink of me, a woman of Samaria?" (v.8).

Though perhaps asked with a measure of sarcasm, her question was perfectly logical. The woman knew that Jews were not supposed to have any contact with Samaritans, that the prevailing opinion among the Pharisees was that the Samaritans were heretics who distorted the Mosaic law. Moreover, they were not considered to be true Jews; they lacked "racial purity". Thus they were to be avoided at all costs. Besides, she was a woman unaccompanied by her husband. Clearly, it struck her as strange that Jesus, viewed by many as a noted rabbi, would enter into a conversation with her. Yet Jesus had taken the initiative. Indeed, he had asked her to help him by drawing water from the well. The water of Jacob's well became a common bond drawing these two people together.

There is an important insight here. God encounters us where we are. He meets us in the present circumstances of our life in order to offer us his mercy and love. Like the Samaritan woman, none of us is worthy; and none of us can make ourselves worthy. God's love is not something we can earn. It comes to us freely in spite of our condition. As Photini encountered Christ at Jacob's well, so too the risen Lord is present in our midst, offering us the mercy and love of our heavenly Father.

The woman's discernment

Jesus responds to the woman's initial question with a challenge: "If you knew the gift of God and who it is that is saying to you, 'Give me a drink,' you would have asked him, and he would have given you living water" (v.10). In a sense this is a call to respond to his initiative, an invitation to open her heart to him. In the dialogue that follows, it becomes clear to the woman that Jesus is speaking not about the physical water which comes from Jacob's well but about "living water", the gift of salvation which brings refreshment, healing, renewal and new relationships. "Everyone who drinks of this water [from the well] will be thirsty again, but those who drink of the water that I will give them will never be thirsty. The water that I will give will become in them a spring of water gushing up to eternal life" (vv.13-14).

Despite her circumstances, the Samaritan woman grasps the significance of the Lord and his words. In the very depth of her being, the child of God responds to the Lord. An interior transfiguration begins to occur and her true self, created in the image and likeness of God, begins to emerge. Wisely she says to the Lord: "Sir, give me this water so that I may never be thirsty or have to keep coming here to draw water" (v.15). This is a moment of discernment, a profession of faith in Christ.

As it continues the discussion gradually becomes more personal. Slowly and cautiously the woman reveals the condition of her life. She acknowledges that she has had five husbands; and when Jesus notes that the man she is presently with is not her husband, she does not deny it but responds by declaring that Jesus is a prophet. In one of his homilies St John Chrysostom pays special attention to this point in the story:

> What then did the woman do? She did not show resentment, nor leave him and run away, nor think the whole affair a disgrace. Rather, she marvelled at him and persevered the more, for she said: "I see that you are a prophet" (*Homily 32 on the Gospel of St John*).

As we follow the dialogue, we find ourselves wondering how she had been treated by her five husbands? How did she cope with the abuse she must have experienced? What little we know about her indicates that her life must have been filled with disappointment and a sense of personal failure. Her series of broken relationships no doubt did little for her sense of self-worth or her ability to trust others. She may have come to expect abuse from others, especially from men.

All of this must have affected her relationship with God. The disappointments and betrayals she experienced, the abuse she suffered at the hands of others and her own tragic choices must have made it difficult for her to believe that she was truly a valued daughter of God. Her trust in God's mercy and her hope in God's forgiveness must have been weak.

Recognizing this, we are struck by the compassionate way Jesus treats her in this dialogue of healing and reconciliation. Jesus takes seriously the person with whom he is speaking. He is able to look beyond the circumstances of her life to affirm her lovingly as a person of intrinsic value and goodness. He asks questions, but he also listens. He is able to convey empathy and respect for Photini as a person who belongs to God the Father. He expresses a love for her which she may never before have experienced.

Although he learns of her tragic situation, Jesus does not stand before her as a harsh judge. He does not reprimand her as a "heretic" or reject her for being "impure" according to the Mosaic law. He does not condemn her for her sins. Rather, he speaks to her as the Good Shepherd, concerned with the well-being of each member of his flock. Jesus recognizes her dignity as a daughter of God.

Yet at the same time Jesus wants Photini to see herself and her situation clearly. Reconciliation and healing require an honest assessment of oneself. Jesus' very respect for Photini provides her with a basis to expose the true condition of her life to him. His presence and his compassion enable her to begin the process of *metanoia*, the deep change which reorients her life towards God. In this encounter at Jacob's well Jesus created a safe place in which the living water could overflow, an environment in which Photini could look honestly at herself and recognize the love of God revealed in Christ.

The dialogue between the Lord and Photini moves on to a discussion of worship. Once again, Jesus is not at all reluctant to discuss such an important issue with a Samaritan woman. Clearly a thoughtful person, Photini immediately points to the debate between the Jews and the Samaritans over where God is to be worshipped. Both emphasized the historical significance of a particular location: the Jews affirmed the centrality of the temple in Jerusalem, the Samaritans believed that the appropriate place was Mount Gerizim.

Jesus declines to be drawn into this old debate. Instead, he explicitly rejects the emphasis on an historic location and emphasizes the deeper character of authentic worship:

> Woman, believe me, the hour is coming when you will worship the Father neither on this mountain nor in Jerusalem... The hour is coming, and is now here, when true worshippers will worship the Father in spirit and truth, for the Father seeks such as these to worship him. God is spirit, and those who worship him must worship in spirit and truth (vv.21-24).

This brief, powerful and authoritative affirmation emphasizes worship which is sincere and authentic, which does not depend on a particular place. Ultimately, this is an approach to worship centred on the revelation which Jesus himself is bringing as the promised Messiah.

Again, the Samaritan woman gains deep insight into the person of the Lord and recognizes the truth of his words. She responds at once to the Lord and his teachings. Despite the burdens of the past, she humbly and faithfully confesses that she is waiting for the Messiah. She acknowledges the deep spiritual longing in her heart. With profound conviction she says, "I know that the Messiah is coming. When he comes, he will proclaim all things to us" (v.25).

Jesus honours this conviction and affirms her faith. When Jesus declares that he is the Messiah – "I am he, the one who is speaking to you" (v.26) – it is truly a theophany. At that very moment the Samaritan woman becomes a privileged witness to the mighty acts of God.

In this encounter at Jacob's well Jesus reveals his own identity as the promised Messiah. In so doing, he reveals also the love and mercy of God and the dignity of the Samaritan woman. Photini responds to the presence of this Christ. Despite her past, despite the abuse she had experienced, she comes to know Jesus as her Lord and is able to see herself as a beloved daughter of God.

We also need to respond to the presence of the Lord and to the love he offers. That response may take different forms depending on our own spiritual journey and the circumstances of our own life. Photini expressed her response initially through a willingness to enter into a dialogue with Jesus, then in her confession of her life's situation, then in her profession of faith. And, as we shall see, she went on to express it in her willingness to be a disciple.

There are different ways of responding to the presence and prodding of the Lord. What is important is that an honest response take place. Because of her response, Photini came to know Christ as the Messiah and her Lord. Our responses to the Lord through prayer, confession and profession of faith also help us truly to know him as our Lord and thus to deepen our relationship with him. In this way Christ becomes for us not a distant figure of the past but a friend and companion in the present.

The disciple and missionary

The story of the Samaritan woman does not end with her own recognition of Christ as Messiah. Her encounter with Christ was a life-changing experience, which she wanted to share with others. After her meeting with the Lord, she leaves her water jar at the well and goes back to the village, where she begins to tell others about Christ. Abuse and rejection and the experience of God's healing and reconciliation gave her the wisdom and courage to share the good news with others. To those in her village she declares, "Come and see the man who told me everything that I had ever done. He cannot be the Messiah, can he?" (v.29).

Photini became an instrument of reconciliation. A woman whose life was out of control became the "enlightened one", a messenger to others of Christ and his light. Many of the Samaritans, we are told, came to believe in Jesus simply because of her testimony. They invited him to spend time in their village, and in turn many more came to believe in him as the promised Messiah. With joy in their hearts they turned to Photini and declared: "It is no longer because of what you said that we believe, for we have heard for ourselves, and we know that this is truly the Saviour of the world" (v.42).

St John Chrysostom affirms the missionary activity of Photini in the strongest terms, referring to the importance of her "apostolic work" by making a comparison (in *Homily 32 on the Gospel of St John*) between her and Nicodemus (John 3:1-21 the subject of the previous homily):

> The woman at once believed and appeared wiser than Nicodemus. Indeed, not only wiser but stronger. For though he heard countless things of this kind, he neither summoned any other person to Christ, nor did he himself speak freely of him, while she engaged in apostolic work, spreading the good news to all and calling them to Jesus, drawing to him a whole city from outside the faith.

Elsewhere, he compares her with the disciples:

> For, as far as she could, she herself did as the apostles had done, indeed with even more alacrity than they. For they left their nets after being called, while she of her own accord, with no summons, left her water jar and did the work of an evangelist with excited elation as a result of her joy (*Homily 34 on the Gospel of St John*).

There is also an important insight here for our own lives. Our relationship with Christ must inevitably involve others. In being drawn more closely to Christ, we are drawn more closely to others. For Photini this meant becoming not only a disciple but also a missionary. She told others of her experience of Christ. Again, how we share with others our experience of the Lord will differ. We are distinct persons in particular situations and blessed with particular gifts. What is important is that our relationship with the Lord, if it is genuine, is bound to affect our relationships with others. Not all of us will become missionaries like Photini. But our experience of God's mercy and love must be expressed in our relationship with others.

The other disciples

An important part of this story is the reaction of the other disciples. Just before the events described in John 4, they had gone to buy food, so they were not present for most of the dramatic encounter that took place at Jacob's well. When they returned, they were astonished that Jesus was speaking to the woman (v.27).

The action of the Lord must have challenged the ethnic and religious sensibilities of the disciples, for as we have noted Jews and Samaritans customarily avoided contact with each other. What Jesus had done, therefore, did not fit with their expectations of how he should behave. Perhaps they were also afraid that this encounter would harm his reputation – and thus their own as well. Moreover, the Lord's action challenged their understanding of the scriptures and their religious tradition. The Mosaic law and religious customs prohibited the contact which took place here.

Perhaps the disciples too learned a lesson that day. Perhaps they learned that receiving the gospel message called them to go beyond what they were accustomed to, beyond their way of thinking, to a genuine *metanoia*, a true change of heart and mind, open to the mighty actions of God and to the surprises of God in the present.

Like the disciples, we too can hold views which do not reflect the reality of the Lord and the gospel. We can have perspectives and prejudices which reflect more of our cultural background than of the teachings of Christ. We must therefore be constantly ready to let the gospel of the Lord penetrate more fully into our hearts and minds. With the help of our fellow believers, we need to be willing to assess our values and our perspectives on others in the light of the gospel.

An example of faith

The story of St Photini, the Samaritan woman, is a story of a person who truly changed for the better because of her encounter with Christ. Despite her difficult past, she was willing to open herself up to the light of Christ. She became a person of faith; and because of this she was willing to be a disciple and to become a missionary. Photini became a bearer of the light of Christ and she shared this light with others. Because of this St John Chrysostom declares:

> Let us then imitate the Samaritan woman. Let us converse with Christ. For even now he has taken his stand in the midst of us, speaking to us through the disciples and prophets. So let us listen and obey (*Homily 31 on the Gospel of St John*).

Growing Up Orthodox and Female

A Story from the Middle East

MAHA MILKI WEHBE

Forty years ago, in a modest house in a village in Lebanon lived three sisters and two loving parents, forming a happy family. In a setting of olive trees against rising mountains, life was simple. The village community, along with the fifty surrounding villages, belonged to the same church, served by a saintly priest who reflected the church to the people for 17 years, before becoming the bishop of another region.

Suddenly, one day the father of this family was gone. The four females of the house were on their own, without material or moral support. The situation was especially grave in a country where a family without a male at the head was marginalized and looked down on, if not degraded.

Because the eldest sister was suffering from a nervous breakdown, the middle sister was forced to the forefront. It was she who had to stand up to greedy neighbours trying to rob them of their land, without effective backing from her sisters and mother, who were ashamed, as "helpless females", to confront tough and persistent male neighbours. This sharpened her vision, directed her ambition and pushed her fears to the background. Thrust into an atmosphere of frustration, she turned it into a will to succeed.

She applied to the best university in the country and was awarded a full scholarship, which took care of her lodging and pocket-money. During the first year in Beirut, the war, which was to last for 15 years, broke out. Unable to reach her home town, she worried constantly about the condition of her elder sister. Under the circumstances, the nearby church and its youth group became her second family (later she would marry one of the members of the group).

The group was a dynamic one, venturing into the mountain villages to meet people, clean their churches, chant in their services. In this new community she learned more about Orthodoxy, both intellectually and spiritually. The group also opened her up to ecumenical activities and endeavours. She felt a sense of accomplishment, and soon became the animator of the group. Her new community became a shelter during the dark days of bombing and sniping, and the shift from the church of the village and her family there to the new setting was a smooth one.

Her years in university not only offered her an academic education, leading eventually to a degree in agriculture, but also deepened her awareness of life and the problems related to dealing with different groups in society. The selfishness of people became clearer to see, and the difficulty of facing life alone posed a problem. In the meantime the war intensified; and when the university had to shut down, she fled under difficult security conditions to her village, where she had to remain for more than a year. There she put her theoretical agricultural studies into practice, getting up before sunrise to go to the fields with the villagers, and coming back to learn knitting and sewing in a local institution.

In the village she applied not only what she learned in university but also used what she had learned in the city church. She became an increasingly active church member, helping the priest in his ministry and church activities. As a result, the village people saw her as a strong person with a well-defined outlook on life – no longer an orphan who was looked on as a burden, but a young woman one could depend upon. She was no longer afraid to confront situations, but always remained ready to serve.

A few months later, when the university reopened, the entire family moved to Beirut. The mother had to work outside the home for the first time in her life to pay the rent for a small apartment and to support the family, now that the youngest daughter was also in university. A new life developed, and they found themselves in a new social milieu, a multi-confessional and a multi-class community.

As the months rolled by and university days were coming to a end, a new relationship with an old friend was intensifying. This was to culminate in engagement a year later and then in marriage. The young man was very attached to his church. Before their marriage, the couple travelled to Greece with a group of students from different churches. At that time they became close friends with a young priest who was to become the bishop of Beirut and who would officiate at their wedding.

Persistently he urged the young man to become a priest under him; equally persistently she resisted the idea: an Orthodox priest was the last thing she wanted her husband to be. She envisaged service in the church in a different capacity.

Meanwhile, the couple moved to one of the Gulf states, where the husband had taken a job in the business community. But the Lord had put his seal on him, so where was he to escape? They went back home, back to the bishop, back to have a baby girl and back for him to be ordained a deacon and later a priest. Over the difficult years that followed, she continued to resist this new situation and declined to belong fully to the church as institution. She was lukewarm, seldom going to church and rarely touching any book related to it. She intensified her own voluntary activities in secular clubs and women's movements, but not in the church.

One day, the bishop appointed her to be a member of the Women's Programme of the Middle East Council of Churches (MECC). This brought her face-to-face with the sudden awareness that she was theologically ignorant. How could she represent her church? Immediately she made a firm commitment to move from relation to action, from being a merely passive recipient to being an active participant. She became aware of a new task, that of being a partner with her husband in the ministry of Christ. The call to ministry was a call to both of them, in accordance with the talents of each. Hence, a process of reshaping had to begin.

The first step was to take up theological training at the seminary of her church in Balamand. She began by auditing courses, one with fourth-year students, one with the beginners and another with a visiting professor. Her studies entailed a 90-minute drive to Balamand and back, spending time away from her husband and daughter and sometimes having to stay overnight at the seminary.

Another step was attending national, regional and international meetings. This exposed her to other peoples and cultures, and she learned more and more to recognize others as they are. Involvement with the women's desk of the World Council of Churches and other related bodies helped to further her commitment to the church worldwide.

On another level, her evolving awareness of her own increasingly deepened church affiliation drew her attention to the other wives of clergy in her diocese. Meetings, activities, trips and social work began to be planned and organized, which led in turn to a widening of the circle to reach out to women at large in the church of Antioch. With the strong support of the patriarch and bishops, the idea of the First Antiochian Women's Convention was born, and when it took place in Syria in August 1996 it was a huge success, bringing together women from the dioceses, all exhibiting one heart and one mind. A healthy new baby had been born, and everyone wanted to help in its upbringing.

On a more personal level, she decided to stop her part-time teaching at high school, a decision which coincided with her being appointed as coordinator of the Women's Desk of the MECC in Lebanon. This was a large responsibility, but her zeal and commitment led her to accept it;

and she was able to put her skills of organization and public relations to more fruitful use. Before accepting the position she sought the advice of the Patriarch, who recounted to her an incident involving a task he had to do as a young boy. When he asked his father if he could do it, the father replied, "Someone else has done a similar chore before you." The answer was Yes – with an affirmation of anticipated success.

* * *

The seeds of leadership are, in many women, sometimes dormant but always exhibiting themselves in indirect ways, developing. It is true that all things work for the best for those who love God. In my own life, all of the past, the sweet and the bitter, was slowly engraving the shape of what was to be. The grace of God and a considerate, open-minded husband, who permitted and encouraged the potential in me, helped me to grow and become active. The church leaders and spiritual fathers, brothers and sisters are still pushing me in the direction of ministry. I learned that to grow up and be effective as an Orthodox meant a deep awareness of being part of the church and not merely a cut-off individual. The church is the place, the dimension in which God manifests himself – the church being the world and not only the neighbourhood, along with all those who have struggled before us. For me, this communal feeling, which always involves belonging to groups seeking the grace of the Lord, has meant that the church is a place of transfiguration.

But growth is always a function of grace, which is the only factor that changes people. Knowledge of God is also experiencing him, and this happens only in a community. Knowledge is togetherness. But this togetherness should never be one-sided or sexist. We are not to create a parallel female body to combat male dominion. All are one in Christ, because each is perfected by the one God, and as such every woman and man is perfected the more he or she comes closer to the centre of the circle – Jesus. The female should never seek to compete with the male but rather to fulfill the potential of harmonizing mind and heart in a unity which she is more equipped to harmonize. She is not a diminished human being longing to become complete according to the male historical model. Christ is her model. He perfects her. Only if this vicious circle is cut can true liberation take place. And true liberation happens only in, through and with the help of God.

Growing Up Orthodox and Female

A Story from the West

VALERIE ZAHIRSKY

The epithet "father of his country" refers to a strong leader who has moulded the early destiny of a nation. It is an impressive title, which indicates clearly that the man to whom it is applied has done significant things. But the church gives us someone who lived in such a way that she was given a far more exalted title: "Mother of God". This one, Mary, is presented as an example not only for women but for all human beings.

A panoply of other women surrounds Mary in the church. In the New Testament we meet Prisca, of whom St Paul writes with high regard, indicating her prominence by sometimes mentioning her name before that of her husband Aquila. She instructed a well-known and dynamic preacher named Apollos to give him a better understanding of the faith. Not only did she have the wisdom and discernment to recognize his need for instruction, but she also felt herself qualified to offer it. Prisca also took an active role alongside Paul and her husband in the trade of tentmaking. Paul also writes with great affection about Phoebe, who is sometimes called a "deaconess", though the word used to describe her would have been recognizable to the Roman Christians of her day as meaning a missionary who is qualified to teach. Phoebe did teach, taking one of Paul's most complex letters to the house church in Rome and interpreting it for the believers there.

Other men appreciated the influence of women on their own lives and the life of the church. In 369 St Basil the Great wrote to Bishop Eusebius of Samosata about his feelings on the death of his mother: "The only consolation I had in life was my mother, and I have been deprived of her through my sin. Do not ridicule me because I, a grown man, complain of being an orphan, and forgive that I cannot bear, in the parting of her soul, to realize that none of her godliness is revived in me."

"Such wonderful sisters and mothers"

Growing up in the Orthodox church meant that I was surrounded by the examples of women who had performed many kinds of service in the church, thus pointing to many possibilities for my own service. A friend once said that the great thing about being Orthodox was to have "such wonderful mothers and sisters" in the faith.

Yet there was another side to the exciting possibilities these women placed before me. For it seemed that many people in non-Orthodox churches were completely unaware of the woman-rich history of the Orthodox church and were conditioned to see Orthodoxy as an oppressive force beating down on women. I wondered why people seemed so determinedly unaware.

As a teenager I was given a book about Mother Maria Skobtsova, a Russian intellectual, activist and divorced mother who became a nun. Mother Maria, who had led an unconventional life before becoming a monastic, continued to be so afterwards. She did not live in a cloister but organized a centre of worship in Paris which also included a house where she and her helpers gave refuge to Jews, offered meals to the poor and provided temporary shelter for many who had no place to live or who came to talk late into the night about theology and philosophy. Mother Maria was a familiar figure in the fish and vegetable markets of Paris in the early mornings, looking for bargains on the food needed to nourish the numerous denizens of the house on Rue Lourmel.

Mother Maria was arrested by the Nazis and eventually died in Ravensbrück. Several survivors wrote that they were sustained in those terrible days by the Bible studies and prayer meetings she conducted. They remembered her absolutely unshakable faith in God, her ability to comfort others even as she suffered, and the sense of humour that still occasionally bubbled up in a comment she would make in the midst of horror.

The Diary of Anne Frank was a popular book among girls of my age at the time I was reading the story of Mother Maria. A short time later, we were all reading another account of a family who hid people and was finally captured during the Nazi years — *The Hiding Place*, by Corrie Ten Boom. The author wrote about her sister Betsy's wonderful efforts to comfort and instruct fellow prisoners in Ravensbrück with prayer and Bible study. She described those efforts as unique, the sole spiritual activities in the camp. Certainly this work was admirable and courageous, but if Mother Maria's work was going on in the same place at the same time, could it have been unknown to the Ten Booms? There must have been underground communication among the camp's Christians, or Betsy would not have been able to gather people as she did. It seemed to me the Ten Booms' story would have been richer had it acknowledged the ministry of an unusual woman from a Christian tradition so different from their own, who yet felt moved in the same way they did to offer people hope in hopelessness.

A Western feminist theologian, speaking at a large gathering of women, gave me another example of the sometime "invisibility" of Orthodox teaching. She said that the church leaves women caught between two unacceptable models: Eve, who is considered to be the source of all sin, or Mary, the impossible ideal who is in any case unrelated to the lives of real women.

Listening to her, I found the image of an icon coming into my mind again and again, the icon of the resurrection in which Christ is pulling Adam and Eve up from death with his two powerful hands. In some versions his face is towards Adam; in others it is turned towards Eve. But it is clear that he is saving them both. If they were equally guilty in the Garden of Eden (as most Orthodox hymnography suggests), they are now equally drawn to the light of his presence. How did a well-educated theologian so totally miss this, I wondered?

As for the speaker's view of Mary, it was clear that it was very strongly shaped by the Roman Catholic teaching of the Immaculate Conception. Mary was removed from the realm of human existence and had become irrelevant, unnecessary. She had no place in women's struggle to find their proper ministry in the church. All this was far from the Orthodox idea that Mary, born as we are, gives all of us a fully realized and blessedly imitable example of how to use our human nature to glorify God in every moment of life.

It was not only people in other churches who had a skewed idea of Orthodoxy. Francine du Plessix Gray, a writer who has travelled widely in Russia and interviewed many Russians, quotes with approval another writer's words in her book *Soviet Women: Walking the Tightrope*:

> Byzantine Christianity may have been more repressive of women than Roman Catholicism... because the region was more vulnerable to the goddess-centred fertility religions of the Near East, and the Orthodox church had to contend with unusually powerful matriarchal patterns. Furthermore, its ascetic obscurantism was never counterbalanced by a tradition of chivalric love, or by the liberating secular influence of a Renaissance or an Enlightenment.
>
> And so Russian culture remained totally deprived of that idealization of marital sex which prevails in much of the Roman Catholic tradition. The Orthodox clergy, which referred to women as "those cursed by God" continued to look on the female sex as the source of all spiritual danger. Faithful to Tertullian's view of women as "the devil's gateway" Orthodox theology emphasized women's mental inferiority and their powers of witchcraft.

Reading this, I was amazed to think that the Orthodox church with its long tradition of married clergy could be thought less likely to "idealize marital sex" than the Roman Church which so carefully sequestered its clergy from marital encounters of any kind. I tried hard to think when my priest husband had last referred to me as being "cursed by God". Who, I wondered, had decided that the influence of the Renaissance and the Enlightenment were necessarily "liberating"? Why do so many people assume, mistakenly, that Tertullian is an Orthodox saint? And what in the world does "ascetic obscurantism" mean?

Becoming an "Orthodox apologist"

My reaction to all this was to decide to become a sort of "Orthodox apologist" and to try, when I could, to talk about the teachings of the church as they really are and as they really affect the experiences of women. This has given me the chance to talk with many people from many backgrounds. It has also shown me that our own clergy and laymen sometimes need to be reminded of the precedent set by women like Phoebe, Prisca and the many others who have taught, preached, evangelized, studied and ministered during the centuries. Nobody can be allowed to stifle the work of women through attitudes that have little to do with Christianity and everything to do with chauvinism.

Trying to be true to the faith and witness to others is a daunting task. But as I grew up in the church, it seemed to be the most exciting challenge imaginable. The letter to the Hebrews reminds us that we are surrounded by a great cloud of witnesses. As they stand with us, we can take strength from their example. We can show other women how many kinds of work and ministry are open to them, and so desperately needed from them, in this ancient church that will light our way into the next century and far, far beyond.

Growing Up Orthodox and Female

A Story from India

SHANTI VERGHESE

The healthy growth of a child depends on its environment, the nourishment it gets, the mental, physical and spiritual stimuli it receives during its formative years. The church, our mother, nurtures us and we in return give her our love and loyalty.

I belong to the Malankara Orthodox Syrian Church in India, which is believed to have been established by the apostle Thomas in A.D. 52. As an ancient church, it is a storehouse of traditions and customs – some good, some not so good. The topic of "growing up Orthodox and female" might be analyzed from the angle of a girl child who is born into the church, grows up learning its doctrines, accepts its traditions and customs and does not question the teachings of the church or her position in it, as this is part of her life and thought. On the other hand, a young woman who comes into the Orthodox faith at the time of her marriage must learn many things and accept a new tradition. The church is often very apprehensive about these "late-comers". As members of non-Orthodox, mostly Protestant denominations, they come with different ideas and beliefs. Their influence on the family and their reservations about the Orthodox church may cause genuine concern among the church leadership.

I belong to this second group. I came into the Orthodox fold at the age of 23. When my future husband and his father invited their bishop to our wedding, he seemed at first upset that a promising young member of his flock, from a family of staunch Orthodox believers, was about to marry someone from outside the Orthodox faith, the daughter of a theologian and priest of a non-Orthodox denomination of the Syrian church. Even strong embankments around a rice field sometimes crack and crumble due to the continuous lashing of water against them, he noted. His worry was that the onslaught of my non-Orthodox ideas could cause cracks in the walls of my husband's Orthodox faith. However, he said, he took comfort in the knowledge that in this particular case the walls were extra-strong.

While such fears are less common in the more ecumenical climate of the present day, they are still present. I believe it is necessary for women who come from non-Orthodox traditions to be given a proper induction into the Orthodox faith. The doubts and questions that arise in their minds, as they did in mine, about some of the teachings are sincere and genuine. Leaders of the church, clergy and laity, should be trained to listen with sympathy and answer with conviction. Here the lack of theological knowledge, especially among the laity, is a major obstacle. The sacrament of confession, prayers to Mary and the saints and special prayers for the dead were all new to me and difficult at first to accept. With encouragement from my husband, a visible exposure to the faith of hundreds in the church and a growing belief in the efficacy of such prayers, combined with an openness of mind inherited from an early liberal background, it has been possible for me to accept these teachings and practices.

The beauty and meaning of the Orthodox eucharistic liturgy is always a means of attracting others to its fold. This act of worship lies at the centre of the life of the community, blending families together in the expression of their common faith. As Leslie Brown says in his book *The Indian Christians of St Thomas*, "this service kept the Syrian Christians together down the centuries, even when they could not fully understand the meaning of the prayers and readings, sermons were infrequent, the Bible unknown and their customs and social life influenced by their non-Christian surroundings". However, to a new entrant in the church, certain prayers used during the worship on Good Friday are difficult to accept. I believe that the passages in which those who crucified our Lord are cursed are uncharitable in the light of Christ's teachings; and I hope and pray that a change will soon be made in these.

For the new recruit as well as for those born and brought up in the Orthodox faith, private confession has always been difficult. Confession in itself is good provided the priest who listens can counsel with knowledge, understanding and authority. He should have the insight and ability to understand and analyze the feelings of fear, sorrow, repentance or guilt of the one who confesses. If the priest is not adequately equipped, psychologically or spiritually, to deal with these problems, confession becomes meaningless. In the last few years our church has made concessions in allowing persons who wish to take part in holy communion to do so without private confession but after receiving absolution.

As I grew up further in the Orthodox way, I began to be more impressed by the place given to the Virgin Mary in our prayers and supplications. The position given to the mother of our Lord is next to the Lord himself. We have a large number of churches and cathedrals established in her name. We observe Lent in her memory and have long periods of fasting invoking her intercession. The entire church, clergy and laity alike, observes all this with great devotion and piety. The position of Mary as the Mother of God is accepted without question. But I fail to understand how a church which gives so much respect and veneration to the woman Mary is not inclined to give any place or position in its ministry and work to half its members just because they are women. Let us not forget that it was the women who waited at the cross on Calvary when the men ran away. It was to them that Christ appeared on that first Easter day. It was to them also that he gave the mission of spreading the message of his resurrection.

As an Orthodox woman and especially as a mother, my interest and concern is in upholding my faith and values and handing them down to the next generation. I see today strong cross-currents of new ideologies and views blowing across the church. The young people are being exposed to these intellectual onslaughts, which may be contrary to Christian values and traditions, and many succumb to them. The clergy, no matter how strong and well-prepared to deal with such matters, is not numerically adequate to meet these cross-currents. Wars are not won by generals alone. The ordinary soldier needs to be trained to fight. Women are good fighters for a worthwhile cause, but they need the weapons and the skills. They need a thorough knowledge of church history, doctrines, the faith and order of the church, the position of their church vis-à-vis other churches, the strong and weak points in its tradition and culture. Our women should be given the facility to study in their own theological seminaries. The correspondence course in religious education offered by our church is definitely not enough. Women need to attend classes in which they can listen to the views of knowledgeable people in their specialized areas in order to formulate their own thoughts and develop their own ideas. The women in our church have not yet started asking for ordination. They want only to learn and equip themselves so that they can impart their knowledge to the younger generation.

Through meetings of church women in different parts of the world in recent years, Indian Orthodox women have gained much exposure to the thinking and activities of other churches. We are now reasonably well aware of our responsibilities to the church and the church's duty towards us. We know that conducting Sunday schools and charity drives and attending prayer meetings and organizing visits to hospitals and orphanages – necessary as all these are – are not the only work we are capable of doing.

In the secular world, women are found in all professions, holding important portfolios and positions. Many have excelled in medicine, law, science and administration. They are found to be intelligent, efficient and hard-working, possessing a certain acumen in defusing difficult problems and situations. During the fifty years of Indian independence, the legal status of women has been raised. The state leadership has gained considerably from the expertise of its women officers in development, administration, education and health care.

Does the church not want the contribution that women can make in these fields? Women are capable of contributing positively in church administration, financial management, planning and policy-making at the parish, diocesan and central levels of the church organization. The constitution of the Malankara Orthodox Syrian Church in India declares that "all men and women who have received holy baptism and believe in the divinity of the holy Trinity, the incarnation of the son... are members of the church". However, when it comes to the parish, it is clearly stated that "all men who confess and receive the holy Qurbana and have completed the age of 21 may be members of the assembly". It is from these members that the managing committee of the church, which makes decisions and implements policies, is chosen – and women do not have a chance to be on it.

The Supreme Court of India held in a recent judgment that women could also represent the family in matters relating to church administration. However, our church has not yet accepted this as its policy. It should amend its constitution to include women also in the higher echelons of its organization. As I have grown in the Orthodox way, the gender discrimination shown by the church leadership has become more and more apparent to me. While the systems in the church bureaucracy are difficult to change, small mercies have been shown in the recent past. Now in our church at the end of the baptism service, girl babies are also taken up to kiss the altar; earlier it was only the boys who had this privilege. Women are now allowed to read the Old Testament lesson during the Qurbana. So far, however, not many women have actually done this, since at the parish levels it is still to be accepted.

The Orthodox Syrian Church in India needs to find ways to tap the tremendous energy lying dormant among its women and use this for strengthening its faith and its ministry. We are fortunate in being members of this ancient church – a worshipping church of men and women keeping alive the teachings of our Lord and Master. The traditions are kept and old customs practised. When we repeat prayers and chants that have come down to us from the saints and prophets of old we notice how meaningful they are even in this age and time. Tradition can be invigorating and energizing if changes are allowed to happen as new ideas and viewpoints arise. Such changes can bring a cohesiveness in thinking and unity in action in the community. Traditions and customs should never be outdated, retrograde and inhuman. They should encourage progress and openness.

The members of the Orthodox Church in India are spread out in different parts of the world. They live in alien cultures and societies. Very often they find it difficult to reconcile their traditional beliefs and practices with the liberal and modern trends in such societies. The mother church must be concerned about the growing generation of young people in such countries and how to keep them within the Orthodox faith. A woman who has grown up in this faith is always anxious about her children living away from the family and being exposed to influences which can undermine their faith in the church. I suppose this is a common problem of all Orthodox churches, and an interchange of ideas among our churches can result in some positive action.

The last few years of the Ecumenical Decade – Churches in Solidarity with Women have seen changes in many non-Orthodox churches. We see women being encouraged to develop their potential and accept responsibilities in the church organization. These churches have progressed in all areas as their women have contributed immensely towards it. I feel let down and discouraged when I think of what we could have achieved in our church if only the women were given opportunities to help.

While growing steadfast in the Orthodox faith, I also feel a responsibility to pray and work for the unity of the churches. The ecumenical movement has envisaged the growth of a new community of men and women in the church who believe in partnership and equality, who encourage and sustain one another through love and respect and who work unitedly for justice and peace on earth. When the churches attempt to come together ecumenically there may be many theological issues regarding faith and doctrines facing them which cannot be reconciled. Thus we must think of other areas in which we can cooperate and work together.

Human and life issues can bring people together. This will include confronting all the forms of degradation and violence perpetrated on nature and people. We are sent into the world to proclaim the teaching of Jesus our Lord through our words and our actions. Christian ecumenism should concentrate more on the unity of churches for the mission of Christ in the world. The Decade's call to the churches to practise in their day-to-day activities the values of love, peace, justice and truth will thus be answered.

It will be my prayer and endeavour in the coming years to see that the Orthodox church becomes an active participant in such a movement.

Young Orthodox Women in Russia Today

EKATERINA SHIBAYEVA

When somebody asks me about the particular problems of young women in the Russian Orthodox Church, I am not certain how to answer. In one sense, there does not seem to be much difference between my mother's activity and mine. My mother works on the parish council, I work on the Orthodox students council; my mother is helping our priest to write theological books, I am studying theology and write my own papers; my mother is responsible with some other women for organizing an Orthodox centre for children, I with my friends am organizing a new Orthodox youth centre. In this way, our tasks are the same, but we do them in different ways.

What is the difference between young people and adults? Some youth have had no negative experiences and thus they have more energy. But also they may not have had enough positive experiences or knowledge to work in the best way.

Let me say something about the young women's activities which I know about and in which I as a young woman have taken part.

The first and the most important duty of youth is to study. There are now two theological universities in Moscow, two in St Petersburg and a few in other cities where women can study theology. There is also an Orthodox medical college in Moscow, where young women not only study theology and medicine, but also work in the hospital. Often they explain to their patients what Orthodoxy is, teach them how to pray, bring some books and the like. We also have young people who are working in a similar way in prisons, though most of these are young men, because this work is very dangerous and difficult.

Another very important part of the mission of young women is working with people who have been converted. Women, especially young women, help converted women to feel themselves at home, to study and to live Orthodoxy. They help to prepare women for baptism.

There is one more specific youth mission work. When we meet our friends who are unbelievers (we have many of them), we have to "preach" in every situation: in lectures, in students' meetings and even at discotheques.

My focus is on this kind of activity. The main aim of our Orthodox students centre is to direct Orthodox students' activities. Eighty percent of our members are women, and they need a ministry in which they can help others. Our activities are extremely varied. On the one hand, there are Orthodox discotheques, in which we use music of Orthodox composers, which sounds like popular music but whose words have an Orthodox meaning, to bring young people to a thinking process. On the other hand, we organize students conferences, where we can discuss and explain our Orthodox views to people who call themselves "intellectual". We also organize summer camps for youth, restore churches in the summer and arrange pilgrimages to holy places.

Orthodox young women play the main role in organizing all of these events. Nevertheless, our primary duty is to study and prepare ourselves to be teachers, mothers, priest's wives, members and presidents of parish councils, church finance officers, lawyers, journalists, ecologists, doctors, nurses and so on – and what is most important, to be real Orthodox adult women.

Orthodox Women in Theological Education

CHRISTINA SHAHEEN REIMANN

As my husband and I entered the church hall after his ordination service, a man whom I did not know came up to me and blurted: "Please do not be offended by my question, but why would a woman go to seminary?" In introducing us to the parish as a newly ordained priest and his wife, the bishop had mentioned that I have a bachelor's degree in theology and education from Hellenic College, the undergraduate programme of Holy Cross Greek Orthodox School of Theology, and a master's degree in theology from St Vladimir's Seminary, but I had not expected my seminary experience to be the focus of events at a reception for my husband's ordination. Taken aback – and trembling with some strong dormant emotions – I managed to respond: "To learn everything I can about my faith and to share it in every way, so I can grow in Christ and live in the faith." I wished I had the courage to add, "Why wouldn't a woman go to seminary – and furthermore, doesn't every Orthodox Christian want to study theology?"

That unspoken response is rooted deeply in my heart and confirmed by my experience in the Orthodox church, which holds emphatically that "if you pray, you are a theologian, and if you are a theologian, you must pray". In contrast, this man's doubtless sincere question grew out of a simple equation – "seminary" equals "place where people study to be priests" – which does not correspond to the Orthodox Christian tradition though it obviously reflects many people's understanding of seminary.

Both men and women have been asking me this question ever since I first told people I wanted to study theology. Why would a woman study theology? You cannot become a priest – are you going to be a nun? During the course of my studies and afterwards, these questions conjured up many different emotions, but the most difficult part of responding to them is that I do not share the understanding of theological education on which they are based. My definition of seminary is far broader. For me, "seminary" equals "place for growing in the love and knowledge of God, in faith, truth and maturity in Christ". Going to seminary was a way for me to respond to God's call to serve him.

To me it was crystal clear why I wanted to study theology: I was called to it, personally and universally. As a baptized member of the Body of Christ, I am a vital part of the church, a means of communion with God, a sign and manifestation of the kingdom of God. Therefore, I have a responsibility to fulfill my calling as disciple and apostle, which is to communicate the gospel and to strive towards the growth, sanctification and well-being of the body. And the church has been commanded to be in continual mission by proclaiming, announcing and teaching the gospel to the whole inhabited earth: "Go therefore and make disciples of all nations, baptizing them in the name of the Father and of the Son and of the Holy Spirit, and teaching them to obey everything that I have commanded you" (Matt. 28:19-20). The church is made up of both men and women called to continue the saving acts of Jesus Christ for the salvation of humanity and the whole of creation. St Paul best articulates who and what the church is:

> There is one body and one Spirit, just as you were called to the one hope of your calling... But each of us was given grace, according to the measure of Christ's gift... The gifts he gave were that some would be apostles, some prophets, some evangelists, some pastors and teachers, to equip the saints for the work of ministry, for building up the body of Christ, until all of us come to the unity of the faith and of the knowledge of the Son of God, to maturity, to the measure of the full stature of Christ... Speaking the truth in love, we must grow up in every way into him who is the head, into Christ, from whom the whole body, joined and knit together by every ligament with which it is equipped..., promotes the body's growth in building itself up in love (Eph. 4:4-16).

St Paul goes on to say in 1 Corinthians 12 that the body has many parts and that each part is essential for the body's proper functioning. This belief was fervently practised in apostolic times. In the church of the first three centuries, clergy and laity constituted an organic whole within the ecclesiastical organization. Clergy and laity held an equal, responsible, active position in the church. We have the testimony of countless women who served as apostles, teachers and deaconesses during these times, witnessing to the theology of our church which teaches that as Christians and Body of Christ we are a royal priesthood, which is the foundation out of which the holy priesthood is called.

Let us not forget:

St Mary Magdalene – one of the Myrrh-Bearing Women, equal to the apostles, who was a faithful follower and servant of our Lord during his earthly ministry. She preached the gospel alongside St John the divine, theologian and evangelist.

Thecla – the disciple of Paul, holy martyr and equal to the apostles, who also preached the gospel and brought many people to the faith.

St Phoebe – prototype and first deaconess of the church, who is described by St Paul as "a benefactor of many and of myself as well" (Rom. 16:2).

St Nina the Enlightener of Georgia – who was a great missionary, travelling to Georgia, where she baptized the king, his family and many souls.

St Macrina – eldest sister of St Basil the Great and Gregory of Nyssa, who educated all of her siblings in the faith. Gregory himself named her "the teacher".

St Olympia – the deaconness of Constantinople and companion of St John Chrysostom, who theologized with one of the greatest theologians.

St Melania the Roman – who travelled through many lands doing good works and converting many to Christianity.

Our holy mother Xenia the deaconness – who educated many women in the faith.

The lives and ministries of these women show clearly that, by virtue of their relationship with Jesus Christ and thus their communion with the life of the holy Trinity, they not only knew their theology and faith but, each being a ligament, doing her part, they supplied growth for the body, building itself up in love.

So why would a woman go to seminary? Why would a woman want to study theology? Asking these questions only underscores that we need women and men to go to seminary to learn and live out their faith in the uniqueness of their persons and gifts. Each woman called to seminary studies knows why she is there. Some may be able to articulate it more clearly: "With my seminary education I want to be a youth director, or a pastoral assistant, or an iconographer, or a writer, or a missionary, or a choir director, or a pastoral counsellor, or a professor or..." Others may not so easily find words to describe their calling to study theology, but their commitment to the arduous and challenging life at seminary speaks for itself.

The kinds of women who study theology vary widely. The universal message of the gospel draws women from the four corners of the earth. At both Hellenic College and St Vladimir's Seminary I studied with women from all over the USA as well as from Canada, Greece, Turkey, Russia and Finland. They included:

– Women who have been active in their parishes since childhood, who are seeking to deepen their faith and understanding of the teachings of the Orthodox church, in order better and more fully to serve Christ.

- Converts who are striving to learn all they can about the faith so that they can better articulate and witness to it.
- Apostate women who left the church for varying lengths of time and returned convinced by the teachings of the Orthodox church, strengthened by their own "conversion" stories. They come back to the church with the fervour of one newly converted, whose only desire is to requite the love initiated by God, the lover par excellence.
- Wives of priests or seminarians, seeking to enrich their ministries.
- Daughters of priests, nieces of bishops, sisters of priests and bishops, nurses, geologists, mothers, historians, librarians, performing artists, linguists, musicians, iconographers, authors, teachers, single women, married women, nuns and theologians – to mention a few.

Pioneers, entrepreneurs and martyrs go to seminary. The experience of seminary for each woman is as unique as she is. Her response to her call will manifest itself in the person that she is in her given life conditions, where she is in relation to God, herself and her neighbours. And her work at seminary will also reflect these conditions.

However, the general ethos and *phronema* of seminary will be experienced in the same way by all women. And that experience can be summed up very succinctly: *the seminary is a place for men*. Women do not belong at seminary. This message, born out of our brokenness, is crystal clear and permeates every aspect of seminary life. Only rarely does seminary become a place for women. This happens when men turn towards the women and recognize, affirm, support and encourage them, acting out of grace and not brokenness, welcoming women as partners and vital members of the body instead of fearing and hating them.

My experience as an undergraduate was different from what it was in the master's programme. When I was in the college, all but two of my closest companions were in the school of theology. These friends experienced the same things I did: women's presence and involvement in the life of seminary was confusing. Similar to the puzzled man who asked me about seminary, most of the faculty and administration asked: "What do we do with women at seminary?"

Women were treated as second-class citizens who did not have a valid voice. They were not taken seriously for their desire to study theology, and could be patronized and even abused. Barred from certain classes, they were deprived of the full seminary experience. For example, it was thought that women should not attend the liturgics laboratory class because it does not apply to their work in the Body of Christ. However, that class contains theology that is not taught in other classes. It is essential for a proper theological education to be as well informed as possible about what we believe and practise.

At the time I attended Hellenic College, no women were permitted to take Byzantine chant classes. However, the dean of the school of theology encouraged me to come to the psalterion for the various services. "If you come," he said, "the others will feel they can too." Never mind that when I did chant some of my male classmates would leave not only the psalterion, but the chapel itself, insulted that they had to share it with a woman. Now these classes are open to seminarian wives and to others who wish to learn to chant.

Other classes could also be a cross to bear. Often a woman would be made to feel militant, feminist or invisible simply because she did her homework and contributed to class discussion. Her voice was not embraced as a vital part of the discussion, but was perceived as a threat to her male peers' masculinity and identity as seminarians. A woman has to fight to be heard, to be recognized, to be; then she has to put up with inane questions like "Why are you so defensive?" A woman's response to this broken reality can be manifold. If a woman is afforded the luxury of community with one or more classmates or faculty members, she can thrive. She will enjoy the many blessings that can come from being in the unique environment which seminary provides for the student of theology. She will succeed. If she does not have this *koinonia*, she may retreat, isolate herself, become paranoid and eventually turn on herself and others, fulfilling the prophecy that she does not belong at the seminary. Or she may internalize and repeat the abuse which daily attacks her.

There were few role models and no mentors for women at seminary. When we did have them, they were chased out. More often than not, the women studying theology were doing so without the spiritual blessing or financial support of their bishops. Nevertheless, many women who have been called to study theology at seminary endure. Though not seeing the light at the end of the tunnel, they keep their lamps lit and keep their focus on Christ, the light, who is our way, truth and life. Not knowing what the end result will be, what fruit it will bear, they simply answer the call to "follow me" and thereby fulfill the vocation of apostleship which comes to all who labour to announce the gospel – and among them were women.

As a student at Hellenic College I found the experience of the liturgy and the sacraments to be the unifying forces that heal, teach, transfigure our life. In the chapel, although the language used was not my native tongue, everything became clearer and illumined all relationships and work done on campus. Fortunately, my undergraduate experience did not crush my desire to study theology at the graduate level. At St Vladimir's Seminary, I enjoyed quite a different experience. Here, women were treated as persons and vital members of the body of Christ. Professors answered their questions and encouraged the women to express themselves. Women were respected for being who they are. Women participated in all aspects of seminary life, contributing to the multi-faceted workload that was primarily student-run. Hearing the services in English, my native language, I was able to learn the theology of our church and understand it. Chanting is done by a choir which everyone is expected to join. Still, there are few women to serve as role models to the women and even fewer women on the faculty.

The seminary experience for women is definitely the way of the cross. Yet we do not shun that cross. Rather, we recognize the seminary as a place where women as well as men are able to work towards acquiring the mind of the fathers whose

> main characteristic of theology was the living connection between their thinking and the Bible. Their whole theology was a living homiletic, dogmatic, pastoral or liturgical interpretation of scripture, which was for them a mystical encounter with the person of the Incarnate Logos, with Christ.[1]

We struggle, in the words of Dumitru Staniloe, to "make theology what it is, penetrating beyond dogmatic definitions to the reality itself by our direct and living contact with Christ as a person and with the Holy Trinity as a communion of persons", so that we can maintain the true theology of our church which, as Alexander Schmemann reminds us, "has always been pastoral, missionary and prophetic".

Seminary can and should be a place that assists the whole body in actualizing itself in the world. And like our fathers and mothers before us, we strive "to make theology an essential belief and a creative function in the lives of all, to make the *ekklesia* a genuine depository as well as an expression of love, sacrifice and an unselfish struggle for society" (A. Schmemann).

NOTE

[1] Fr Dan-Ilie Ciobotea, "The Tasks of Orthodox Theology Today", *St Vladimir's Theological Quarterly*, Vol. 33, no. 2, 1989.

Orthodox Women as Writers

LEONIE B. LIVERIS

A visitor to Constantinople from the new world, the diaspora of Australia, can only feel a novice pilgrim in the steps of the great women saints, martyrs and those known only to God who in their own way discerned the signs of their own time and witnessed to faith in both adversity and security. This empathy for the past is balanced by the struggle of the present, "living on the edge" in solidarity with contemporary women who seek equality in all aspects of life within the church, the family and community. Their work and struggle continue, despite the attitudes and practices of the church which define woman as distinct, different and diminished by her gender, notwithstanding the carefully affirming statements of their worthiness and special place in the church by laymen, clergy and bishops.

At the end of the 20th century, Orthodox women must take courage from the past to speak our concerns and our passions for and within the church. And when we do not have the opportunity to speak or to be heard, then we must write, as historians, sociologists, theologians, community workers, academics, mothers and daughters. Our voices have much to convey at a time when the world has never been so open to communication, both local and global. We have the skills; we need only the fortitude and commitment to our faith and to ourselves as Orthodox women.

Mary/Martha

Over the past decade, there have been efforts to raise the consciousness of Orthodox women to issues of concern through the written word. Most newsletters or journals produced by women, particularly in the United States, have until very recently been local or diocesan publications or for a specific interest group, such as the *Clergy Wives* newsletter. With experience of many other church women's groups which lack a network to share information, the women's desk of the World Council of

Churches has been instrumental in assisting Orthodox women to establish a universal network through a small journal published in Australia. Let me say a few words about the background and creation of the journal *MaryMartha*, for which I have been responsible since 1991.

During the 1980s, I was for some years the Orthodox woman member of the Australian Council of Churches Commission on Church and Society. Out of this emerged the Commission on the Status of Women, which was mandated to research issues such as domestic violence, poverty, ministry and inclusive language in worship. The reports were powerful. For the first time, a serious study of violence revealed truths to the churches which they were most unwilling to hear.

In 1988, the commission was relocated from Sydney to Perth, and I was appointed executive officer in addition to my work as coordinator of the women's desk for the state council of churches. The work of the commission was often "on the edge". Financial support from the churches for women's concerns was not always forthcoming. The church was accustomed to a situation in which women were kept busy providing the money for the work designated by the parish council, usually for "bricks and mortar" or mission societies. It was the federal government which provided funds for research on domestic violence and the women's department of the state government of Western Australia which funded the initial production of a quarterly journal, *Voices from the Silence*, and a yearly calendar. For the calendar we found hundreds of women, both secular and tonsured, living and departed, from churches and from other religions, to honour and relate their achievements and struggles for justice and thus to provide role models and icons for women of today.

The Ecumenical Decade – Churches in Solidarity with Women was launched in Perth in late 1988 with a liturgical service in which all the gifts of women were offered to the service of the church. We asked the bishops and clergy present to act for the full participation of women and to acknowledge all the gifts they were offered. In addition, the heads of churches were reminded of the presence of young women, who are barely visible in the church of today, for they can see more clearly than their mothers and older sisters how excluded women are from responsibility, ministry and equality with men. Regrettably, although the Orthodox are members of the council, no Orthodox priest was present.

In 1989, I was invited to be a member of the steering committee for the Orthodox women's consultation to be held in Chania, Crete, in 1990. We met in Cairo to discuss the theme "Church and Culture", with three sub-themes: human sexuality, ministry and participation and decision-making. At that meeting we realized how limited is the circulation of papers concerned with the issue of women in the church. I had not heard of the historic inter-Orthodox women's meeting in Agapia, Romania, in 1976, with its well-thought-out recommendations for the Orthodox churches until nearly ten years later. The meeting in Crete reviewed the work of Agapia and made most of the same recommendations again.

One outcome of the Crete consultation was a grant from Ecumenical Decade funds to launch an Orthodox women's journal that would publish papers about issues important to women, to be distributed across all Orthodox jurisdictions without control or direction of one specific church. I was delighted to take on the challenge of editing the new journal. The first issue was distributed at the WCC assembly in Canberra in 1991; and by July 1997 sixteen had been published. The papers and articles have been interesting – sometimes controversial, sometimes a bit conservative, but always providing much-needed information for Orthodox women around the world. *MaryMartha* has been widely distributed, not only to individuals, but also to college libraries, seminaries and bishops. Yet during the first six years there was not a single acknowledgment of it by a priest or bishop – not even a complaint!

MaryMartha has not only provided a forum for many Orthodox women to express their opinions, ideas and historical and theological research but has also been the medium to disseminate reports, addresses and recommendations from several Orthodox women's meetings. Without this modest journal, few Orthodox women would ever know of their Orthodox sisters working for change in both liturgical practices and traditional community attitudes.

The title *MaryMartha* was chosen to reflect the two potentials within us all: the church of Marthas, serving others, always busy with chores and family, symbolizing the role of servant and nurturer; and the church of Marys, acting beyond that idealized image of woman, affirmed by Jesus Christ who said "she has chosen the better part" (Luke 10:42). Mary and Martha do not represent either/or possibilities for women; rather they represent the potential in all of us.

The need for networking

The network of information among women in the Orthodox church is essential. Many of those in the diaspora have the privilege of access to the Internet with the World Wide Web and electronic mail. But those of us who have these possibilities should not forget that for most Orthodox women in Eastern Europe, Africa, the Middle East and Asia, the printed word remains the most important medium for access to ideas and challenges for change.

In addition, we have a responsibility to share ecumenically who we are, what we believe and how we practise our faith with our sisters in other Christian churches. For too long Orthodox women have stepped back from dialogue with other Christian women, as though we fear being changed by exposure to different dogmas and traditions. Many Orthodox women have not realized that our participation at ecumenical women's seminars has been promoted by the insistence of women staff of the WCC and often financially supported by the generosity of Protestant churches. We have much to be thankful for: their desire to hear our voices and to read about our life experiences, the diversity of our spiritual journeys and our liturgical traditions. Such involvement not only allows for dialogue and sharing, but also anchors us more firmly in our tradition. We should not be afraid or suspicious of ecumenism.

My own country takes pride in its unique concept and practice of multiculturalism. We strive to create a cohesive community that integrates different religions, languages, cultures and races. Certainly we do not always succeed, and within the community there are bigots, racists and intolerant people who are ignorant and sometimes dangerous in their hatred of those perceived as different. However, nowhere in the community are relationships better than among women working together against violence and discrimination, for equality in and access to the workplace, for adequate child care and simply for friendship. When Laotian, Italian, Turkish, Greek, Chilean and Lebanese women meet for English lessons, they do not sit apart because one is Catholic, one Buddhist, one Orthodox or one without faith. Drawn to each other by a common need, they share their personal strengths and concerns for the future with each other. The women are encouraged to write their stories, to sing their songs and to share their traditions and religious beliefs. Women enjoy learning and reading of each other's experiences and dreams for the future. The need to participate in the future for the sake of their family over-rides any suspicion that the "other" is someone to avoid, someone who might weaken our beliefs and tradition. This obvious and powerful example of the universal sisterhood of women convinces me that what women share in common is far greater than what separates us.

The challenge of scholarship

Orthodox women scholars like Elisabeth Behr-Sigel in France have written of the need for Orthodox women to break the silence imposed on them not by the genuine tradition of the church, but by social customs and convention.[1] Nearly twenty years later, she appealed once more to Orthodox women "to widen their horizons beyond the bounds of the narrow parochialism within which they are often tempted to remain".[2] Eva

Topping from the United States, a Greek and Latin scholar, challenges Orthodox women "to re-examine the androcentric prejudices in Orthodox tradition that have determined attitudes and praxis of the church even in these times".[3] More recently, Eva Adamziloglu, the first Greek Orthodox woman to attend the international conference of the Association of Women in Theological Research, stated that "feminist theology clearly concerns all areas of theology", and cited her own thesis, "Women in the Theology of the Apostle Paul" and the recent thesis of Constantinos Yokarinis on the ordination of women as examples of the application of feminist theology within the Orthodox church.

In addition to the more scholarly work undertaken within academic departments in Europe and the United States, other journals and newsletters are being published. Some are parochial and within a particular "ethnic" church; others are slowly gaining a wider readership. Journals such as *St Nina's Quarterly* and more recently *The Handmaiden* are addressing issues for women in the Orthodox church. Orthodox women are also contributing papers to professional journals in history, theology, anthropology and sociology. Some publications by women specifically address historical and social aspects of being in the Orthodox church, but the voice of Orthodox women still remains small compared to that of men – regardless of whether the message is conservative or confrontational.

Too few Orthodox women are willing to write for either public or ecumenical forums, particularly taking up issues raised by feminist theology or feminist scholarship in other disciplines. I do not accept the interpretation of this relative silence from Orthodox women as proof that all is well within all our communities and parishes. I cannot be convinced that, especially in the diaspora, there are only conservative voices, content with the situation of women in the church. When we so strongly deny being feminists, or having anything to do with the feminist agenda, we need to be reminded that it has been the feminist agenda and struggle, in both society and the churches, which has opened the opportunities for many women to be educated.

As I noted earlier, despite the series of formal meetings of Orthodox women promoted by the women's desk of the WCC since 1976, there has been little progress. The recommendations seem to go only as far as the desk of the bishop. My own observation is that most of these recommendations do not fully reflect the group discussions, keynote addresses or plenary sessions, much less the discussions around the coffee table. They do not truly relate, in bold, challenging and expectant words, what has taken place at the meeting. And the cautious language of the recommendations means that the final document can be easily ignored. There is no evidence that the church will actively and consistently promote such consultations for women nor give freedom to women to organize such consultations themselves. And we have not yet learned to claim the freedom ourselves and organize regardless. We need to take an example from our Catholic and Anglican sisters, who have claimed the right to meet and discuss issues of women in the church as an essential and urgent matter. We need to keep in mind the wise words of Kathleen Bliss, the first secretary for the WCC Commission on the Life and Work of Women in the Church, in 1952: "To say that women's powers to educate and succour have found an outlet in an immense variety of ways is not the same thing as saying that the church has made use of even a tithe of the vast reserve of talent and devotion which lay to hand in the persons of its women members."[4]

In order to discern the signs of the times, more honesty, more research and more commitment are demanded from us than from women in the past. It is necessary to acknowledge that we do not live in religious societies in these times, nor do we live in the fourth century. We have to admit how difficult it is to accept without question those writings of the early fathers which disparage women and their purpose in this world. When debated in the context of their times and knowledge and society, they can perhaps be understood, if not entirely accepted. However, at the end of the 20th century, it is definitely unacceptable that many priests still only refer to those biblical texts about women which affirm submissive and secondary roles for them, attitudes too often adopted by fathers and husbands. In order to stay in place with the Christian faith, many women absent themselves from the liturgical and eucharistic life of the church because they find no refuge, no solace and no appropriate pastoral care.

As women who remain in the church, we hope to contribute ideas and constructive programmes to the church. Orthodox women have much to offer with our scholarship, our research, our writings, our words and thoughts and, dare I say, "our theology". Many Catholic, Anglican and Protestant feminist scholars and writers are raising issues about which we are silent. Christian feminists debate the uncomfortable and confrontational issues of women's ordination, birth control, abortion, homosexuality, pre-marital sex, clergy abuse, domestic violence, in order to inform, assist and support those members of the church who are suffering and in spiritual need, in order to cope with the tragedies and dilemmas of everyday life. All too often, the response of our church and our bishops to these issues is either silence or condemnation without discussion.

I look forward to the day when many Orthodox women writers and scholars will enter the debates on these issues, acknowledging the reality of social problems that affect women and courageous enough to move beyond the esoteric and obscure theological theses that fill the shelves of academic institutions. Like Orthodox women, Catholic women concerned for the integrity and truth in the practice of their faith are also denied access to participation in the decision-making structures that determine their place in the church. Why are the writings of feminist theologians and historians so readily dismissed only because they are not Orthodox? Why the hostility to Orthodox women who challenge the canon laws and traditions that are derogatory to women, demean us because of our life-giving biology or exclude us from participation in the full sacramental ministry of the church?

As women's scholarship continues to grow in both secular and religious feminist writings, we must learn to discern from the wealth of material available what is relevant to our own lives and experiences, and learn to apply that to our own private personal and spiritual needs. The experiences of women from the past continue to come before us as women scholars, using their research skills and linguistic abilities, peel away the layers of the centuries. We are by turn dismayed and outraged, challenged and excited by the knowledge and writings of women who came before us and who lived lives of such noble action and faith.

It may well be time for Orthodox women to speak and write more frankly of their faith, their calling, their ministry and their sense of social justice in a world where we have not been heard or read. Perhaps we as Orthodox need also to be mindful of the critical words of John Chryssavgis about our typical practice: "We open the Scriptures and interpret with such certainty in ourselves and our supposed piety; we read the Fathers and use them to condemn our neighbour; and we learn the canons by heart in order to stigmatize those around us."[5] The church and our communities are surely capable of accepting questions from women, listening to their doubts and their challenges by reading their research articles without the automatic accusations of heresy and wrong practice. I hope that journals such as *MaryMartha* and *St Nina's Quarterly* will mark the beginning of opportunities for Orthodox women not only to write about the well-known women saints and celebrations of the church, but also to examine more closely the legacy of these stories for today. If the example of the saints, martyrs and ascetics is to guide women in their daily lives and faith journey, then the telling of the story must relate to the experiences of today.

Throughout the centuries the skills of reading and writing have been in the control of men, the church and the wealthy. Women were not so privileged unless the male members of the family deemed it suitable for them to be educated. It is not surprising to learn from new scholars and translators that, from the times of the early church, the monasteries were filled with women who wanted the freedom to read the Scriptures and live a prayer life in full knowledge of their faith. I suggest they may well have wanted a longer life as well, childbirth being the notorious cause for the early death of women. In this century, women are increasingly well educated and work in professions. We may have found an acceptable niche in the parish or diocesan office, we may teach in the theological seminary, we may even be given responsibility by the church to undertake particular roles, but we are not protected by the laws of the land nor are we considered by the laws of the church. We still require the "patronage" or favour of the clergy, the bishop or the male laity of the parish council. Without such patronage, we are like the women of centuries ago, deprived of the right to read and write.

If we are to withstand the criticisms against the emerging voices of Orthodox women, whom too many dismiss as caught up in "Western feminist rhetoric" that distorts the truths of Orthodoxy, we must reflect on the example of the courageous Kassiane, a sharp observer of human frailties, who expressed her opinion of those who lacked courage and commitment in a memorable phrase: "I hate silence when it is time to speak."[6] Kassiane defied the edict against the veneration of icons. By defending women against the slurs of an emperor, she lost any claim to the throne of Byzantium. How fortunate we are to have inherited her words and music twelve centuries later! An independent woman, abbess, hymnographer and poet, Kassiane encourages us from the past to speak out, to write, to push to the edges the definition of our place in the church.

In a paper on Kassiane, Eva Topping wrote: "It is time for Orthodox women to speak openly, to claim our history through research, writing and publication, to claim our equal rights in the church. Unlike Kassiane, there is no imperial crown at risk; rather, we stand to gain full participation and responsibility in the church."[7] At the point when women feel most keenly their exclusion from so much of the life of the church, when they believe their God-given talents, intelligence and faith are being ignored and diminished by the church, then it is time to listen to Kassiane and act. We can no longer be silent, for it is time to speak and to write.

Metropolitan Anthony of Sourouzh has said that the debate on women's roles of participation, and even ordination in the church, should take place "in a spirit of intellectual honesty and spiritual integrity... while hammering at the intellectual inertia of the Orthodox and the humiliating situation of women."[8] At no other time in history have women, as teachers and scholars, had more opportunity to contribute their intellect, their scholarship and their spiritual integrity. Let us dare to be wrong as we struggle to write our thoughts and our understanding of theology. We are all called to be theologians. Let us dare to dream our place in the church as one of full acceptance of women, created equally in the image of God. Let us dare to be prophetic voices, as we dare to discern the signs of the times.

NOTES

[1] Elisabeth Behr-Sigel, *Orthodox Women and their Participation in the Church* (report of the Agapia consultation), Geneva, WCC, 1976, p.17.
[2] Report from the Levadia meeting on "Orthodox Women in a United Europe", Nov. 1994.
[3] Eva C. Topping, *Holy Mothers of Orthodoxy*, Minneapolis, Light and Life, 1987, p.127.
[4] Quoted by Susannah Hertzel, *A Voice for Women: The Women's Department of the World Council of Churches*, Geneva, WCC, 1981, p.18.
[5] John Chryssavgis, *Homily* on Luke 8:41-56.
[6] Cited in *The Lives of the Spiritual Mothers*, Buena Vista CO, Holy Apostles Convent, 1991, pp.373-81.
[7] Eva C. Topping, "It is Time to Speak", in *MaryMartha*, Vol. 1, no. 4, 1992, p.8.
[8] Cited by Elisabeth Behr-Sigel, *The Ministry of Women in the Church*, Redondo Beach CA, Oakwood Publications, 1991.

Human Sexuality and the Body

An Orthodox Perspective

DESPINA D. PRASSAS

In his *Divine Names*, St Dionysius the Areopagite calls on us to "contemplate a certain one and simple nature of the peaceful Union, unifying all things to Itself and to themselves and to each other" (10.2). While the unity referred to here is that of God, Dionysius outlines a framework of how to relate to all that is around us. We are called to unify our thoughts, actions and relationships and to direct them towards God. All things must be understood in relation to God, to oneself and to those around us. This framework in fact closely resembles the Orthodox understanding of the holy Trinity. Each person of the Trinity exhibits a different hypostasis while maintaining the same essence. Father, Son and Holy Spirit relate to one another by way of mutual indwelling – *perichoresis*.

Just as Orthodox trinitarian theology applies to all aspects of church life, so too it applies to an understanding of human sexuality. The Orthodox tradition would disagree with those who think that sexuality has no place in Christian anthropology. For many, the problem here begins with the fact that sexuality is directly related to the body. A misguided understanding of the human body has grown out of remnants of Greek philosophical dualism combined with misinterpretations of scripture fostered by Gnostic influences and bolstered by selective reading of monastic texts. By contrast, Orthodox worship and life have always seen the person as a whole, well-integrated being though not complete in any sense, since perfection always awaits us.

Especially in the dialogue *Phaedo*, Plato draws a sharp distinction between the body and the soul. The body is the tomb of the soul (65d), leading it astray (65b). The contemplative life of the soul is better without the distraction of the body (65c). While there are times when Plato sees the harmony of beauty in the body and soul,[1] he more often describes the body as inferior to the soul.[2] It is a source of evil and an impediment to the soul's attaining of truth (*Phaedo*, 66). The soul is superior to the body (*Phaedo*, 94; *Timaeus*, 34c) and in opposition to the body (*Phaedo*, 80, 94).

Inevitably, this understanding of soul and body influenced many of the fathers of the church, who had been schooled in the writings of Plato and the Greek philosophers. Moreover, some passages in the New Testament might be read in a way that would lead to seeing the body as distinct from the soul and a cause of sin. Consider, for example, one of the gospel accounts of Jesus' teaching on adultery:

> You have heard that it was said, "You shall not commit adultery." But I say to you that everyone who looks at a woman with lust has already committed adultery with her in his heart. If your right eye causes you to sin, tear it out and throw it away; it is better for you to lose one of your members than for your whole body to be thrown into hell. And if your right hand causes you to sin, cut it off and throw it away; it is better that you lose one of your members than for your whole body go into hell (Matt. 5:27-30).

This passage refers back to the Ten Commandments. While the consequences of Jesus' message here were not meant to be taken literally,[3] this passage can be interpreted in different ways. One understanding could simply be that it is the members of the body which are the cause of sin and therefore unnecessary if one truly wants to be saved. It is possible to see in this passage the beginnings of a disembodied understanding of the human being. A distinction is being made between the body and something else – whether that "something else" is the soul, Jesus does not say. So, even though the passage concludes by referring to the desire to save the whole body, it is easy to see how it could be misconstrued as supporting the inferiority of the body.

The writings of St Paul have also been interpreted as denigrating the body or the flesh. A number of passages portray the passions of the flesh as contributing to the death of the individual (cf. Rom. 7:5; 8:5,8; 2 Cor. 10:3; Gal. 5:16,24). The flesh is set in opposition to the work of God, for "the mind that is set on the flesh is hostile to God" (Rom. 8:7). Through the teachings of the Desert Fathers and the 4th-century Christian anthropologists a clear distinction between "flesh" and "body" would come about.

But a closer reading may reveal a more nuanced understanding of what St Paul was trying to say in these passages. Many of them are set within the context of a relationship with Jesus Christ. In the passage just cited, for example, Paul has been speaking of a breach in one's fellowship with God:

> Those who live according to the flesh set their minds on the things of the flesh, but those who live according to the Spirit set their minds on the things

of the Spirit. To set the mind on the flesh is death, but to set the mind on the Spirit is life and peace (Rom. 8:5,6).

The mind which is set on the flesh is the mind which has no relationship with God. This mind idolizes the flesh or the worldly way rather than the way of God. And the mind cannot attain salvation without God. Thus the term "flesh" in these texts should not be understood as a denigrating term for the body but as a reference to one's vulnerability to temptation.

The flesh is fallen and sinful human nature rather than the human nature which was originally created to dwell in communion with God. This is supported by Galatians 5:18-21, which outlines the "works of the flesh" as including idolatry, jealousy, anger, selfishness, envy and dissension. The flesh is seen as the body/soul structure which has fallen.

> "Flesh" is not the same as "body". The term flesh... signifies whatever within us is sinful and opposed to God; thus it is not only the body but the soul in fallen man that has become fleshly and carnal.[4]

The desires of the flesh are the desires of the creature. The spirit is seen as the body/soul structure redeemed, or even better, the desires of the Creator.

St Paul would agree with this understanding of the human person. He portrays the body/soul structure as an integrated unity in 1 Thessalonians 5:23: "May the God of peace himself sanctify you entirely; and may your spirit and soul and body be kept sound and blameless at the coming of our Lord Jesus Christ." According to St Paul, the body, soul and spirit working together make up the whole human being. Or, to quote Bishop Kallistos Ware again, "the body... is an integral part of human personhood".[5]

Yet Christian writers partial to dualistic Platonic or Neo-Platonic philosophy have introduced a distinction between soul and body, denouncing any physical or material aspect of the nature of the human being. Augustine wrote that "whoever desires to restore himself to the state in which he was made by God... should condemn all corporeal things... There is simply no other way of saving the soul or of renewing it, or of reconciling it with its maker."[6] Similar comments can be found in the Gnostic literature: "Salvation belongs only to the soul; the body is by nature corruptible"; "The human body [is] an hindrance to gnosis with God."[7]

A selective reading of the monastic literature could also affect one's understanding of the unity of body and soul. St John Climacus refers in his *Ladder* to the body as enemy and the flesh as ungrateful and treacherous friend (Step 7 and Step 9); elsewhere he calls the body a gross and savage monster (Step 26). St Maximos the Confessor says the soul is nobler than the body (*Centuries on Charity*, 1.7); and Ilias the Presbyter urges his readers to reflect on the wretchedness to which the body is subject (*Gnomic Anthology*, 3.8).[8] According to St Thalassios the Libyan, it is the soul's task to guide the body; and St Peter of Damascus says the soul must use the body according to its own wishes.[9]

Such a selective reading misinterprets the monastic writings as a whole. From the earliest days of monasticism, we find St Antony acknowledging that the body is neither evil nor responsible for its misuse, but created for a good purpose, so that it needs only to return to its original nature. At the same time the movements of the soul include pride, self-glorification, insolence, hatred and envy.[10] Thus, while distinguishing body and soul, St Antony maintains the unity of the person, since both body and soul have their faults. Since all monastic texts refer back in one way or another to the teachings of St Antony, a closer examination of the writings of the above-mentioned fathers would reveal that they are functioning within the tradition of the church and, more specifically, were referring to the fallen body.

By the end of the fourth century, several very important Christian anthropological texts had appeared. The two most valuable were perhaps those by St Gregory of Nyssa: *On the Making of Man*, a completion of the *Hexaemeron* of his brother St Basil, and *On the Soul and the Resurrection,* a dialogue with his sister St Macrina. A third, *On the Nature of Man*, by Gregory's less well-known contemporary Bishop Nemesius of Emesa, was considered well into the mediaeval period also to be a work of St Gregory. All three texts look into the human person in the light of the growing medical understanding of the time – St Gregory from a more scriptural and philosophical perspective, Bishop Nemesius from a more systematic point of view.

While the fathers of the church may differ on whether the human being is tripartite (body, soul and spirit) or bipartite (body and soul), their understanding of the unity of the person is the same. St Gregory writes:

> For our purpose was to show that the seminal cause of our constitution is neither a soul without a body nor a body without a soul, but that from animated and living bodies, it is generated at the first as a living and animate being, and that our humanity takes it and cherishes it like a nurseling with the resources she herself possesses, and it thus grows on both sides and makes its growth manifest corresponding in either part (*On the Making of Man*, 30.29).

Body and soul are viewed as an integrated unity which expresses human life. The physical body is not a component of the person, but the total person's mode of existence. And this unity is important for the place of the human being in the world. In the words of Bishop Kallistos Ware:

> Man is able to exercise a mediating role [between the noetic and material realms] only because his human nature is essentially and fundamentally a unity... If his body were not part of his true self, but only a piece of clothing which he will eventually lay aside, or a prison from which he is seeking to escape – then man could not properly act as mediator. Man spiritualizes the creation first of all by spiritualizing his own body and offering it to God... In spiritualizing the body, man does not thereby dematerialize it; on the contrary, it is the human vocation to manifest the spiritual in and through the material... The body is an integral part of the human person.[11]

But this is no news to Orthodox Christians, given the importance of icons in the life of Orthodox churches.

The soul does not reject the body, but uses it for "every good work".[12] Body and soul work together for the salvation of the human being. Sin is the result of poor choices, not the result of the physical nature of the human being.[13] But most importantly, sin is defined as a separation from God.

If the body is not sinful in and of itself, what does this say about sexuality? Much of our conversation on sexual love is tainted not so much by wrong ideas and practices, as by "dissection of life, where physical activity is detached from the life of the spirit or the life of the spirit is detached from bodily experience".[14] We must look at sexuality or sexual life as an activity that involves the whole person, body and soul and spirit, rather than simply as an activity that involves our biological self. And here we return to St Dionysius the Areopagite: our sexual actions involve not only ourselves, but also our relationships to those around us and to God.

By not allowing God to take his proper place in our decision-making, we run the risk of sinning, of separation from God. When we exclude God, we will eventually replace him with something else, either a physical love or lover, and we engage in a form of idolatry which leaves no place for God. God becomes incidental to our life, taking a back seat to all our actions and to our desire to have more and more, a desire which really is reserved for love of God. Thus we start down the road of sexual obsession.

But sexual activity viewed in the context of love, in which God is not only the witness to but the source of our ability to love, is not obsession but a healthy expression of who God has created us to be. To love truly, in body, soul and spirit, is to move beyond oneself and beyond the other person to embrace God – which is the same as embracing the whole world. Our ability to engage in physical love is an activity sanctioned by God, since we are his creation and our body is "the temple of the Holy Spirit" (1 Cor. 6:19).

Our sexual actions also involve others besides ourselves and God. We need others in our life in order to know ourselves. God created woman so that man would not be alone (Gen. 2:18). To behave in a promiscuous way, to engage in sexual activity with just anyone, is to see the other person as an object, not as a person. When we see sexual activity as simply an action, devoid of any relationship with the other person, we are reduced to an animalistic state. We are reduced to a series of parts instead of the unity which is called person. There must be a meaningful, committed relationship between two people if sexual activity is to be that which works for the betterment and not the degradation of the person. Therefore sexual activity must be placed within the full sacramental context of personal relationship, this relationship being defined as a unity of thoughts and actions which takes into consideration one's relationship with God, oneself and the other person.

One of the clearest affirmations of sexual activity can be found in the prayers recited during the service of crowning:

> Holy God,
> who formed man from dust
> and from his rib built up woman,
> whom you yoked to him as a helper for him,
> for it seemed pleasing to your Majesty
> that man should not be alone on the earth;
> Now, Master, stretch out your hand
> from your holy dwelling place,
> and join your servant and your servant,
> so that by you woman is betrothed to man.
> Yoke them in oneness of mind, crown them in one flesh,
> give freely to them the fruit of the womb,
> the enjoyment of fair children.[15]

Sexual activity, the coming together of man and woman as one flesh, is crowned. If this activity were seen as sinful, it is doubtful that it would have been included in this prayer, much less the biblical text from which it comes (Gen. 2:24).

We need to reclaim our own Orthodox understanding of sexuality, which differs from that of other Christians. For those of us who live in countries where Orthodox Christians are in the minority, it is easy to be influenced by teachings on sexuality which are neither patristic nor liturgical in origin.

In the churches, the most common ways of dealing with sexuality seem to be silence and censorship. Either the topic is not addressed (apparently in the hope that it will go away) or strict rules and regulations regarding behaviour are imposed. This moralistic approach is simply not Orthodox. Our approach must always be relational, following the teachings of St Dionysius. How we live affects our relationship with others, with ourselves and with God. This is the framework in which we will find the freedom and love that come from God.

NOTES

[1] Cf. for example *Republic*, 3.402d.
[2] Cf. *Epis.*, 8.355b, *Laws*, 5.728d, 743e, 10.892a, 12.959a.
[3] Cf. James L. Mays, ed., *Harper's Bible Commentary*, San Francisco, Harper & Row, 1988, p.957.
[4] Bishop Kallistos Ware, *The Orthodox Way*, Crestwood NY, St Vladimir's Seminary Press, 1990, p.79.
[5] *Ibid.* p.64.
[6] *On the Greatness of the Soul*, 3.4.
[7] The former is a Gnostic teaching described by Irenaeus in *Adv. Haer.*, 1.24.5; the latter, from the *Hermetic Tractate* 7, is cited by Bentley Layton, *The Gnostic Scriptures*, New York, Doubleday, 1987, p.462.
[8] Translation from *The Philokalia*, Vol. 3, trs. G. Palmer, P. Sherrard, K. Ware, London, Faber & Faber, 1984, p.48.
[9] St Thalassios, "On Love, Self-Control and Life in Accordance with the Intellect", tr. in *ibid.*, Vol. 2, 1981, p.308; St Peter, "The Sixth Stage of Contemplation", tr. in *ibid.*, Vol. 3, p.135.
[10] St Antony, *Letter* 1,49; 1,74; tr. in S. Rubenson, *The Letters of St Antony*, Minneapolis, Fortress, 1995, pp.200,202.
[11] *Op. cit.*, pp.63f.
[12] St Peter of Damascus, "The Knowledge of God", ch. 16 in *Twenty-four Discourses*, tr. in *The Philokalia*, Vol. 3, p.255.
[13] Gregory of Nyssa, *On the Soul and the Resurrection*, ch. 3, tr. Catherine Roth, Crestwood NY, St Vladimir's Seminary Press, 1993, p.57.
[14] John Chryssavgis, *Love, Sexuality and the Sacrament of Marriage*, Brookline MA, Holy Cross Press, 1996, p.2.
[15] Mikro Euhologion, tr. Fr Evagoras Constantinides; publ. by the author, 1989, p.116.

Orthodox Women in Ecumenical Dialogue

TENY PIRRI-SIMONIAN

Not long ago I was invited as a staff member of the World Council of Churches to speak to a mixed audience of ecumenical partners and others about the ecumenical journey of women since 1948. I saw my role as *communicator*, interpreting to my audience how women in the ecumenical movement have discerned their place and role in church and society. It was clear to me that my primary loyalty on that occasion was to the movement as a staff member of the WCC.

At this gathering of Orthodox women, I see myself as one of the actors in the ecumenical process of discerning women's place in church and society. My own ecumenical involvement started in 1970 with the World Student Christian Federation and in 1972 with the World Council of Churches. As I sought to define my role in the ecumenical movement, one possibility was to adopt the agenda of my Western sisters in the movement. The alternative was to start from where the majority of Orthodox women in the churches were. It was clear to me that my relationship as a women to the ecumenical movement was conditioned by the ethos of the Orthodox tradition and the way Orthodox churches responded to a fellowship designed on a Western Protestant model. I opted for the second role, knowing this meant I would sometimes distance myself from current trends in women's thought and groups of solidarity.

I do not believe that these two roles – as "communicator" and as "actor" – are incompatible for one person. In essence, these two roles recount two different readings of the "signs of the times" in the ecumenical fellowship. They come out of the same quest of women to offer their gifts to the church and society. Each is motivated by the desire of women to affirm their vocation in this world as persons created in the image of God. In other words, they are two different ways of telling the same story, two sides of the same coin. When conducted with integrity, these efforts are equally valued by God. Our goal is to hear what the master said to his slave in Jesus' parable of the talents: "Well done, good and trustworthy slave; you have been trustworthy in a few things, I will put you in charge of many things; enter into the joy of your master" (Matt. 25:21). Our question is: after journeying together for several decades as Orthodox and other Christian women in the ecumenical movement, how can we recognize and multiply the "talent" we are given by God? We do this by using the gift of being created as women in God's image, and by assuming the responsibility that is ours by being called, together with men, to become co-creators with him.

Our journey has shown that we can put our common coin into proper use only by learning about each other, by understanding each other's concerns regarding the journey, by respecting the different speeds with which we move in our common quest, and, finally, by discerning an ecumenical journey for the glory of the triune God and for the imperative of standing up together as Christians for life-giving values and issues. Sharing with each other means listening to each other's stories – the ecumenical story and the Orthodox story. Discerning an ecumenical journey means setting together the common vision arising from our understanding of the church and being part of the church, that is part of the body of Christ the risen Lord.

The ecumenical story

Already at the time the World Council of Churches was founded in 1948, visionary women had put the issue of women's participation on the agenda. Two Orthodox women were present at the first assembly in Amsterdam, one from the Russian Orthodox Church, the other from the Syrian Orthodox Church in India. It was the latter, Sarah Chakko, who presented a report to the assembly on the "role and status of women in the church". As an outcome of this report, women's concerns became part of ecumenical thinking; and several years later Sarah Chakko was the first woman to be named as one of the presidents of the WCC.

For the next 25 years the main ecumenical issues for women were "integration of women's concerns into the whole life of the church" and the related issue of the "cooperation between women and men". Several study processes and consultations were organized during this period, which aimed at attributing a new significance to the understanding of community of women and men from ecclesiological and confessional perspectives. In preparation for the fifth assembly in Nairobi in 1975, a world consultation entitled "Sexism in the 1970s – Discrimination Against Women" was held in West Berlin in 1974. Its final report brought together the reports of working groups on women in politics, women in economic structures and education.

The Berlin meeting raised awareness of women's situation as a universal concern despite differences in cultural, racial, economic and political backgrounds. This awareness led the WCC to recognize that a new understanding of community was needed. In response to this consultation the Central Committee agreed that:

- public support should be given to the United Nations International Women's Year;
- adequate representation of women from member churches should be assured on all WCC boards and committees;
- a fund should be set up for the political, social and cultural development of both urban and rural women, especially those living at the subsistence level;
- a task force on sexism and language should be appointed to help eliminate sexist language, concepts and imagery from all WCC speeches and documents, beginning with the preparatory materials for the fifth assembly.[1]

Nairobi was the first WCC assembly to devote a plenary session to the question of women in church and society. As one of the speakers at this plenary, I had been invited to give a witness as an Armenian Orthodox woman living in war-torn Lebanon. My story was different from the other presentations. I spoke of the spiritual turmoil I felt as a person victimized by a meaningless civil war and incapable of contributing to its peaceful resolution. My voice was the voice of all peace-loving women and men. At the assembly I began to feel that my priority – which was the priority of men and women in the Middle East – was not an urgent priority for women's concerns at that point in time.

In response to the plenary session, the Faith and Order Commission was asked to incorporate into its study on "The Unity of the Church and the Unity of Mankind" a new emphasis on "The Community of Women and Men in the Church",[2] to be undertaken jointly with the sub-unit on women. This decision was also a call to the churches to start a theological and biblical enquiry into women's insights.

Within the WCC structure, the sub-unit on women in church and society encouraged reflection on spirituality, theology, ecclesiology and community – vital issues for the Orthodox churches as well. The mandate of the study on "The Community of Women and Men in the Church" (CWMC) was to encourage reflection on questions of theology and ecclesiology, participation and relationships which would lead to the unity and renewal of the church. Unfortunately, no Orthodox women were included on the advisory committee which the Central Committee appointed to oversee the work.

In 1976, a consultation in Agapia, Romania, on "Orthodox Women: Their Role and Participation in the Orthodox Church" brought together Orthodox clergy, lay women and men to discuss the questions raised by the CWMC study. The keynote address, "The Meaning of the Participation of Women in the Life of the Church", was given by Elisabeth Behr-Sigel, the prolific French Orthodox historian and theologian. The Agapia meeting identified several concerns, among them training the family for its missionary and liturgical role; the parallel life-style of monastic communities; the limited role women play in church and society and the need for further training so women can increase their skills; the lack of adequate religious training for women, which hinders them from participating effectively in parish councils and Sunday school teaching. Noting that women have always been active in serving the church, the consultation said they should be given the opportunity to participate in the decision-making bodies of the church. Regarding the ordination of women, the consultation recommended that the office of deaconess be studied and "re-activated".

As part of the CWMC process, the WCC distributed to member churches and other constituencies a study guide intended to stimulate sharing and reflection in groups beginning on the local level, then moving into a process of national and regional meetings. So far as I know, the Orthodox Church in America was the only Orthodox church which responded to the questionnaire and prepared a similar study book. The Middle East regional meeting was the only place where Orthodox women were visible and made an input into the study process.

The CWMC study culminated with an historic consultation in Sheffield, England, in 1981, which brought together a tremendous wealth of insights from different cultures and traditions related to the day-to-day life of the churches. Among the key speakers was Elisabeth Behr-Sigel, who gave a paper on the Orthodox tradition as a resource for the renewal of women and men in community. Sheffield concluded with a series of recommendations and a letter to the churches describing a new life in Christ.

The recommendations urged further WCC attention to such issues as the nature of ministry, authority and worship, inclusive community and attitudes in education. The consultation realized that preparing women to participate in the life of church and society is not enough; guidelines were needed to ensure the partnership of women and men in decision-making processes. Sheffield's letter to the churches recognized the situation of women in different churches without attempting to give a "normative theological judgment".

A month after the Sheffield meeting, the WCC central committee met in Dresden. Very few Orthodox women were present at this meeting.

Besides responding to the various Sheffield recommendations and endorsing the follow-up by WCC units, the central committee recommended that the CWMC study be incorporated especially into the Faith and Order programme on "The Unity of the Church and the Renewal of Human Community".

In this connection, a consultation in Prague in 1985 focused on what new understandings of the community of women and men in both church and world mean for the unity and renewal of the church. The consultation explored the continuing significance of the CWMC study, looked at new approaches to Bible study from the perspective of women, shared experiences of churches from diverse contexts and considered "fundamental ecclesiological and confessional perspectives", such as the Orthodox and Roman Catholic.

Some participants expressed frustration and pain over the ecumenical discussion of issues related to women and men in the church, arguing that the process was moving too slowly. Others expressed their appreciation of the development of the concept of *koinonia* – "a true community of women and men" – by the Orthodox. They said that "the concept of *koinonia* as a communion in Christ, a community based on relationship to God, where love rules, offers a theological basis for a vision of a community of women and men living in mutuality in the church".

The recommendations from Prague acknowledged that some voices had not been heard in the CWMC process. To stimulate discussion in those circles, it was proposed that "'case studies'... be carried out among Orthodox groups in different parts of the world". A study guide should be prepared, including "issues such as marriage, family life, the role of Mary, monasticism, etc. This study guide should be oriented towards regional groups in order that cultures other than Europe and North America be taken seriously." Furthermore, explorations of ecclesiological issues should "listen to and incorporate the experience of the church where it lives as a minority in the midst of people of other living faiths". Finally, Prague recommended, Faith and Order should consider how the ground-breaking work on "Scripture, Tradition, Traditions" from the fourth world conference on Faith and Order (Montreal 1963) could be developed "in such a way as to contribute to a fuller theological framework for ecclesiology".[3]

During the United Nations Decade on Women (1975-85), the WCC had encouraged member churches to give public support. However, when the UN Decade ended, there was a recognition that the churches had not sufficiently addressed the injustice within their own bodies and that an impetus was needed to encourage the churches to overcome the barriers to expressing solidarity with women. Thus on Easter 1988 the Ecumenical Decade – Churches in Solidarity with Women was formally launched as a way of reaffirming the WCC's commitment to "work for the full equality and partnership of women and men in the churches". The aims of the Decade were the following:

- empowering women to challenge oppressive structures in the global community, their country and their church;
- affirming – in shared leadership and decision-making, theology and spirituality – the decisive contributions women are already making in churches and communities;
- giving visibility to women's perspectives and actions in the struggle for justice, peace and the integrity of creation;
- enabling churches to free themselves from racism, sexism and classism and from teachings and practices that discriminate against women;
- encouraging churches to take actions in solidarity with women.

A second Orthodox women's consultation sponsored by the WCC, entitled "Church and Culture", was held in 1990 in Crete. Its aim was to provide Orthodox women an opportunity to discuss the goals of the Decade and to link these goals with their own situation in church and society. Three broad areas were discussed: ministry, human sexuality, participation and decision-making. The following is a summary of the recommendations:

- Ministry: A renewal of the diaconate is needed. The diaconate as practised in the early church, which was identical for women and men, has disappeared. The female diaconate has completely disappeared, and the male diaconate has come to be restricted to liturgical functions. Renewal of both will enrich the ministry of the church.
- Human sexuality: The church should acknowledge and study the sexual double standard for women and men, particularly the cultural implications of this for questions of human sexuality. The church should also address this double standard in its counselling of young people.
- Participation and decision-making: Conciliarity is the essential characteristic of the church's communal life. In the conciliar process, each baptized member of the church is responsible for the church and the unique gifts given to each person are necessary for building up the church. The gifts of all baptized should therefore be respected in the church. The church needs to clarify the scope of women's participation in its communal and liturgical life and, in its understanding of participation and decision-making, to separate the requirements of the faith from the tangled web of tradition, custom and culture.

Since 1990, the dialogue between Orthodox women and their sisters in other parts of the ecumenical family has continued through a series of seminars organized by the WCC Education office and the Ecumenical Institute in Bossey. These seminars (in 1992, 1994 and 1997) sought to provide a forum in which a constructive dialogue on spiritual and ecclesiological issues and matters concerning worship and the community of women and men in the church could take place. The themes of the seminars were (1) Feminine Images and Orthodox Spirituality; (2) Orthodox Spirituality and Spirituality Expressed by Feminist Theologians; (3) Authority and the Community of Women and Men in the Church.

The seminars proved challenging and enriching for both the Orthodox participants and other Christian women theologians. Since Orthodox churches displayed some reservations about the CWMC study and the Sheffield recommendations, these seminars have offered Orthodox women an opportunity both to reflect on and clarify the questions and concerns raised by the study and to hear the points of view of their Christian sisters.

This, then, is the historical context for the two consultations of Orthodox women in Damascus (1996) and Istanbul (1997). The immediate context was the mid-Decade process of assessing how the visions and hopes of the Decade were being expressed on local, national and regional levels. Two consultations were organized in order to recognize the cultural diversity of Orthodox women and to provide an opportunity for women representing all Orthodox churches to participate.

Many of the recommendations from the first consultation in Damascus reaffirmed those made in Agapia and Crete. The participants celebrated the fact that more women were being allowed to study theology and teach in Sunday schools. They noted with satisfaction that some women were participating in decision-making bodies in parishes. However, they regretted that the re-establishment of the order of deaconesses – though accepted in principle by several churches – was not moving fast. The participants also acknowledged with pain that the response of the church to questions of human sexuality within the framework of faith and culture seemed to be stalled.

The restatement and reaffirmation of earlier recommendations indicates the slowness of the reception process both by the churches and the women themselves. Nevertheless, it is important that the participants expressed the need to continue such meetings, organized in the future by the women from Orthodox churches themselves.

The Orthodox story

Orthodox participation has been marginal to the life of the WCC and the ecumenical movement. In addition to the problems arising out of their social and political situation, especially in Central and Eastern Europe, the former Soviet Union and the Middle East, the Orthodox churches have had reservations about the WCC's programmatic priorities. This has been further complicated by a tendency within the WCC to treat Orthodox participation as a token presence rather than an enriching resource. Naturally, then, the contribution of Orthodox women has remained limited as well.

Statistical information on the participation of women in WCC events is limited, and there is even less about the participation of Orthodox women. As noted earlier, there were two Orthodox women at the WCC's first assembly in Amsterdam in 1948. Thirteen attended the sexism consultation in Berlin in 1974. At the WCC's fifth assembly in 1975, 22 percent of the delegates were women, and an assembly plenary session was devoted to women for the first time. As mentioned above, I was the only Orthodox woman to take part in it. There were apparently three women on the delegation of the Russian Orthodox Church. The participation of Orthodox women in Sheffield consisted of one keynote speaker (Elisabeth Behr-Sigel), one WCC staff member (deputy general secretary Marie Assaad, from the Coptic Orthodox Church), some women from the Middle East and the USA and a man and a woman from the Russian Orthodox Church.

Intensified participation by Orthodox women as assembly delegates began with the sixth assembly (Vancouver 1983), where there were at least one or two women on every delegation, depending on its size. Here we may note the evolution of the participation of Russian Orthodox women in WCC assemblies. At the fourth assembly (Uppsala 1968), there was one woman, Nina Bobrova – a staff member of the Department on External Relations and a longtime member of the WCC central committee. At the fifth assembly (Nairobi 1975) there were three women; and in Vancouver there were ten women.

One Orthodox response to the CWMC study and to the Ecumenical Decade came in an inter-Orthodox theological consultation on "The Place of the Woman in the Orthodox Church and the Question of the Ordination of Women", organized by the Ecumenical Patriarchate in Rhodes in 1988. Its conclusions highlighted theological approaches to the mystery of the Incarnation and the church, the priesthood of Christ, the "Adam-Christ" and "Eve-Mary" typologies, the male character of the "sacramental" priesthood, and Christ and the Theotokos in the recapitulation of humanity. It also singled out two special concerns: the equality and distinctiveness of women and men; and fuller participation of women in the life of the church. The report ends with a section on the challenges posed by feminist theology in non-Orthodox churches, written by the US Orthodox woman theologian Kyriaki FitzGerald. Unfortunately, the Rhodes consultation did not set up a process to follow up the implementation of its recommendations, nor did it establish procedures to measure their impact on women at the parish level.

Within the ecumenical movement the contribution of the Orthodox churches to ecumenical thought – through the concepts of *koinonia* and laity, through trinitarian theology, through their understanding of the sacramental nature of membership in the Body of Christ, of the priestly nature of the Body of Christ, of one spirituality in the Body of Christ and of the saintliness of all the baptized – is widely acknowledged. All of these Orthodox ecclesiological and theological approaches shed new light on the understanding of the community of women and men in church and society. Unfortunately, these important contributions have not been sufficiently and substantially pondered by Orthodox women and men in recent times.

Orthodox women are aware that it is thanks to the WCC that women from the two families could come together to affirm the common basis of their theology, to reflect together, to deepen their faith together and to raise sharp questions which will help them continue their pilgrimage in this world. It is also thanks to the WCC that all Christian women can discover their differences and commonalities and grow together.

Discerning together ecumenically

What can be learned from the two "stories" – the ecumenical and the Orthodox? The first point I would underscore is that trust-building is the precondition to planning a journey together, both among Orthodox women and ecumenically. This means assuring one another that we know who we are, what our histories are, what our traditions say to us and what our stereotyped images of one another are. It also requires expressing our respect towards one another irrespective of differences in thinking and acting. Finally, it involves affirming that we are all committed to building a community in diversity among women.

Personally, I have learned many things through my contacts within the ecumenical movement and in inter-Orthodox relations. These contacts have pushed me to study more deeply the ecclesiology, theology and tradition of my own church, to seek answers to the questions coming from the ecumenical movement within my own tradition and within the larger Orthodox family, and to discern ways of enriching my commitment to women's concerns in church and society. My ecumenical contacts have helped me to understand my own roots better; and they have also made me more tolerant towards other points of view.

For example, the ecumenical concern for the ordination of women led me to research the question of the diaconate in my church. I discovered that the diaconate of women as an ordained ministry continued into our century. Similarly, I have been helped to understand the Orthodox concepts of ministry and laity in the church.

The search for spirituality through images and symbols in the church has encouraged me to find out more about my patron saint, St Herepsimé. Recently, I discovered with joy that St Nina and St Herepsimé started their journey together. St Herepsimé and another companion, St Kayané, who remained in Armenia, were the first Armenian Christian martyrs; from their blood the Armenian Christian nation was born in 301.

I am sure as we continue this journey together, first as women representing the two Orthodox families together, we shall discern our vocation in this troubled world. I am also convinced that our discernment cannot be complete unless we show good will and love to our sisters in the ecumenical movement and seek to learn from their experiences.

The Orthodox women's meetings in 1996 and 1997 have taken place on the eve of the 50th anniversary of the founding of the WCC and in the context of the conclusion of the multi-year study process on the Common Understanding and Vision of the WCC and preparations for the Council's eighth assembly (Harare 1998), with its theme "Turn to God – Rejoice in Hope". The coming together of all this with the end of the Ecumenical Decade – Churches in Solidarity with Women, and the need to set new priorities in this area make this an ideal moment to discern the future together and a great opportunity for Orthodox and other Christian women to give value to our common gifts by setting a common agenda for the next period.

To arrive at a common agenda, I propose two steps. The first is to deepen our reflection on certain concepts and themes. The ones I will suggest here come out of my personal experience, study and reflection. Some of these are common to all Christian women, but need prior reflection separately in their confessional families. Some are pending questions arising out of the 1981 Sheffield report. Some arise from various Christian confessions and have been raised by women during the Bossey seminars mentioned earlier. My discovery of the different interpretations given to these themes and concepts has enriched my ecumenical experience.

1. Ecclesiology. What is the church? What is the place of inclusive community – of lay and feminist paradigms of community – in the church? What do Orthodox perspectives on these have to say to women in the ecumenical movement?

The WCC's Vancouver assembly (1983) called for "the development of a community of healing and sharing within the WCC and the member churches where women, men, young people and children, able and disabled, clergy and laity, *participate fully* and minister to one another". "Participation" was defined as implying "encounter and sharing with others, working and making decisions together in styles that enhance inclusiveness, and living together as people of God".[4] Some women within the ecumenical movement have criticized this definition of participation as too broad and too weak. Personally, I find it to be very close to the Orthodox women's experience of church and community. Would an interpretation of this statement by Orthodox women bring a new dimension to the understanding of participation? Furthermore, the phrase "living together as people of God" suggests the beginning of the journey towards salvation. According to the Orthodox understanding, salvation happens in community with God and in relation with others and God. Would a discussion by women on these two approaches contribute to the better understanding of the community of women and men in church and society?

2. *Images and symbols.* Both Orthodox and other Christian women understand the importance of images and symbols in defining oneself in relation to the other. An important first step towards respecting each other's differences and learning from each other's traditions and experiences is understanding what these images and symbols represent and what they mean to different women. Some of the issues that come up in this connection are inclusive language (the symbolism and power of language); the place of icons in the church and in the lives of Orthodox women; the Mother of God, Theotokos, the beginning of new humanity; the Orthodox women saints, prophets, martyrs and what they say to women today.

3. *Understanding each other's ecclesiology within the context of the world today.* Ecumenical reflection on church unity has shown that many tensions around such important issues as scripture and community in fact arise from different understandings of ecclesiology. To what extent do these tensions influence women's solidarity in the ecumenical movement?

4. *The centrality of the eucharist*, especially for our discussion on building community in the church. How does this contribute to the understanding of ministries in the church in an open ecumenical women's dialogue?

5. *The Orthodox understanding of the "sacramentality of all the baptized"* in the context of the ministries of women in the church. How does this concept relate to the notions of hierarchy and authority in the church?

6. Faith and culture. This issue has been on the ecumenical agenda since the early days of the movement. It has been extremely controversial in relation to certain practices of the church regarding women. How can women break through these tensions?

7. Story-telling as a method of learning. Talking to the past tradition (through liturgy and through the lives of the saints) and using that tradition to gain insight into the present and the future are important elements of how Orthodox women live and express their faith in different cultural contexts. Other Christian women theologians may affirm identity within the framework of community through three-generation story-telling. How similar or different are these two approaches? It could be helpful to look into these two approaches and discover the types of "spirituality" they engender.

These are just a few examples from my experience of possibilities for discerning together. I am sure that the moment real dialogue begins between Orthodox and other Christian women in the ecumenical movement, the learning experience will be enriched by many new themes and concepts. Such dialogue should help us to discover similarities and affirm differences; and it should help to move the ecumenical process further ahead. To assure the success of this dialogue, it is absolutely necessary that the reflection take place in mutual trust and within a space where differences can be stated frankly and heard properly.

The second step I would suggest reiterates a recommendation from the Vancouver assembly which has not to my knowledge been implemented:

> The Orthodox churches should take the initiative to provide simple study material and information on the Orthodox church and the role of women, for the benefit of non-Orthodox women and men. This information would greatly strengthen the understanding and sisterhood between women of different confessions. The WCC should assist in this exercise. While the position of Orthodox women needs to be respected, the ordination of women must still be kept actively on the ecumenical agenda.[5]

In order for women's participation in church and society to become a concern of the whole church, the women in the ecumenical movement must not drag Orthodox women behind them. Nor should Orthodox women feel isolated from the movement. The WCC should provide the space for open and sincere dialogue among women. At the same time, no matter how limited our resources are, we Orthodox women should start discussing among ourselves. As recommended in Vancouver, women should work together to produce study materials that will help women in the fellowship to build right relationships with one another.

NOTES

[1] As summarized by Ans J. van der Bent, *Vital Ecumenical Concerns: Sixteen Documentary Surveys*, Geneva, WCC, 1986, p.199.
[2] Cf. *Minutes* of the 29th meeting of the WCC central committee, August 1976, p.96.
[3] Cf. Thomas F. Best, ed., *Beyond Unity-in-Tension: Unity, Renewal and the Community of Women and Men*, Geneva, WCC, 1988, esp. pp.162f.
[4] David Gill, ed., *Gathered for Life* (official report of the WCC's Vancouver assembly), Geneva, WCC, 1983, p.255.
[5] *Ibid.*, p.58.

Defining Ourselves as Orthodox Women

MARIE ASSAAD

The topic assigned for this presentation – to survey recent developments and challenges related to the participation of women in church and society – is of course an impossible one, especially perhaps at a time when women and their role in development is a central issue in international discussions. Those who have followed the five major United Nations conferences of the 1990s – Rio de Janeiro (environment and development), Vienna (human rights), Cairo (population and development), Copenhagen (social development) and Beijing (women) – know that the most intensive discussions and disagreements during the deliberations in these international forums have centred on women, their rights and responsibilities.

To make the assignment manageable, I shall limit myself here to comparing what was revealed by two 1985 studies of the World Council of Churches with the preliminary results of the extensive programme of team visits the WCC undertook in 1994-95 at the midpoint of the Ecumenical Decade – Churches in Solidarity with Women. I will then share some of my experiences from working with women at the grassroots since my return to Egypt from Geneva in 1986.

Few signs of change

The 1985 studies were undertaken in connection with the end of the United Nations Decade for Women. One, based on a set of questions sent to the churches, was designed to assess the nature and extent of women's participation in the churches. The second, entitled "Women, Religion and Sexuality", sought to discover how various world religions define the role of women and deal with women's bodies and women's sexuality. The eight women – from Africa, the Americas, Asia, Australia-New Zealand and Europe – who took part in this study were adherents of eight different religious traditions (Buddhist, Hindu, Jewish, Muslim and Christian – Orthodox, Protestant and Roman Catholic). They were theologians, ordained priests, social scientists and activists. Besides meeting together several times, each spent a year researching original sources to find out how the teachings of her own religious tradition approached these issues.

The mid-Decade reports I have used here covered visits to about 250 WCC member churches and some 500 women's groups. Subsequently, about 80 more churches and 100 more women's groups were visited. The visitation programme concluded with a team visit to the offices of the WCC in Geneva to reflect on the Council's own commitment to follow up the goals of the Decade.

In short, the reports of the mid-Decade visits have largely reconfirmed what was discovered in the 1985 survey by the WCC women's desk: that in all the member churches of the WCC – Western and Eastern, Protestant and Orthodox – women constitute more than half the congregations or parishes, but their number decreases as we move up the church structure, almost disappearing at the top of the hierarchy. Although many Orthodox churches were still to be visited at the time of this report, my own experience leaves me little doubt that few Orthodox women are present even in local church boards. Yet despite how little churches take account of the concerns of women, the reports told again and again of the deep love women have for their churches and their readiness to commit themselves to the service of the churches.

The mid-Decade reports have also confirmed what the 1985 study on "Women, Religion and Sexuality" found regarding the role of culture and its impact on religious teachings: namely, that "cultural and political contexts play a more influential role in determining the practice of the churches towards women than do theology and tradition".

The study revealed how all religions have been interpreted by men. The researchers were surprised to note that although their religions were different in nearly every other aspect, there was a great deal of similarity when it came to the definition of women, their bodies and their sexuality. All religious traditions include teachings which in theory elevate women to the highest level; in practice, women are relegated to a lower position in both church and society. The researchers could not help concluding that when it comes to teachings about women, all their religions were influenced by the patriarchal values that have always dominated relationships, particularly in religious institutions.

The mid-Decade reports on women's involvement in theological education have confirmed what was learned in 1985. Although the number of women enrolling in theological schools is steadily increasing, the percentage of women in faculty and administrative positions remains extremely low. Should we not agree then with the team report that now that women are becoming more *visible* in theological institutes, they should also become more *audible*? The libraries of too few theological schools include feminist literature; and the curricula of too few include courses on theology from women's or feminist perspectives. As far as Orthodox theological schools are concerned, in Egypt I know of a few women theology teachers, but teaching feminist literature or teaching theology from a feminist perspective would be anathema.

We may agree with the report of the visits that "there is a significant increase in awareness of women's concerns". But there is also a backlash, exacerbated by increasing religious fundamentalism. The first victims of the tendency to interpret scripture literally are women. They are the first to be told to take a secondary position and to confine their role to that of wife and mother. We need to read scriptures in the context of the present, being aware of the difference between the cultural and historical setting of the past and the present. Women in particular have an active role to play in re-reading scripture according to our new awareness of ourselves and our role in society.

Where are Orthodox women in all this change? How do others define us and how do we define ourselves? Where do we take our struggles for gender equality and justice for women?

It is recognized that most of the women in our Orthodox churches are very faithful and loyal to the church and are ready to serve it at all times, in humility and obedience. Anca-Lucia Manolachi, a Romanian Orthodox theologian, has written, "the Orthodox woman is by far more Orthodox than men, more submissive, more full of mercy towards the poor and more faithful to the message transmitted by the clergy".[1] Building on this statement, Elisabeth Behr-Sigel, an Orthodox professor in Paris, writes:

> Women feel at ease in the warm liturgical atmosphere of the parish; they are in a comfortable cocoon and ask no questions as if the social life outside had no connection with the rituals of the liturgy. It is out of laziness rather than Christian humility on their part that women do not bother to ask themselves whether their Christian responsibility does not require them too to play a more active part in the spiritual guidance of the community.[2]

Are these descriptions of our situation as Orthodox women overstated? How do we truly define ourselves? Do we not tend to adhere to a theology of sacrifice and suffering, and if we are ever victimized by our husbands or menfolk, we are admonished to be patient and pray. Poor women in particular are often asked to be patient, to pray, to bear their cross until they get their reward in heaven. Is this not one expression of our Orthodox spirituality?

Many of us, though deeply rooted in our Orthodox faith and identifying profoundly with it, are frustrated by this emphasis on obedience and submission. We cannot help reacting, perhaps with anger, to the many forms of inequality and abuse on the basis of gender. The team visit reports have confirmed what we see and hear around us of "the unspeakable violence that is being perpetuated daily".

Fortunately, some women have now decided to break the "culture of silence". Women around the world, inside and outside the churches, are learning to share their suffering and to encourage one another to overcome apathy and obedient submission to teachings that alienate and subordinate us. We are learning to say No to whatever is denigrating and unjust, especially to helpless women who have been economically and educationally deprived.

Regarding the theology of sacrifice and suffering, the team report expresses well what many of us feel:

> A theology of sacrifice and suffering when applied only to women, imposed on women and taught in order to keep them subjugated, is harmful to women and dangerous for the theology of the church. It hinders women's liberation and in turn men's liberation, and it distorts the purposeful will of God.

When the churches do not support women in their struggle against patriarchal values, some of these women, although remaining faithful to the church as their spiritual home, will take their struggles outside church structures. They join other men and women in civil society who believe in their mutual liberation from the shackles of patriarchy that has ruled the world and our religious life for far too long. We need to help free our gospel teaching from the cultural influences that have shrouded its true message as "one gospel that frees us all, men and women, and makes us precious and equal in the sight of God".[3]

Pain and hope at the grassroots

My present ministry is serving with women at the grassroots level, listening to their stories of pain. Working together with them for our mutual empowerment has become a very rewarding task. Yet I do not perform it under the aegis of my church. The Coptic Orthodox Church remains my source of spiritual nurture, but it is not my place of involvement in society. I do this work as a volunteer in a local non-governmental organization, in which we are able to relate to women of other denominations and other faiths.

The work in which I am involved is among the most downtrodden Egyptians in Cairo – the household garbage collectors known as the *Zabbaleen*. For more than fifty years, these people, who now number around

25,000 in several settlements around Cairo, have earned a meagre living by collecting and sorting the refuse of the rich. They have toiled in silence, accepting life in hazardous conditions, living among the animals they breed on the remains of the food they collect. And they give fresh value to the growing amounts of refuse from a consumer society by carefully sorting it for recycling and returning the raw materials to the industrial stream.

The women are the worst victims of the difficult environmental and social conditions of this area. For in addition to the burden of an unhealthy environment, unhealthy work, neglect, illiteracy and poverty, they bear the full burden of harmful traditional practices derived from the patriarchal values that victimize women and men alike.

Let me relate some small vignettes from a typical life story of a girl growing up in Mokkattam, one of the settlements of garbage collectors. A mother gives birth to a girl child. Her neighbour, who has just had a boy, is celebrated by the family, and the neighbours offer her all kinds of food. The mother of the girl is left to herself to lament her fate and accept the blame for it.

On the tenth day, the *daya* or traditional birth attendant comes to circumcise the girl, using a razor blade to remove her external genitalia partially or completely, so that she may grow up sexually subdued and thus rendered acceptable for marriage some day.

When the girl is seven or eight years old, she cannot go to school, because the family is poor and preference is given to her brother, the future bread-winner. Moreover, she has to help her mother with the many household chores, particularly in caring for her younger brothers and sisters, who keep coming at a rate of one a year.

By the age of 14 – two years below the legal age of marriage in Egypt – she must marry. On the wedding night, she has to undergo a virginity test, which consists of the breaking of the hymen, either by the *daya* or by the bridegroom himself. The blood is then publicly displayed to the wedding guests.

From the first month of marriage, the girl is expected to become pregnant, and is blamed for every month of delay. And woe to her if she gives birth to a girl.

The young wife lives in constant fear of being forsaken by her husband or losing him due to premature death before her sons are old enough to care for her. She has never been given any education or skills which would enable her to work outside the home. She lives in an extended family setting, under the rule of her mother-in law who, having herself been oppressed as a female, now perpetuates the oppression on this newcomer to the household. Any act of disobedience or protest on the girl's part earns her a violent beating from her husband or his father. If she has the courage to complain to the priest, she will be told that it is her duty to be obedient to her husband and his family.

While the misery of these women appears shocking to us, it is simply an extreme form of the patriarchy that is prevalent in our societies and affects us all. It appears in other, more subtle ways in the means by which women are marginalized and excluded from decision-making in the church and society.

Yet despite the violence manifested against the young girls of Mokkattam and the painful lives that await them, they are full of hope and faith. Seeing their enjoyment of the few gifts of life and their enthusiastic response to new opportunities has been a most rewarding experience to those of us who are privileged to work with them. Both we and they learn to define ourselves better and are empowered to remove what Mercy Oduyoye has called the "stone of fear of human sexuality, the stone of men's power over women and the stone of violence against women".

For how long will we allow the church and society to socialize boys for domination and girls for subjugation? Should we not – for the sake of every poor and oppressed woman – work together to challenge our churches to break the shackles of patriarchy and to help raise the prophetic voice of the gospel of justice and liberation? Should we not as women and men liberated by Christ work in partnership, each according to her or his God-given gifts, to free ourselves, our churches and our societies from the gender prejudices that are so rampant in our world?

NOTES

1 Anca-Lucia Manolachi, in Jeanne Becher, ed., *Women, Religion and Sexuality*, Geneva, WCC Publications, 1986, p.176.

2 Elisabeth Behr-Sigel, in *ibid.*, p.187.

3 S. Wesley Ariarajah, *Did I Betray the Gospel?*, Geneva, WCC, 1998, p.47.

Women Deacons

A Brief Review of Ancient Evidence

KYRIAKI KARIDOYANES FITZGERALD

Biblical evidence

The earliest references to women deacons are found in the writings of St Paul. As with all the ancient orders of ministry, however, it is difficult to trace in a clear and comprehensive manner the historical development of the order of the woman deacon or "deaconess", especially during the first four centuries of the church.[1] The limited number of documents which mention this order are not comprehensive. Moreover, it is evident that in the early church practices regarding all orders of ministry differed from place to place and from one historical period to another.

We do know that by and large the order of the women deacons flourished in the Christian East until the Middle Ages. In Western Christianity, on the other hand, this order was generally discouraged (and so is even more difficult to trace). Evidence suggests that various aspects of the ministry performed by the ordained deaconess in the Christian East were taken up in the Christian West by other women, especially by widows and later by nuns. Nevertheless, there are noteworthy examples of this order surviving in some form in parts of Western Europe well into the Middle Ages. However, since references to the deaconess are largely absent from the Western fathers, historians have often identified this ministry as an "Eastern usage" which was accepted in certain parts of the church in Western Europe. Clearly there was no practice or understanding of the responsibilities, position and qualifications of women deacons which was universal throughout the early church.[2]

We do know that the order is traced to the apostolic period especially by the Eastern fathers. The New Testament provides us with some limited references to the ministry of women deacons. One is in the first letter to Timothy:

> Deacons likewise must be serious, not double-tongued, not indulging in much wine, not greedy for money; they must hold fast to the mystery of the

> faith with a clear conscience. And let them first be tested; then, if they prove themselves blameless, let them serve as deacons. Women [in this office] likewise must be serious, not slanderers, but temperate, faithful in all things. Let deacons be married only once, and let them manage their children and their household well; for those who serve well as deacons gain a good standing for themselves and great boldness in the faith that is in Christ Jesus (1 Tim. 3:8-13).

Because of differences in manuscripts and interpretations, not all commentators or translations recognize a reference to women deacons in this passage – in contrast to a number of early Christian commentators, including St John Chrysostom.

The other significant New Testament reference to a woman deacon is St Paul's commendation of Phoebe, to whom he clearly refers as a deacon (*diakonos*) of the church of Cenchreae:

> I commend you to our sister Phoebe, a deacon of the church at Cenchreae, so that you may welcome her in the Lord as is fitting for the saints, and help her in whatever she may require from you, for she has been a benefactor of many and of myself as well (Rom. 16:1-2).

While some would argue that the Greek term *diakonos* here should be understood as a "helper" or "minister",[3] the early commentators, especially in the Christian East, do not support this, clearly recognizing the significance of Paul's affirmation of the presence of women deacons and his reference to the ministry of Phoebe. As St Stephen became the prototype for male deacons, St Phoebe came to be seen as a prototype for female deacons.

Patristic evidence

Writing during the third century, Clement of Alexandria, one of the first commentators on Paul's letters, clearly recognizes the importance given by the apostle to Phoebe's ministry and to the order of the woman deacon. Speaking more generally about the women who accompanied the apostles, Clement says the apostles

> took with them women, not as wives, but rather as sisters, so that they might serve as their co-ministers [*syndiakonous*], serving women who were confined to their homes. Through them the Lord's teaching was also able to enter the restricted domains of women, without causing ill will. We are also aware of all the things the noble Paul prescribed on the subject of women deacons [*peri diakonon gynaikon*] in one of the two epistles to Timothy.[4]

In his commentary on the letter to the Romans, Origen affirms even more forcefully the order of the woman deacon and the significance of the ministry of Phoebe. Romans 16:1-2, he says, teaches with the authority of the apostle that even women are instituted deacons in the church. This was the function which was exercised in the church of Cenchreae by Phoebe, who was the object of high praise and recommendation by Paul. He enumerated her outstanding works; she assisted everyone, he said – that is, she helped them in their needs – she also helped me in my needs and my apostolic work with a perfect devotion...

Also this pious Phoebe, while giving assistance and rendering service to all, deserved to assist and to serve the apostle himself. And thus this text teaches at the same time two things: that there are, as we have already said, women deacons in the church, and that women who have given assistance to so many people and who by their good works deserve to be praised by the apostle ought to be accepted in the diaconate. He also exhorted that those [women] who are active in good works in the church receive likewise in return from their brothers consideration and be treated with honour, in whatever matter is necessary, even in material services.[5]

St John Chrysostom echoes these opinions, referring to Phoebe as a deacon of the church of Cenchreae and praising her for her goodness and sanctity. Moreover, St John affirms that both men and women should imitate her.[6] His commentary on 1 Timothy again notes that women were called to be deacons and insists that 1 Timothy 3:11 is referring not simply to women in general:

> Some have claimed that this was said of women generally, but this is not so, for why should he introduce anything about women to interfere with his subject? He is speaking, rather, of those women who have the dignity of the diaconate [*alla peri ton to axioma tes diakonias echouson legei*]. "Let deacons be the husband of one wife." This is fitting to say of women deacons [*peri gynaikon diakonon*] as well, as this order is also in the highest degree necessary, useful and proper in the church.[7]

It should be remembered that St John Chrysostom was writing at a time and in a place where the order of female deacons was flourishing. It is noteworthy that in this commentary he does not feel the need to prove or to justify the existence of the order of the women deacon. His concern is rather straightforward. He is simply taking note of Paul's affirmation of the significance of the ministry of Phoebe and of the importance of the order of the woman deacon in the life of the church.

Theodoret, the bishop of Cyprus, born about forty years after St John Chrysostom, also makes an important reference to St Phoebe and her ministry:

> Cenchreae is a prominent suburb of Corinth. The effectiveness of the preaching there is to be admired: in a very short period of time, not only were the cities filled with piety but the countryside around them as well. The church assembly at Cenchreae was already so considerable as to have a prominent and

> noble woman deacon [*gynaika diakonon*]. She was so rich in rendering good works as to have merited the praise of Paul.[8]

In his commentary on 1 Timothy 3:11, Theodoret writes:

> The women "likewise", in other words, the [women] deacons, "must be serious, no slanderers, but temperate, faithful in all things". What he prescribes for men, he also prescribes in the same or similar manner for women. Just as he says that deacons must be "serious", so he also says that the women must be "serious". Just as he forbids the men to be "double-tongued", so too he forbids the women to be "slanderers". And, as he forbids the men to be "addicted to much wine", so also he commands the women to be "temperate".[9]

Because of the significance Paul and his subsequent commentators attached to the ministry of Phoebe, the church began to refer to her as being "equal to the apostles". As we have already noted, St Phoebe came to be viewed as the first deaconess of the church and thus the prototype – the example of faith and service – of the woman deacon.

For this reason, early ordination prayers for women deacons refer to St Phoebe; for example, the second ordination prayer for the woman deacon in the Byzantine tradition implores God to "fill her with the grace of the diaconate just as you gave the grace of your diaconate to Phoebe whom you called to the work of ministry".

Mounting evidence

In addition to the early commentators on St Paul and the subsequent liturgical tradition, inscriptions on tombstones offer additional evidence of the presence of women deacons in the early church. Numerous examples of this archaeological witness are scattered throughout the Christian East. One important example of the significance of Phoebe for the early church is found in the epitaph of a 5th-century Byzantine tombstone on the Mount of Olives: "Here lies the servant and bride of Christ, Sophia the deacon, the second Phoebe [*Sophia he diakonos, he deutera Phoibe*], who fell asleep in peace on the 21st day of March."[10] From the same period, another well-preserved tombstone in Cappadocia commemorates a deacon named Mary who, "according to the text of the apostle, raised children, practised hospitality, washed the feet of the saints and distributed her bread to those in need".[11]

Another important reference to the ministry of early deaconesses comes from a non-Christian source of the second century, the *Letters of Pliny the Younger to Trajan.* Some time during A.D. 111-112, the emperor Trajan sent the lawyer Pliny on a fact-finding mission to the inadequately managed province of Bithynia. The poor state of temples in the region was being blamed on Christians; and Pliny found it expedient to arrest, torture and even execute Christians in conjunction with his investigation of the situation. In *Letter 96*, he writes: "So I thought it... necessary to enquire into the real truth of the matter by subjecting to torture two female slaves, who were called deacons [*ministrae*]; but I found nothing more than a perverse superstition which went beyond all bounds."

This letter attests to three important points. First, Pliny's comments in the original Latin text reveal that the word *ministrae* is the title given to these women by their fellow Christians. While we would wish we knew more about the ministry of these women, it is important to bear in mind their ministry was distinct enough to be recognized by persons outside of the Christian community. Second, Pliny clearly believed that these women were important enough to be captured and tortured in order to extract from them "inside information" unknown to those outside the body of believers. Third, a number of scholars maintain that these women may have had particular responsibilities in worship, since Pliny was actually hoping to extract useful information regarding the practices of Christian worship.[12] It is also worth noting that the Latin *ministrae* used by Pliny to refer to the two captured women deacons is essentially the same word used to describe Phoebe in the Vulgate translations of the Bible.[13]

NOTES

1 In what follows the older and more traditional term "woman deacon" is used interchangeably with the term "deaconess".

2 Cf. Evangelos Theodorou, *Herōides tés Christianikēs Agapēs* ("Heroines of Christian Love"), Athens, 1949, p.37; *Hē Cheirotonia' ē Cheirothesias' tōn Diakonisōn* ("The 'Ordination' or 'Appointment' of Deaconesses"), Athens, 1954, p.37; Janet Grierson, *The Deaconess*, London, CIO Publications, 1981, pp.12f.; Aime Georges Martimort, *Deaconesses: An Historical Study*, San Francisco, Ignatius Press, 1986, p.204.

3 In English, the King James Version (1611) translated *diakonos* here as "servant"; the Revised Standard Version and the New Jerusalem Bible use "deaconess", the New Revised Standard Version (1989) substitutes "deacon". A number of ancient manuscripts of the Greek refer to Phoebe as "being also" [*ousan kai*] a *diakonos*. On this see also Constantina Peppa, "Die Töchter der Kirche Christi und die frohe Botschaft des Sohnes Gottes" (Univ. of Bern dissertation, 1994), pp.22-30.

4 *Stromata*, 3,6, 53:3-4; cf. Theodorou, *Herōides*, p.31; Roger Gryson, *The Ministry of Women in the Early Church*, Collegeville MN, Liturgical Press, 1976, p.30; Martimort, *op. cit.*, p.77; Grierson, *op. cit.*, p.3.

5 *Commentary on Romans*, 10:17, cited in Gryson, *op. cit.*, p.31; cf. Theodorou, *Hē 'Cheirotonia'*, pp.18f.

6 *Homilies on Romans*, 30,2.

7 *Homily 11 on 1 Timothy*; cf. Theodorou, *Herōides*, p.28; Gryson, *op. cit.*, p.80; Martimort, *op. cit.*, p.118.

8 *Interp. Epist. ad Rom.* 16:1-2; cf. Martimort, *op. cit.*, p.117; Gryson, *op. cit.*, p.87.

9 *Interp. Epist. 1 ad Tim.* 3:11; cf. Gryson, *op. cit.*, p.87; Martimort, *op. cit.*, p.118; Grierson, *op. cit.*, p.3.

10 Cited by Theodorou, *Herōides*, p.79.

[11] There is probably a reference here to 1 Tim. 5:10; cf. Martimort, *op. cit.*, pp.125f.; Theodorou, *Herōides*, pp.78f.; Gryson, *op. cit.*, pp.90f. Martimort includes citations from Greek monographs published in the first half of this century through 1957 (pp.143-45).

[12] Cf. Bonnie Bowan Thurston, *The Widows*, Minneapolis, Fortress, 1989, p.73; cf. Theodorou, *Hé 'Cheirotonia'*, p.18; Gryson, *op. cit.*, pp.14f.; Grierson, *op. cit.*, p.4; Martimort, *op. cit.*, pp.25f.

[13] On the nature of the ministry of the deaconess see also the introduction to this book. A fuller investigation of this order is found in Thomas Hopko, ed., *Women and the Priesthood*, Crestwood NY, St Vladimir's Seminary Press, 1999, and in my own study, *Women Deacons in the Orthodox Church: Called to Holiness and Ministry*, Brookline MA, Holy Cross Orthodox Press, 1999. The most extensive collection of primary source material translated into English on the topic of women deacons is perhaps the World Wide Website *www.womenpriests.org*, maintained by the Roman Catholic theologian John Wijngaards.

The Priesthood of Women

A Look at Patristic Teaching

CONSTANTINOS N. YOKARINIS

The ordination of women is certainly one of the most controversial issues in the Christian world today. The admission of women to the ordained ministry by more and more churches in the West has been the source of deepening ecumenical disagreement, particularly since the official decision of the Church of England in 1992 to ordain women.

When we try as Christians to resolve these disagreements, we immediately face the question of which criteria should be used to decide them. Do we appeal simply to the words of the Bible? Or to the authority of two millennia of Tradition embodied in the church? Or to the working of the Holy Spirit in the church today? Or to our God-given powers of reasoning about such matters? And if we appeal to more than one of these criteria, which if any are to have priority? For all Christians, these are theological questions.

The priesthood of women has had a long history. It arose as a serious issue in the Christian community for the first time during the period of Gnosticism and Montanism. It was revived in the divided Christian church eighteen hundred years later. A century after that, the question still has a dynamic in the life of the church which threatens to undermine all efforts to restore church unity.

During most of church history there has been little serious discussion of the admission of women to the ordained ministry. The debate is a contemporary one, raised by the decision of some Western communions to admit women to the priesthood. Although the Orthodox church has never faced the priesthood of women as an existential problem, this does not mean that the issue has been ignored. The Orthodox church wants "always to be ready to make its defence to anyone who demands an accounting for the hope that is in us" (1 Pet. 3:15). Orthodox views on the subject have been articulated in special conferences, especially the inter-Orthodox meeting held in Rhodes in 1988.

Discussion of the priesthood of women cannot be limited to academic theology, because of its potential to open up a frightful chasm within the whole church. I believe we have a long way to go in examining these theological issues before we arrive at the truth. Consequently, declarations of an absolute character regarding the ordination of women, made without exhaustive theological research, can only damage the effort for church unity. Especially in the divided world in which we live today, Christian churches must be cautious and wise when debating or acting on such an extremely sensitive issue.

I have been invited, in the context of this consultation on "Discerning the Signs of the Times: Women in the Orthodox Church", to present the findings of my own research on women's ordination to the priesthood and episcopacy. This research, carried out over six years, was the basis of the doctoral thesis I submitted to the faculty of theology of the Aristotle University of Thessaloniki in 1992. Entitled "The Priesthood of Women in the Context of the Ecumenical Movement", this was the first work of its kind in the Orthodox literature to treat the issue from an historical and dogmatic perspective from the time of the early church to the present day. All the aspects of and arguments around the issue which have been presented in the past by all parties involved in discussions about the exclusion of women from the priestly office were closely scrutinized in the light of patristic and dogmatic teaching.

The multi-faceted nature of the issue of the priesthood of women creates additional difficulties. Yet trusting the Lord's promise that wherever two or three are gathered in his name, he will be among them, I believe he will finally lead us in the right direction, so that, under the illumination of the Holy Spirit, the true answer will be found and the obstacles to unity overcome.

My research has been based exclusively on the patristic and dogmatic teaching of the Orthodox church. I should make absolutely clear at the outset that I am not going to answer the question, "Should women be accepted into the priestly office or not?" I believe that a decision on such a disputed fundamental issue belongs to the church. Consequently, any disagreement on it can be overcome only after long and exhaustive theological research. What is needed is theological common ground, and I believe my research can contribute positively to this quest.

The exclusion of women from the ordained ministry over twenty centuries of church history is a fact that no one can ignore. In seeking to understand the existing situation and the reasons for the impasse, I asked myself four questions:

– Are the arguments which are presented theologically irrefutable?

- Do these arguments correspond to the nature and substance of the problem?
- Do these arguments agree with revealed truth, so that they can be accepted as an indisputable teaching?
- Why have all the theological arguments failed to give an answer which is universally accepted?

These questions demand careful answers. In approaching them, I had to examine concurrently every possible aspect of the issue, in order to test whether the arguments and views expressed were in line with the faith and teaching of the early church and the patristic tradition. In this examination it emerged clearly that the critical point of the dispute is the "male character" of the incarnated God-Logos. I recalled the words of Maximos the Confessor: "Because of the mystery of the incarnation of the Logos, all have the ability to comprehend all biblical enigmas and types, as well as the ability to know every phenomenon and intellectual thing which occurs."[1] Here was patristic advice to leave aside all that has been written about women's ordination and take the dogma of Chalcedon as a challenging point of departure for examining the issue. My thesis is therefore based on the theology of the Council of Chalcedon (A.D. 451). As far as I know, it is the first to approach the issue of women's ordination from this promising standpoint.

A dogma is an absolute principle of faith in the life of the church. Its authority cannot be denied. And the dogma of Chalcedon is the cornerstone of the Christian church, as it was taught by the apostles and the church fathers, and exists as the revealed truth experienced in human history.[2]

Having decided to approach the entire issue from a christological perspective, I had to examine a range of critical questions such as these: What is the content of biblical anthropology?

- How did the fathers understand human nature?
- How did the fathers understand the division of the first Adam into male and female form?
- What is the meaning of the expression in Orthodox dogmatic teaching that the Son of God was "perfect human being"?
- What is the meaning of the male form of the human nature of our Lord; and was this a theological or historical necessity?
- What are the implications of maleness in the divine economy?
- In what way are biological realities – male or female identity – connected with our salvation?
- Is the teaching of the church that a divided humanity and the whole world are recapitulated in the person of the God-man to be understood as an eschatological reality, an ideal "beyond" the actual existing church?

- If we define the nature of priesthood in terms of the sacrifice of Jesus Christ, are we referring to the sacrifice of his perfect human nature or his maleness?
- Adam and Eve were created in the image and likeness of God. The image of God is the Son, the archetype of all human beings. Consequently, the image is only one, and it was redeemed and renewed through the sacrifice of Jesus Christ. Is this one image of God male or female?
- Do we understand salvation in terms of ontology or in terms of biology?
- If we believe that the content of the sacrifice of Jesus Christ was reconciliation and the restoration of unity, how can the priesthood be offered under the conditions of the division between male and female?
- If the Holy Spirit "blows where it chooses", what theological support is there for saying that the characteristics (male-female) of a sinful world can be obstacles to the Spirit when the cross and the resurrection speak of a new creation?
- When we speak of the bearers of Christ's priesthood as acting in his place and being in his type, are we understanding priesthood in terms of natural resemblance?
- Priesthood functions and is expressed in the eucharist. The church is a sacramental body; and the sacraments are a real participation in the incorruptible life of the body of Christ. Can we, while experiencing our union with Christ, invoke conditions of sin – the division between male and female – to justify theologically the exclusion of women from the priestly office?

A careful look at these questions makes it obvious that research into this subject involves a great number of topics and perspectives – the anthropological, the trinitarian, the christological, the ecclesiological, the eschatological.

The mystery of incarnation

Leaving aside for the time being all the arguments pro and con, let us focus on the mystery of incarnation. The incarnate Word is the founder of the kingdom of God, the reason of our salvation and our eschatological hope. What does the Orthodox church believe and teach about incarnation according to the dogma of Chalcedon, which is the cornerstone of the church?

Because both sides, for and against, focus on the male character of Christ, we must take the fact of God's incarnation as our starting point, basing this theologically on the dogma of Chalcedon. In other words, the answer to the problem is connected directly with the human nature of

Christ, because the male character of his incarnation is at the heart of the problem.

The patristic understanding of the elements of the human nature of the incarnate Logos was summarized succinctly by John of Damascus: "all the attributes of the first Adam, save only his sin, these attributes being body and the intelligent and rational soul".[3] According to biblical anthropology, Adam's human nature consisted of the following elements and properties:

- The image and likeness of God. Here the question is to which part of Adam's nature, body or soul, these divine properties belong. According to John of Damascus, "'after his image' clearly refers to the side of his nature which consists of mind and free will, whereas 'after his likeness' means likeness in virtue, so far as that is possible."[4] Such an understanding implies that biological elements or characteristics are absent from the image and likeness, and that the image is only one for both sexes, male and female. This point is crucial for any theological approach to human nature. Theological anthropology must be constructed from the top down, beginning from trinitarian and christological dogma, in order to discover in human reality the unity of nature and the multiplicity of created hypostases.
- The first Adam – one and undivided human being and nature – has been "torn" into forms of existence, male and female. This distinction was added provisionally at the end in order to enable the human being as created to survive in the conditions after the fall.[5]
- One of the most important divine properties was the ability of the human person to exercise a form of leadership and power over the creation. The grammatical form of the verb *archetosan* is plural. This means that both sexes have received from the Creator the authority *in equal terms* to exercise sovereignty over the creation. This demonstrates in a clear and convincing way their equality as human beings and bearers to the same degree of the special properties, qualities and abilities assigned to both of them.

After the fall, the implications of this division or distinction into sexes change. They lose their sovereignty over creation and their equality and unity disappear. This is the starting point of their division in ontological terms. Their life is now miserable; fear, conflict, pain, deterioration and death appear as tragic consequences of their misuse of freedom.

Let us now take a synoptic look at the patristic teaching on *what* the God-Logos actually assumed, in regard to his human nature, in his incarnation.

1. According to John of Damascus, "'the nature of the Word' means neither the subsistence alone, nor 'the common nature of the subsis-

tence', but 'the common nature viewed as a whole in the subsistence of the Word'"[6] – in other words, body and soul. Human nature as a whole, both male and female, has been assumed by the incarnate Logos. If Christ as human being had belonged to the divided or "torn" human nature, he would not have been able to offer any healing to the human race, because he himself would have needed healing – and the female would have been excluded from his salvation.

It should be noted that the perfection of the human being does not exist in Adam or Eve, nor in the Virgin Mary, nor in John the Baptist, but only in the incarnate Word, who is the archetype of humanity, the image of perfection of all human beings, male and female.

2. Theologically, his conception by the Virgin Mary and from the Holy Spirit, not from man's sperm, is interpreted as abolishing the division into male and female, because in himself Christ has "recapitulated" humanity and creation.
3. The male character of his becoming human has been taken on "in order that his individuality *(idiotes)* might endure",[7] even on the level of his humanity, thus proving how genuinely he is co-essential *(homoousios)* with our human nature. Thus his being male attests to a relationship, just as his hypostasis as "son of God" does. Furthermore, his male character indicates that we were given by grace what God has by nature.
4. There are two reasons for saying that the male character of his incarnation has nothing to do with any concept of human sexuality. First, he has taken on himself the pre-Fall nature of the first man, who at that stage had no awareness of his biological differentiation as male or of his sexual functioning – remembering here that the division into male and female was to serve the post-Fall conditions of the human race, while the incarnate Logos assumed the human nature without sin.

   Second, the human nature of Jesus Christ has no previous existence. The human nature Christ assumed in the womb of the holy Virgin was not a complement of his mother's humanity in the way that the first Eve assumed the nature of Adam in order to be his complement. Christ's human nature was unique, because it came to existence from the pure blood and holy flesh of the Holy Virgin and from the Holy Spirit. So, the incarnated Logos became *he aparche tou phyramatos*, "the beginning of a new essence", the second or "new" Adam, which means the one and undivided human being.
5. The hypostatic union produced certain results for human nature. According to patristic teaching, the incarnation of the Logos had the consequence of salvation and even taking on divine properties.[8]

6. The first Adam was created "in the image and likeness" of God, but in the case of the incarnation, the aforesaid elements are not dynamic properties in the God-man, but are fulfilled reality, since the Lord himself was made man in order to make man God. The Lord did not raise "the previously fallen image" in his God-man hypostasis, but united it to his own by grace. This is a new element, which did not exist in the human nature of the first Adam, because in the context of incarnation there is a substantial difference: we move from "in the image" to the "image", which is the Son of God.
7. The son of God is the archetype of man and woman. Consequently, it is imperative to have a clear understanding of the nature of the christological archetype, which the person of grace and salvation is invited and challenged to imitate (cf. 1 Cor. 11:1), in order to become a child of the kingdom of God.

Our aim is to obtain the possessions of his sacrifice, because he is the only High Priest and the priesthood belongs exclusively to him.

The traditional view that priesthood belongs exclusively to men because the incarnate Logos was a male human being reduces the archetype of all human beings to the level of a *natural resemblance*. This is understandable in terms of our sexuality, which is characterized by polarity, conflict and passion and related to the situation after the fall. But patristic teaching is more than clear on this point. Jesus Christ united humanity, and the difference between male and female has been taken away by the Spirit in a mysterious way.

Priesthood has an ontological content. It is a gift and function of the Holy Spirit and cannot be related to biological elements. In its ecclesiological dimension the priesthood cannot be linked to any form of division or particularity known as male or female.

The sacrifice on the holy cross is a sacrifice of the God-man, not of his maleness. Therefore the male character of his humanity cannot be used as a criterion for excluding women from the priesthood, because this would completely contradict the dogma of Chalcedon. There is no dogmatic decision that would justify such an exception based on the distinction of sexes; the only reasons for doing so are connected with the human weakness for understanding and living the mystery of the divine economy, because, according to Maximos the Confessor, "[Christ] is seen and understood by many people as flesh and not as Logos, although truly he is Logos".[9]

Of course, it cannot be denied that some fathers rejected female ordination as emphatically as possible, basing their claim that a woman is unsuited to ministerial orders on the fact of her subordination to the man – particularly if one takes into consideration God's intervention to define the structure of human relationships, fixing the duties and rights of male and female, so that by definition woman is seen as incapable of receiving the divine grace that would empower her to perform the duties of the ministry.

Our human weakness has been aggravated by negative historic conditions such as social stratification, the domineering role of men, the disadvantageous position of women. Interpersonal relations between the two sexes throughout history have been kept in a climate of conflict and division. The tradition of the church as an expression of how we live our faith is formed in the reality of its historical context. The church has grown up and organized itself in the realm of history; it is not an extraterrestrial community. So it is not surprising that it has been influenced to a certain extent by the dominant patriarchal structures and ideas of the Graeco-Roman world in which Christianity emerged. The church has always struggled to get rid of any form of sin. Only in this context can the survival of such elements of division as the exclusion of women from priesthood be understood.

It is theologically inconsistent to believe in Christ, who "recapitulated" the divided human being and the creation in his God-man hypostasis, and at the same time to support views such as the exclusion of woman from the priesthood because of her sex. It is ironic that this exclusion is based on the heart of our salvation, Christ's sacrifice – which is precisely the restoration of the unity of a divided world as a presupposition of the restoration of our communion in God.

The church has an eschatological destiny and character, but it is very often forgotten that there can be no *eschaton* without a reference to our presence in history. As the church struggles to make the kingdom of God a reality, the first thing to be overcome is every form of division. John Chrysostomos specifically says: "See the dignity of the church, the angelic condition! No distinction there, 'neither male nor female'. I would that the churches were such now!"[10] The Christian church serves the kingdom of God. Its duty is actively to prepare its members in the present historical setting to overcome the division which marks the presence of sin. If we really want the kingdom of God to come, as we pray, then it is imperative to abandon our sexist views. This idea is not mine; it belongs to our Lord, as Clement of Rome says in the *kyriakon logion*.[11]

If our theological research has clarified the common position of our dogmatic and liturgical tradition that Christ is "the offerer and the offered" and that in the holy sacrament "God, the Father, the Son and the Holy Spirit, dispenses all, while the priest lends his tongue and affords his hand",[12] then a convergence of views and attitudes of the churches is possible within the framework of the ecumenical movement.

For academic theology, therefore, the dogma of Chalcedon would seem to offer a key that can unlock the impasse in which we find ourselves and open up new horizons for approaching this issue. Let me finish this brief summary of my research by quoting another distinguished father of the church, Gregory the Theologian: "There is one Maker of man and woman; one debt is owed by children to both their parents."[13]

An ecclesiological perspective

The church is the work of the Son and of the Holy Spirit, sent by the Father into the world. Just as it is the new unity of human nature purified by Christ, the unique Body of Christ, so too it is the multiplicity of persons, who all receive the gift of the Holy Spirit.

The object of the work of the Son is the common nature: this is what Christ redeems, purifies and recapitulates. The work of the Holy Spirit is directed to persons, communicating the fullness of grace to each human hypostasis in the church, making each member of the Body of Christ a conscious co-worker with God, a personal witness to the truth. This is why the Holy Spirit appeared on the day of Pentecost in a multiplicity of flames resting on each person present. The relation between the work of Christ and of the Holy Spirit in the church might seem to have the character of an antinomy: the Holy Spirit diversifies what Christ unifies. Yet what is supreme in this diversity is its perfect concord, what is manifested in this unity is its infinite richness.

But even more must be said: without this diversity of persons, the natural unity could not be realized, and in its place would come the abstract, administrative unity of blind submission by members of a collective. There would be no place for the development of persons; and diversity would be transformed into its opposite: the mutual oppression of individual and limited beings. There can be no unity of nature without diversity of persons, and no persons fully realized outside natural unity. The meaning of the church as one and catholic demands a perfect harmony of two terms: unity and diversity, nature and persons.

There are thus two dogmatic reasons why the divine grace of the Holy Spirit cannot be prevented by the biological elements of human nature such as maleness or femaleness: the christological unity of human nature, and the pneumatological diversity of the human person. Priesthood as a spiritual gift and power belongs only to persons.

NOTES

[1] Maximos the Confessor, *Kephalaia peri Theologias, Hekatontas* A,66; *PG* 90, 1108A.
[2] While the Oriental Orthodox churches do not include Chalcedon among the ecumenical councils, they do fully accept its theological conclusions regarding the incarnation of Christ.
[3] John of Damascus, *Exposition of the Orthodox Faith*, III, 13 (*Nicene and Post-Nicene Fathers*, 2d series, Vol. 9, p.57).
[4] *Ibid.*, II,12 (*NPF, ibid.*, p.31).
[5] Cf. Gregory of Nyssa, *On the Making of Man*, 16,14 (*NPF*, 2d series, Vol. 5, p.406): "... following out, or rather perceiving beforehand by his power of foreknowledge what, in a state of independence and freedom, is the tendency of the motion of man's will – as he saw, I say, what would be – he devised for his image the distinction of male and female, which has no reference to the Divine Archetype, but, as we have said, is an approximation to the less rational nature."
[6] *Op. cit.*, 3,11 (*NPF, loc. cit.*, p.55).
[7] *Ibid.*, IV,4 (*NPF, ibid.*, p.75).
[8] See John of Damascus, *ibid.*, IV,18 (*NPF, ibid.*, p.66): "He therefore assumed the whole man, even the fairest part of him, which had become diseased, in order that he might bestow salvation on the whole... Therefore, God the Word, wishing to restore that which was in his own image, became man. But what is that which was in his own image, unless mind?"; cf. Athanasius, *Against the Arians*, Discourse III, para. 33 (*NPF*, 2d series, Vol. 4, p.412): "As we are all from earth and die in Adam, so being regenerated from above of water and Spirit, in Christ we are all quickened; the flesh being no longer earthly, but being henceforth made Word, by reason of God's Word who for our sake 'became flesh'."
[9] *Op. cit.*, *PG* 90, 1152A.
[10] St John Chrysostom, *Homily III on Acts* (*NPF*, 1st series, vol. 11, p.18).
[11] Clement of Rome, *Pros Korinthious*, B'XIII, 1.44.
[12] St John Chrysostom, *Homily 86 on John*, para. 4 (*NPF*, 1st series, vol. 14, p.326).
[13] Gregory Nazianzus, *Oration*, 37,6 (*NPF*, 2d series, Vol. 7, p.338).

Women, Power and Social Movements

NICHOLAS K. APOSTOLA

The issue of the place and role of women in the church has been raised to a new degree of importance largely because of the changing roles of women in civil society and the development of modern political and social analysis. This is not to downplay the significance of the issue. For the first time the church has been obliged to begin to think about the nature of gender roles in its structure and decision-making institutions. However, the church is a unique institution in society, and for believers these issues have a meaning beyond the immediate, even though the need to address them is very immediate and very real.

For many people – both men and women – this issue raises questions of justice and the equality of persons. And while these ideas have gained new meanings as a result of the political and social struggles beginning with the Enlightenment, they are not foreign to Christianity or in fact to the entire Judaeo-Christian tradition. Many would say that the very claim that there is an intrinsic and inalienable character to "human rights", to the dignity of the human person, is due in large part to this tradition. Who of us would say that God is not just; that God does not demand justice? Who of us would say that God does not love each of his children equally? Thus it seems to me that the question is not whether the church believes in the equality of and justice for all persons. It is what does equality mean? And how does God effect justice?

The difficulty for many within the church today is that these questions are being raised in a language and style that seem foreign. Arguments and rationales have been borrowed from modern political and social thought and given only the slightest veneer of theological language. In itself the fact that the ideas have been borrowed, that developments in civil society are forcing the church to look anew at the underlying principles of its own beliefs, is not bad. But it would become problematic if these forces were to direct not only the church but also society as a whole to an understanding of the nature of creation, human beings, social interaction and even salvation that in the long view is destructive.

The 20th century will leave a legacy of many ironies. Perhaps the greatest is that this century, when awareness of the rights of human beings both collectively and individually has been raised to a level without parallel in history, has seen killing, war, abuse, social dislocation and the general degradation of humanity and creation in proportions hitherto unknown. In short the principles and presuppositions that we as civil society espouse carry within them hidden contradictions. We need to look at these. We also need to look at the teachings of the church of Christ, which will perhaps give us a different trajectory to follow in addressing these very important questions that have been presented to us.

In this paper I will highlight what I consider some of the major presuppositions underlying modern criticism of the institutional structure of church and suggest what I believe to be the "way out" of this cycle of abuse and sin, a way offered to us by our Lord Jesus Christ in the example of his life.

Power and human interaction

Simply to speak of "power" is to arouse a range of visceral reactions, especially perhaps from those who perceive that they have been the victim of an abuse of power and those who have been accused of some excess of power. No matter at which end of the power equation one might find oneself, the probability is that power has been objectified as a kind of force that can be contained, possessed, transferred. Most political theory has this sort of understanding of power. Hence, democracies and other "constitutional" political arrangements claim to distribute power according to agreed formulas; totalitarian, autocratic, monarchical political systems seem to concentrate power in a few or even in one person. Political struggles have as their focus taking power from one centre to another. Leaving aside the issue of the justice of one cause over another or of the power configuration of one system over another, the common characteristic is that power is objectified.

Consequently, power becomes a commodity that can be bought, sold and bargained for. I believe that its primarily negative connotation is rooted in this objectification of power as a commodity – for what is actually being bought and sold is not the objective commodity of power, but we ourselves.

Power is one way to describe the dynamic at work in a relationship. Defined in this way it is the exercise of influence or force by one person over another person. It is not inherently negative, even though it usually tends to be, because most human relationships fall short of true communion and become "abusive". This use of the word "power" has very little in common with its use to refer to non-personal forces such as energy. Power as a non-personal force has an objective character; power as the interaction between persons has a relational character. To objectify power is to objectify relationship, and consequently to misunderstand its true nature.

We interpret the power an impersonal force exerts over us differently from the way we look at the power of a personal agent. A natural disaster might arouse a sense of injustice, but hardly the sense of outrage we feel over disasters caused by some personal agent. In fact, the impersonal forces of nature are often personified as "acts of God" in order to give some personal focus for our sense of injustice. Injustice at the hands of persons is of a different order simply because persons are moral beings capable of moral behaviour. Impersonal forces have no moral capacity. The current that electrocutes a little child has no moral character; we look for culpability in the negligence of someone. An impersonal force that causes a tragedy or presents an obstacle is something that has to be worked around or changed or corrected; a person presents a completely different matrix of difficulties, if that person is to retain his or her character as person. Persons can be, and often are, "dealt with", but once having been handled in this manner they become objectified and cease to be persons.

In order for one person to encounter another person, a relationship between the two is required. Anything short of this risks reducing a personal relationship to one between objects. This, I believe, is the main thrust of Martin Buber's philosophy. It is certainly in harmony with the Orthodox understanding of persons and relationships, while it falls short of a complete understanding of the human in relationship with the rest of creation and with God.

For Orthodox Christians, the person, and especially the person in communion, is central to any notion of power. Anything which depersonalizes, which abstracts the concept of power from actual persons in relationship with one another, violates the very foundation of Orthodox cosmology. It also violates any organic understanding of society as community, whether or not one accepts Orthodox cosmology.

At least one other aspect should be mentioned here. Power does have what appears to be an objective character.[1] Persons have particularities; and these specifics, which make each person different from every other, have a certain objective quality. The danger to avoid is that of seeing these particularities as separate from the person. Nor should the whole person be reduced to the sum total of all the particularities. The particularities are synthesized in the person. Similarly, we should not confuse what have come to be called the "resources of power" with power itself. These resources do have a certain objective quality in that they are at the disposal of any number of persons and can, to a certain degree, be bought, sold, traded, shared, redistributed or exclusively possessed. In that sense, they have a certain commodity-like quality. However, they are not power itself. The same resource in the hands of different persons does not have the same effect. It is synthesized differently.

Having observed that certain people, or even classes of people, have, because of their social standing, accumulated "power" – that is, the resources of power – modern social ethics faces the challenge of presenting a programme that would distribute these resources in such a way that personhood is not diminished and that society as the community of persons is enhanced. This will require an understanding not only of the resources of power, but also of persons in community – with each other and with God.

I shall focus on three aspects of this problem: (1) philosophical presuppositions underpinning much of the modern discussion of power and powerlessness; (2) the nature of the self and identity in relationship to power; (3) how these issues are taken up and addressed in the Orthodox Christian understanding of the Cross. A discussion of power that excludes God is, from an Orthodox Christian perspective, bound to be partial and incomplete. If power is in the final analysis relationship, then God is intrinsic to any discussion.

The philosophical presuppositions of social analysis

The philosophical presuppositions of any dominant system are rarely questioned. Michael Parenti describes at length how reality is shaped and defined by the classes in power so as to retain and expand their power, how the less powerful support this by their acquiescence and how institutions encourage this. While Parenti's analysis could be described as "leftist", his fundamental presuppositions would probably be accepted by many on the "right" as well. He operates from a modern, scientific, post-Marxian worldview, in which God is not so much denied as relegated to irrelevance.

From an Orthodox perspective the denial of the centrality of God in any discussion concerning the world is certainly considered to be a mistake of the highest order. However, much of what is said concerning the world and human nature from the modern perspective can nevertheless be appreciated and accepted. The Orthodox believe that truth is one and that all ideas contain, in varying degrees, elements of the truth. Nothing is to be rejected out of hand or as totally devoid of worth. The essence of philosophical dialogue is to find points of agreement and to continue to discuss hoping to expand the field. In this way the process is both deductive and inductive.

At the heart of the modern worldview are two principles, one epistemological and the other hermeneutical. The first says that everything, all of reality, can be measured. While the natural sciences have become less and less certain that various methods of measurement are either truly accurate or universally applicable, the underlying hope has not faded that someday we will be able to "understand" how things work. Implicit in this approach is that in order to understand, one has to dissect and measure. The second principle, which is based on the first, says that all "reasonable" people, once fully informed of the *facts*, will come to the same conclusion. This is at the heart of the Marxian doctrine of "mystification", as well as almost every other modern political and philosophical system. But since the facts as presented are rarely "conclusive", we are left to search for more and better facts, or to dismiss those who disagree as either irrational or ill-informed.

Now the difficulty with questioning these two principles is that they are so compelling. It is very hard to argue with facts. As empirical data they have a "seeable" quality. To deny what we *see* in front of us, especially when it is verified by those around us, is to forfeit any hope of knowing anything. To dismiss those instruments which extend our "sight" as fundamentally flawed is to question our ability to perceive reality at all. While reality might be (the Orthodox would say "definitely is") more than what we see, it certainly does include that which we see. And while reality might be (again, "definitely is") more than what we see, what we do not see is not any "more real" than is the world around us which we do see. The empirical can be accepted as real and legitimate without accepting it as constituting the whole of epistemology and hermeneutics.

However, one of the great drawbacks to an entirely empirical approach is that an understanding of systems needs to be reconstructed from data dissected out of an organic whole. Such a synthesis tends to be artificial. In short, while the empirical is an extraordinarily compelling way of looking at the world, it does not necessarily have priority.

One could even say that the empirical forms the beginning point for all dialogue, simply because it is more easily verifiable than other methods of knowing. In order to have any discussion we need to be convinced that something exists to be talked about. We need to agree on what we will both be referring to. However, the empirical – and the epistemological and hermeneutical principles based on empiricism – do not form the beginning point for knowing. They form the middle point between how we first experience an object and how we then synthesize it into our whole understanding of reality.

Along with the belief that the empirical forms the basis for all knowing comes another implicit assumption, almost universally agreed upon in the modern worldview, but also fundamentally flawed: that value is socially or culturally derived and is added to our empirical observations. One reason a discussion of "only the facts" can appear to be a common denominator is that facts are assumed to be neutral – totally without intrinsic value. Value is seen as something defined or given by a society, a class, a philosophy, a political system, a person. In this conception, the family, for example, has no intrinsic worth. It has a culturally given worth. Different societies define it and value it differently. Therefore in most discussion of public policy, of social restructuring, everything is negotiable because everything is seen as a human construct. And while one might use the phrase "inalienable rights", these rights are in reality only seen as a figure of speech tied to a specific socio-political construct.

Discussions concerning the objectivity of a certain study or the bias of a given scholar presuppose that things in themselves have no value until they are given some, and, similarly, that value can be taken away. So, for example, when Parenti discusses the impossibility of keeping "empirical descriptions free of normative consideration",[2] it is not because he thinks that there are intrinsic values in things which political theory must accommodate, but rather because he believes that every political theory is replete with its own value system, that different political theories have different value systems, and that to suppose that people are capable of ridding themselves of their politics is not only totally naive, but part and parcel of the mystification that keeps the ruling class in power.

Valuation is however prior to all thinking, to all systems, to all culture. This is not to deny the social context of thinking about the value of one thing or another, or that thinking itself is not to a large degree a social or cultural artifact. Different people and different cultures have thought about and valued things differently. To say that valuation is prior to thinking is not yet to say that everyone perceives the same value in a given thing, much less to say that the value of a given thing remains static. For now, it is only to say that, for example, when we promote a certain public policy, we promote it because we believe it is good; we do not believe it is good because we promote it.

Robert Neville develops this idea that valuation is prior to thinking in what he calls the axiology of thinking.[3] I believe that he is essentially correct in saying that valuation is prior to reason; that valuation supplies and justifies the norms that guide thinking to be rational when it is; and that when reason is a function of false consciousness, it is founded on a deeper valuation.[4] Valuation – what we define to be good – underlies all "ideological" struggle. This points to the hopelessness of eliminating "value judgments" from the study of the problems of society and redistribution of power. It also urges systematic thinking about the values intrinsic in what is being promoted, and what relationship this has to the "good". In short, it encourages holistic thinking.

To summarize the discussion thus far:

- At the heart of the modern worldview is an epistemological and hermeneutical assumption that there is a fact/value distinction.
- It is assumed that the facts pertaining to a given object can be separated from its value and measured, although there is generally less faith that these measurements can achieve universality.
- Since values are virtually immeasurable, they have been increasingly seen as cultural or ideological interpretations of an object, relative at best, irrational at worst.
- Although the distinction between fact and value is flawed, the hypothetical neutrality of facts does provide a common ground between cultures and ideological systems, as a kind of "middle point" between our first experience of an object and its synthesis into a whole cosmology.
- What now needs to be understood is that valuation is not incidental nor merely culturally conditioned, but is rather the foundation for all thinking; therefore, value and valuational thinking must be at the forefront of discussions about social theory.

Personal identity and power relationships

One objection raised against grounding an understanding of power in interpersonal relationships is that people start out with unequal standing vis-à-vis one another. Instead of a communion of persons there is generally a relationship of exploitation. This is at the heart of Parenti's critique of the "exchange" theory of power relations. He says that habit and custom generally blind us to the elements of asymmetry and coercion involved in most social relations.[5] A related criticism is that in order for inequality in a relationship to be rectified, the weaker party must have some standing, some self-esteem. But the weaker party, almost by definition, will have little if any self-esteem; usually it has been beaten out of him or her. Thus, the argument runs, any attempt to define power in terms of relationship tends inevitably to perpetuate the current power configurations.

Before taking up the basic question of inequality in power relationships, I would like to discuss the idea of the self and personal identity.

The Christian tradition universally condemns pride – generally understood as self-love – as the worst sin. Humility, the chief virtue, has often been understood as self-denial. Without entering into a detailed discussion of pride and humility, let me simply say that the spiritual writings of Eastern Christianity understand pride as self-love in the sense of believing oneself to be autonomous and self-sufficient. It is a denial of the need for communion with God and other people. Humility, on the other hand, is not self-hatred, but the constant willingness to be open to the other. Pride and humility have to do with the self in communion with others. As vice and virtue they establish normative behaviour for persons in community.

Orthodox Christianity has always defined person-in-community as normative. God, the ground of all being, is understood as having revealed himself as a triad of Persons-in-community. While one could argue that this is arbitrary and mistaken, at the very least the empirical data support the norm of persons-in-community. It is not possible for any living thing to come into being without having been touched in some way by another living being. Even the self-dividing amoeba is a being-in-relation. How two amoebae relate to one another is different question, but we do not in any case consider amoebae as persons. Persons are of a higher order of being. Human beings require the communion of two persons, male and female, to come into being. Medical advances have not taken away the need for a male sperm and a female egg; and a "test-tube baby" still needs to be reared by someone. The structure of creation as we know it tends to support the idea that we are not self-sufficient beings, but that all of humanity, all of creation, is interdependent.

Identity may be a more useful term than self. Neville says the identity of a thing is rooted in both its "conditional" and its "essential" features. The former are the features which things share in common: other-relatedness, the sameness that things share which relates them to one another, the features that *condition* a thing. This is what the Orthodox call nature or *ousia*. Essential features, on the other hand, are the unique elements of a particular thing – the features that make *this* thing different from every other thing. This is what the Orthodox would call an *hypostasis*. "An account of identity would express sameness in its self-identity, and difference in its other-relatedness. Being or reality is that which has both self-identity and other-relatedness, sameness and difference."[6] Identity, then, has a dyadic character; to be something is to be *this* rather than *that*. It also is to be *something* rather than *nothing*. Neville emphasizes that "it is important not to hypostasize 'nothing' as if it were a funny 'other thing' in relation to which the determinate thing has cosmological contrast. Nothing does not condition determinate things. Most important, nothing is not real; it does not exist."[7] Here he is laying the foundation for his conception of creation *ex nihilo* as the primary conditional feature which all things hold in common.

A determinate thing then is what Neville calls the "harmony" of conditional and essential features. Every thing is a composite of both essential and conditional features. Neville denies that this harmony "is some kind of determinate 'third thing' over and above the features which integrate them... The 'third thing' argument is typical of idealism, supposing that any two or more different things require yet another to give them position or relation relative to one another."[8]

From an Orthodox perspective, this dyadic argument for self-identity can be accepted in an elementary way. All determinate things are *this* rather than *that*. And the most basic notion that things have been called by God from "non-being" into "being" – creation *ex nihilo* – is also accepted. Neville's argument that things are harmonies follows very closely the Orthodox idea that "nature" or *ousia* does not exist in the abstract, but is always "en-hypostasized". For example, we do not know human nature in the abstract, we only know it in given, determinate human beings. Neither do we know God, or the divine *ousia*, abstractly; rather, we encounter the divinity hypostatically through one of the divine Persons.[9] And while Orthodox theology has not generally been as systematic as Neville about locating identity (and especially the identity of "things" as over and against "persons"), there is agreement that every *created* thing is a composite, that its unity is a harmony of these composites and that this unity is not a "third thing" but rather is the thing itself. On this view, every thing is composed both of elements that connect it to other things (and in some cases to every other thing) and of elements that make it unique. Thus, identity, self-identity, cannot be conceived of as a kind of self-sufficiency, but as an interconnectedness without loss of uniqueness.

To admit the dyadic character of self-identity is not to say anything about the triadic character of reality, which finds its fullest expression in the tri-hypostatic relationship of the holy Trinity. Orthodox theology claims that the dyad in terms of relationship quickly becomes self-referential. Ideally, Orthodox theology does not think of a community as simply two, but as three or more. As opposed to the "vicious infinite regress" which Neville attributes to the idea of the "third thing",[10] Orthodox theology posits the concept of *perichoresis* (mutual indwelling), in which the three are totally united in love without the unique aspects of each hypostasis disappearing. This act of communion constitutes the true nature of being.[11]

If the self is based not on a kind of individualistic self-sufficiency but on communion with the other without loss of identity, and if the true nature of reality is this triadic conception of persons in communion, then all modern political philosophies and theories of power are inadequate. Each in its own way posits the atomistic self, which either contracts with (Rousseau), or is at war with (Hobbes), or individualistically universalizes towards (Kant), or holds commonality of empirical experience with (Locke, Hume) other human beings. On the other side are the Hegelian and Marxian dialectics which tend to swallow up individuals in the sweep of historical progress or class struggle. Of course, these are gross generalizations. Each of these systems does attempt to harmonize individual and society. But all of them fall short in maintaining the integrity of the individual person in relationship with others.

The victory of the Cross

While it is not possible here to explore how the different understandings of the Cross in Eastern and Western Christianity have influenced their different interpretations of power, suffering, good and evil, and their effect on human relationships and on the relationship between humans and God, I will outline what I believe to be the uniqueness of the Orthodox perspective and its important implications for this discussion of power.

First, and most importantly, the Cross is understood only as the Cross of Jesus Christ the incarnate Logos. His suffering is different because Christians understand him as having no sin. The other aspect of his sacrifice is that it is totally voluntary. What he does, he does out of love for humanity and all of the creation. He is not a "victim" who has been taken and sacrificed against his will.[12] Rather, he is the one who has chosen this path out of love for the other. He allows himself to be taken. It is his outstretched hand towards even his enemy that lifts up the other. Also, because of who this Jesus is, his suffering is of an entirely different order from any other, and is capable of repairing the relationship between God and the creation.[13] In this sense the Cross is intrinsically bound up with an entire Christian theology of salvation and redemption. And while this theology may not be persuasive to non-Christians, I believe there is a principle in harmony with the above discussion of relationship and community that may be helpful in understanding a place for "taking up the Cross" in order to set relationships aright even for non-Christians.

The Romanian Orthodox theologian Dumitri Staniloae builds on Buber's idea of I-Thou relationships as the dialogue between subjects. True dialogue is that which lifts each of the participants from the status of an object to that of a subject. The "word" is the means by which this dialogue takes place; and it is through the word that the one subject recognizes the integrity of another subject and speaks to the other, as first person to second person. This is the true communion of persons which is necessary if a relationship is to be without abuse of power.

Yet this is not the norm in human interpersonal relationships. Rarely is a true I-Thou dialogue established, and few if any would even recognize this as the norm to which we are called. Abuse, violence, subjugation of the one by the other are by definition a refusal to recognize the status of the other as subject. We are blinded by a total egocentrism which refuses to acknowledge the other. All struggle by oppressed persons against oppressors – against being oppressed – is this objection to having been relegated to the status of an object. It is typified by the slogan "We want to be heard". In order to be heard, the other person has to be willing to listen.

The tragedy in most social struggle is that in order to make their point, those struggling for liberation, having been objectified themselves, must objectify the oppressor. Dialogue between subjects is impossible – first because those in power have objectified the subjugated, then because the subjugated, denied their status as subjects, strike back. Of course, those in power have no status as subjects. Having objectified other persons, they have objectified themselves. It is the double-edged sword of having refused to dialogue. This gives those in power their "unfeeling" quality, and in some sense allows the oppressed to justify their striking back at what are no longer persons, but objects who hold power. In this configuration liberation never occurs; there is only the tragedy of people speaking past each other, of doing violence to one another.

True liberation requires breaking this cycle of violence, this violation of one person by the other. It is clearly not broken by revolutionary political struggle as it is commonly understood. Nor is it broken by democratic processes in which the minority can be easily subjugated by the majority in very subtle ways. And in every system, institutional inertia tends to support those in power – power defined here not as dialogue but as objectification.

The Cross is the breaking of this cycle of objectification. It is the unilateral recognition of the subjectivity of the other, frozen in the objectivity of egocentrism. Staniloae says:

> But the way in which we gain the overwhelming and earth-shaking insight which reclaims a subject to the status of a second person is not through his or her word, rather it is through her or his sacrifice. Your sacrifice is for me the most jolting word you could speak. It raises me to the highest ethical standing; it imposes the most intense obligation on me; it completely and radically removes from me any thought of individualism or egoism that I might have as towards things and places me in a relationship of service towards the other.[14]

This requires from me an act of love for the other, an act of love which might even require my life. St Paul speaks of the difficulty of doing this when he declares, "Indeed, rarely will anyone die for a righteous person – though perhaps for a good person someone might actually dare to die" (Rom. 5:7). In order to be able to sacrifice ourselves for the sake of the other we have to remove from ourselves any thought of our own self-interest and focus on the love of the other, who might even be our enemy. This is the uniqueness of Christ's sacrifice, devoid of any self-interest, any sin.

For our part, it is difficult enough to remove selfishness from even normal relationships, much less to take up love of enemy. The usual state of relations between husband and wife, parents and children, points to the lack of true communion, the extent of the objectification of subjects, even within the family. In order for us to be able to sacrifice ourselves for the other there has to be no agenda in us. In order for us to shake the consciousness of the other, to wake them up, there must be a purity on our part. Power struggle as currently defined is totally incapable of purity of intent.

The dilemma for the typical analysis of power is that the burden is placed on those already oppressed and there is no incentive for the already powerful, those who have the upper hand, to share their power, to cease their objectification of the powerless. It is the powerful who can afford to reach out and lift up, but because of their own selfishness they refuse to. And nothing changes. The powerful remain powerful and the oppressed remain oppressed.

From the Christian perspective, this is sin and the cycle of sin. To attempt to rectify sin with more sin is not possible. In those instances where political arrangements have become less oppressive, it is precisely because the level of objectification has decreased and the recognition of the other as a subject worthy of communion has increased. Staniloae says that the sign of the Cross has been imprinted on the world – on the world as the gift of God. It stands before us as the way towards the fullness of relationship. The victory of the Cross is that it breaks this cycle of sin. It re-establishes communion between one human being and another, between God and creation.

NOTES

[1] Michael Parenti, *Power and the Powerless*, New York, St Martin's Press, 1978, p.7. This is what Parenti calls the "resources of power"; however, he tends to distinguish these from the interpersonal responses that create power relationships.

[2] *Ibid.*, p.33.

[3] Cf. Robert C. Neville, *Reconstruction of Thinking*, Albany, State University of New York Press, 1981.

[4] *Ibid.*, p.12.

[5] Parenti, *op. cit.*, pp.9-10.

[6] Robert Cummings Neville, "Recovery of the Measure: Interpretation and the Philosophy of Nature", unpublished manuscript, 1988, p.15.

[7] *Ibid.*, p.47.

[8] *Ibid.*, p.54.

[9] According to Orthodox theology, the divine *ousia* remains totally outside the human capacity to comprehend. What is encountered are the divine energies through one of the divine Persons. St Gregory Palamas articulated this distinction between "essence" and "energy" in the 13th century in reaction to the influence of Thomist theology; on this, see John Meyendorff, *A Study of Gregory Palamas*, London, The Faith Press, 1964.

[10] Neville, *op. cit.*, p.54. The denial of the "third thing" can be accepted if it refers to the identity of a determinate thing. But if all reality is reduced only to dyadic categories, then one has to posit a God that has no discernible relationship to the world except as "creator" in a limited sense (as Neville does, pp.192-94). For the Orthodox, a God that is "unreal except as actually creating" is totally unreal. This, from the Orthodox perspective, is completely unacceptable.

[11] For a fuller discussion of the triadic nature of being, see Dumitru Staniloae, "The Holy Trinity: Structure of Supreme Love", in *Theology and the Church*, Crestwood NY, St Vladimir's Seminary Press, 1980, pp.73-108; John D. Zizioulas, *Being as Communion*, Crestwood NY, St Vladimir's Seminary Press, 1985. For a brief outline of Orthodox trinitarian theology, see John Meyendorff, *Byzantine Theology: Historical Trends and Doctrinal Themes* New York, Fordham U.P., 1974, esp. pp.180-89. For a discussion of the concept of *diastema* (space-time) with regard to the internal relationship among the Persons of the Trinity, see Paulos Mar Gregorios, *Cosmic Man: The Divine Presence*, New Delhi, Sophia Publications, 1980, esp. pp.69-99.

[12] This points to one of the objections which oppressed peoples justly raise against holding up the Cross as a model for dealing with abuse. A victim is someone who is victimized against his or her will. It is not the voluntary act of suffering on behalf of another person, but rather violence and evil directed against someone who is essentially an innocent or unwilling focus for this violence. The nature of evil that delights in the abuse of the helpless is another matter and the subject of much of the spiritual writing of Eastern Christianity.

[13] The theories developed in the West of "justification" and "satisfaction" (such as Anselm of Canterbury) were seen in the East as possible but incorrect understandings of the Cross. They were rejected in favour of the restoration of communion between humans (and all of creation) and God. This theology of "reaching out" is iconographically depicted in the icon of the "Descent into Hades" (that is, the resurrection), in which Christ, having conquered the Devil, is seen as physically lifting Adam and Eve out of their tombs – in contrast to Michelangelo's *Creation* in the Sistine Chapel, where Adam is reaching towards God the Father, but their fingers never touch.

[14] Dumitru Staniloae, *Iisus Hristos sau Restaurarea Omului*, Sibiu, 1943, p.241.

Sexism as Sin

Essential Spiritual Considerations

KYRIAKI KARIDOYANES FITZGERALD

This presentation offers some initial considerations from an Orthodox spiritual perspective regarding the sin of sexism. While Orthodox would no doubt often agree with many outside our tradition in identifying a given situation as a case of sexism, how we understand the nature of this sin may differ because of our differing theological and spiritual assumptions. Thus it is important for us to reflect more deeply on this sin from the perspective of our own theology – which may in turn influence our response to it.

During the final discussions of the Damascus meeting, the participants strongly urged that the topic of sexism be introduced and considered from an Orthodox spiritual perspective and suggested that I deliver this presentation at the Istanbul meeting. What is offered here can of course only scratch the surface. It takes the form of a personal evaluation, drawing on my own spiritual formation and Orthodox theological training, as well my experience as a pastoral counsellor and licenced psychologist.

Being as communion

It can be said that the Orthodox view existence or reality in terms of "being as communion".[1] Reality is established by a God who is both one and triune, a God who himself lives in sublime community "without confusion" among the three Persons, "yet one in essence", Father, Son and Spirit. Each Person of the uncreated Trinity abides eternally in the other in an ecstatic "dance" of loving surrender. In Greek, this is frequently referred to as *perichoresis*.

In a creaturely manner, we have this same vocation for living communion with God. This is because human persons are created in the divine "image and likeness" (Gen. 1:26). This communion consists of at least two realities: (1) a call to grow in the mystery of becoming unique human persons, a process which is particular to each human being and is therefore unrepeatable; and (2) a call towards the infinite depths of intimacy with God. Some would see these two elements of our vocation as contradicting each other; the Orthodox, however, pointing to the uncreated Trinity, would affirm that each leads and bears witness to the other. Because of this "theanthropic" reality, we are also created to grow in communion with each other as human persons.

Through this paradox, Orthodox theology and spirituality essentially teach that everything in creation ultimately depends on *authentic relationships*. The "good news" of the unfathomable love of God, expressed through the Lord's incarnation, ministry, passion, death, resurrection and bestowal of the Holy Spirit at Pentecost, healed the ancient schism between God and humanity. The essential understanding of this rift is expressed through the biblical story of Adam and Eve and the first human sin, which consisted fundamentally of a willful choice towards unauthentic relationships. Adam and Eve "fell" because they chose to live "independently". They chose to live out of communion with true Life and Reality. They wanted to be god without God. The Orthodox understand "original sin" not as the inheritance of the "guilt" of Adam and Eve, but as the inheritance of distorted relationships, which misdirect humanity away from authentic life with God, with other human persons and creation.

Because of the "Good News", the consequences of this rift can be healed through the establishment and cultivation of authentic relationships. How we "stand before" God (*proseuche*) through *every* relationship and aspect of our daily lives, including our personal and community worship, expresses our response to the divine call to authentic relationship. As this is founded in God, potential growth in this dynamic is without end. Here we recall the famous words of St Athanasius: "God became a human person, so that the human person may become divine." Writing in the late second century, St Irenaeus says: "Not only in this present age but also in the age to come, God will always have something more to teach the human person and the human person will always have something more to learn from God."[2]

We are on a journey on which the living God has invited us to ever greater depths of communion. The further we travel this direction, the more the divinely established personal mystery within us begins to express itself and the more we "know" God, "bear" God and become filled with God. The full experience of this relationship with God is called *theosis* or, in English, "glorification" or "deification". Again and again, human persons experience the mercy and gifts of the loving God. Both consciously and (more often) unconsciously, these persons begin to bear witness to this process in every aspect of their relationships with others and creation. This deepening communion with God shines through their intentions, thoughts, words and actions, indeed, through their very presence.

These holy persons, the saints, who live in healthy communion with God, can best speak for God. It is to them that St Paul was referring when he wrote, "Those who are spiritual discern all things, and they are themselves subject to no one else's scrutiny" (1 Cor. 2:15). As participants in what the Orthodox call "the uncreated glory of God in Christ" they become "the only authorities within the Orthodox church".[3] In other words, those human persons who have the final authority in the church are those same men and women who have been glorified and have become the saints of God. There is no higher honour or vocation than this in the church. It is a call extended to all.

Spiritual assumptions: setting priorities

After this very brief theological orientation, it is important to note here that a *thorough* investigation of the sin of sexism, or any other sin for that matter, is impossible, because doing so would entail engaging the sin in a manner that is dangerous to human persons. Trying to define this sin from God's perspective is a case of the sin of pride – the desire to be god without God. When we judge the sins of others while we are in a state of pride, we run the risk of leading a military campaign to remove the speck from the eye of our brother or sister while ignoring the log in our own. We become "spiritual terrorists". Authentic relationships with God, other human persons and creation cannot exist under these circumstances.

From a spiritual perspective, this sort of campaign may eventually direct us away from our own calling to full human personhood. This is typically marked by a growing inner hardness and lack of compassion, often expressed towards those who are nearest to us. Sometimes this takes the shape of self-righteous judgmentalism or fundamentalism, sometimes indifference or cynicism. For some people, this inner hardening leads to a tragic form of delusion which either rejects the holy altogether or considers oneself as the sole arbiter of holiness.

Any uncritical, undiscerning search for justice can easily entice us away from seeking the "one thing necessary" (Luke 10:42). Almost no one is immune to these temptations. Far too many of us ignore or even betray our own call to holiness and friendship with God as a result of trying to do God's work for him. From this wrong foothold, we run the risk of idolatry. We make an idol of our own conceptions of reality. Soon we ourselves become the oppressors. Rather than seeking to express the will of the Giver of life, we become agents of effacing the life of others.

Ensnared by the very trap we have set for others, we become less than human.

The antidote to this is rather simple. At the root of all of our personal actions, a conscious, peaceful yet discerning and critical spirit is necessary. This is because, as Orthodox theology stresses, any and all sin is bigger than we are. Nevertheless, the Christian good news is that the love of God is far greater than any and all sin.

Putting an end to denial

The sin of sexism, however, does clearly exist. And while we must avoid playing God in our analysis of this sin, we are still bound to unconditional honesty in naming it when we discern that it is occurring, including in our own selves. The prerequisite for naming this and any sin is putting an end to denial.

This is much more difficult than it sounds. Denial may take the form of a complete inability to accept the existence of a sin. If the sin does not exist, then the world is as it should be. Furthermore, if this sin does not exist, then the messenger must be the problem. Denial may also take the form of a partial admission of its existence, which minimizes the ramifications of this sin through ingenious rationalization. In this case, both message and messenger are trivialized. While this partial admission may seem preferable to no acknowledgment at all, it has the same effect of promoting the sin. Wherever the desire to engage the full light of truth is absent, sin will fester in the darkness. Orthodox spirituality teaches that sin is particularly at home with half-truths.

In recent years, I have come to believe that dealing with the sin of sexism is ultimately a matter of life and death. Its presence and effects are insidious and pervasive; and even the visible damage it inflicts on persons is incalculable. Boys and girls, men and women frequently suffer life-long, crippling losses as a result of this sin. And when this sin is active, yet its presence is denied outright or minimized, it gains power and momentum.

Piercing through pride and "hardness of heart"

Sexism is virtually never active alone. It is usually combined with and feeds on a cluster of other sins. The first of these is pride, which as we saw is essentially the desire to be god without God. Pride is immediately associated with other sins: the urge to grasp, control and destroy (manipulation), envy, the insatiable lust for power, glory and honour.

Typically, sexism is also accompanied by the condition Orthodox spirituality calls "hardness of heart". The heart here refers to something much deeper than the physical heart or the romantic connotations of the word or even its use to refer to the base of human emotions. Simply stated, the heart for the Orthodox is the seat of our highest priorities. "Where your treasure is, there your heart will be also" (Matt. 6:21).

Through the heart, the human person grows in communion with God and others. It is essentially through the heart that one is established in humility. It is important not to confuse humility with humiliation – the destructive devaluation of the human person which promotes inauthentic relationships. The shame experienced through humiliation is typically used as a weapon of psychic violence which devastates the soul. While theology teaches that the soul is created to be immortal, humiliation and shaming may be experienced as "soul murder".

True humility occurs when one discovers what is most real: that one's existence and all creation ultimately depend on the love of the living God. Humble persons are deeply "grounded" in this reality; indeed, the Latin root of this word refers to the ground or mud of the earth. The term implies that genuinely humble persons are profoundly aware of what and who they are. They are whole human persons who relate with other human persons in a manner which leaves room for the mystery of God to take precedence within their relationship. Both men and women, equally, are called to be humble in this manner.

"Hardness of heart" refers specifically to the deadening of our deep inner awareness and connection with God, as well as with human beings and creation. Pride and hardness of heart work together symbiotically to affect how persons perceive, act, feel and respond to reality. If God is "frozen out" of our heart, we will also be unable to see or relate authentically with other human beings, creation or even our own selves. Because these "frozen" places cannot be felt from within, persons whose hearts are hard and choose evil often believe they are justified. They truly have no "sense" of what they are doing (cf. Luke 23:34).

On those relatively rare occasions when a person perceives his or her own inner frozen places, it is often as a result of realizing that he or she has inflicted serious harm on another. This may lead to repentance, *metanoia*, a complete change of heart and mind which reflects a thaw in the frozen heart. Short of *theosis*, all human persons have places in their hearts which are frozen or hard. These vary according to our own unique personal history, relationships, inadequacies, sin and, most of all, relationship with God.

The spiritual effects of sexism

Sexism ultimately depends on pride and hardness of heart in order to exist. It is an expression of inauthentic relating based on gender. Sexism is usually subtle. Whether through action or lack of action, the person who is the object of this abuse is reduced to less than fully human from the perspective of the offender. In other words, the victim is de-personalized and objectified. A human-based "relative value" is projected onto the person, and the offender locks the intended victim into this definition, taking no account of how the living God may truly see and value the victim.

From the perspective of the offender, there is no possibility of an authentic relationship with the intended victim, let alone of transformation (*theosis*). There is a profound absence of true humility here. Betrayal and defiance are at the foundation of all sexism, as it is built on the refusal to acknowledge the divinely given and unique "mystery" of another human being. And so in one act, both God and human person are defied and betrayed. This has physical, psychological, social and spiritual ramifications. All too often, this dynamic may develop into ongoing psychological, physical, economic or sexual intimidation and violence, as the perpetrator is in a more powerful position than the victim.

While not necessarily feeling it, the perpetrator is spiritually "frozen". The offender may even be quite content and distracted, persistently chasing rewards thought to lead to self-aggrandizement and worldly success. While this creates its own kind of addictive excitement, the abuser is actually a stranger to the love of God.

This is as true in the so-called secular world as in the religious world. What is different in the world of the church is the profound level of betrayal experienced. When the abuser is a member of the clergy or a leader in the church, the survivor of the abuse often experiences a double betrayal: by the offender and also by God. Typically, the community and the religious leadership fail the survivor. Lacking discernment, they uncritically seek to defend "the ministry". This adds further insult to the most profound of betrayals already experienced by the survivor. In recent years, organizations and ministries have been formed which seek to address the healing of persons and communities affected by this kind of pain.[4]

Sexism subdues and enslaves the other; indeed, enslavement may perhaps be described as the ultimate goal of sexism. It is little wonder that ancient descriptions of young girls and women (and often young boys and men) being "sold into slavery", from pre-Christian times and in the early centuries of Christianity, implied a life of coerced prostitution, devoid of human dignity. They were seen as commodities of relative value.

Think also of how the religious leaders in many of the gospel stories treated others, especially those in apparently weaker positions – the ill, the destitute, women. Women were not treated as persons bearing the same "image and likeness of God" as they. Instead, an arbitrary value was ascribed to them and then, de-personalized and devalued, they could be manipulated for selfish purposes.

The gospel story recounted in John 8:2-11 demonstrates how the religious leaders of the day trapped and used a woman caught in sin as a way to bait Jesus, simultaneously attacking authentic relationships towards both God and a human person. It is worthy of note that according to the biblical account, before Jesus proclaimed the "orthodoxy" of who he was, he first stopped to rescue and restore the woman. The story ends by depicting the woman departing as a friend of God. The Lord's response indicates that God sees affronts against himself and against other humans – women as well as men – as part of the same reality (cf. Matt. 22:37-39).

From a spiritual perspective, sexism is a delusion. It is not based in reality – the will and love of God. But the life-effacing dynamic of sexism can unfortunately take on a kind of life of its own. Survivor and offender alike may live entirely under the sway of this powerful form of "intoxication". Whether this assumes the form of a complete or partial denial of the existence of this sin, it fails to give glory to God and bears witness to "another gospel", whose message inflicts its own "hardening of the heart" within the unique personal history of the victim. This is then internalized in the psyche of the survivor and may be expressed in a number of ways, often resulting in some form of coping, withdrawal or escape mechanism, so as to help protect the victim from further humiliation and pain.

Sexism in daily life

Sexism thus seeks to undermine the sense of personhood of the targeted individual by aiming to break the person's will and sense of God-given dignity. As this person is held in some form of contempt by the offender, attempts to reform a hardened abuser are frequently met with denial, even aversion. Moreover, within this inauthentic relationship, the free will of the less powerful person usually diminishes. This is not surprising, for the survivor has entered the deluded domain of the more powerful offender. Nevertheless, free will can never disappear completely. There are even occasions when the intended victim cannot be ensnared, usually after the person has already experienced some healing. I have seen this in a number of instances, but it normally requires an extensive degree of personal healing.

We must bear in mind that this humiliating, life-effacing dynamic also occurs in many other relationships in which the more powerful can manipulate the less powerful. Parents abuse their children, husbands exploit their wives (or wives may abuse their husbands), teachers mistreat their students, clergy betray those in their care, bosses exploit their staff, the politically powerful oppress the weak, the rich exploit the poor. In all these situations, the more powerful person is blind to the mystery of the person "over whom" they have authority.

Many observers have pointed to the way in which human-based institutional and cultural structures are used as vehicles to oppress weaker members of a society, including women. When oppression is built into structures, the accountability of colluding individuals is blurred, as they too are over-powered to some extent by the delusion within the system and may easily become spiritually "frozen" to the reality of the will and love of God. Instead, many may burrow themselves more deeply into such a system in order to hide from this fact. Or they may seek rewards from the system as a means of escape from truth.

When combatting life-effacing "structures", it is very easy to become "frozen". This happens when we become identified with the system's process of analysis and lose our orientation and grounding in reality – the will and love of God. As in the fall of Adam and Eve, we seek to become god without God. As stated above, authentic relationships with God, other human persons and creation cannot exist under such circumstances. Under these circumstances, the liberators of today become the oppressors of tomorrow. It requires discernment to "fight the good fight" (2 Tim. 4:7) against evil forces while staying grounded in the "one thing necessary" (Luke 10:42).

The most common form of sexism in contemporary society is that directed against women. It may be committed by men or women. Psychological studies have classified the differences between men's sexism against women and women's sexism against women. Briefly, while the abuse towards the intended victim may seem similar, the former tends to be rooted in contempt towards "the other gender", while the latter tends to direct the contempt inwardly, towards "the self: body and soul".[5]

These disordered relationships between women and men affect both in differing yet profound ways. Let me here offer four brief observations about the sexism directed by men against women.

The first of these has to do with what is perhaps the most obvious case, in which sexism causes inauthentic relationships with women presently in a man's life. He projects certain pre-determined assumptions onto women which diminish or ignore the mystery of their person, their dignity and their God-given vocation. Typically, various strategies of shaming are used to coerce compliance. This dynamic extends itself to expectations of the roles of women in the home, society and the church. Projected onto women with little or no discernment, these assumptions may keep women – and the relationship between the man and women – locked into a human-based and hence "fallen" pattern. Sadly, this may also lock out the will of God for the relationship. The dominant culture may foster such "fallen" relationships in numerous subtle ways, maintaining assumptions regarding human relationships which may have little to do with the will of God.

Second, when men de-personalize the other gender through sexist attitudes and actions, a subtle but very deep damage may be occurring within them as well. Professional psychotherapists and counsellors recognize that dynamics from significant past and present relationships with men and women are often deeply internalized in the human psyche. These inner relationships are reflected in the quality of our external relationships as well.

But how does a man grow as a human being if he has only faulty inner feminine images and memories? How does this affect one's maturing sense of masculinity? Certain approaches to psychology have found that when a man has immature associations with internalized feminine relationships or the "feminine", his masculinity suffers reciprocally. This rejection of the "other" deep within him now sabotages his own masculinity.

This may have serious ramifications in terms of his spiritual life as it is understood in the Orthodox tradition. This leads to a third concern: how the saints of the church are approached. I have been to churches where except for the Holy Mother of God, there were few or even *no* female saints depicted either on the iconostasis or in the frescoes on the walls. Icons of male saints were to be seen everywhere. How does this affect the male and female worshippers who attend divine services? What does this say about the vision of the leaders who selected the icons? What does it say about their understanding of the saints, of the nature of the church, even of paradise? Is it not possible that paradise may be made up of at least half women? Are not at least half of the saints women? How is the quality of one's intercessions to the female saints, even to the Mother of God, affected when the presence and dignity of women are diminished not only in everyday life but also in church?

A fourth, more subtle concern is also raised. Assumptions about the Theotokos may arise which do not belong to the church. For example, it is not uncommon today to hear persons refer to the activities of Mary as though her mission were completed: she gave birth to God the Word out of obedience and has now earned her place in heaven. The implication is that all women should do likewise. On the basis of this static view, there is little room left for the activity of the Theotokos, women saints or even all the saints in the church. Why, then, do we Orthodox still pray to her? Why, for that matter, do we still pray to any of the saints?

It would profit us to reflect more deeply on why, through the ages, the church has testified through its prayers that this human being is "more honourable than the Cherubim and incomparably more glorious than the Seraphim". Is her work completely over within the Body of Christ? What kind of a loving Mother would that be? What does this say about the quality of our relationship with the saints? What does this say about us?

* * *

Obviously, this presentation has been able to present only some basic considerations for an Orthodox spiritual perspective on the sin of sexism. Still, these concerns do seek to express a theology which is healing and life-giving and testifies to the importance of authentic relationships. It is evident that more reflection is needed on ways to respond to the sin of sexism. Central to a discussion of the antidote to this sin may be the paradoxical yet powerful criteria of humility, freedom, purity of heart and discernment. The discipline (*askesis*) required for human persons to cultivate these will, with the help of God, develop over a lifetime. This effort will, first of all, facilitate a growing relationship with God. A teaching used by the Lord to identify his true disciples provides us with a small indication of the mystery of communion among the three persons of the Trinity, which has profound implications for the nurture of authentic relationships among all human persons, men and women, and for every human being with God: "the person who finds his life shall lose it; and the one who loses his life, for my sake, will find it" (Matt. 10:39).

NOTES

1 Cf. John Zizioulas, *Being as Communion*, Crestwood NY, St Vladimir's Seminary Press, 1985.

2 Cited in Kallistos Ware, *The Orthodox Way*. Crestwood NY, St Vladimir's Seminary Press, 1985, p.185.

3 Cf. John Romanides, "Church Synods and Civilization", *Theologia*, Vol. 63, no. 3, July-Sept. 1992, pp.20-21.

4 In the USA the Inter-Faith Sexual Trauma Institute (ISTI) is one such organization. ISTI's mission statement "affirms the goodness of human sexuality and advocates respectful relationships through the appropriate use of power within communities of all religious traditions. ISTI promotes the prevention of sexual abuse, exploitation and harassment through research, education and publication. In areas of sexuality, ISTI offers leadership, gives voice and facilitates healing to survivors, communities of faith and offenders, as well as those who care for them." Further information is available from the Office of the Executive Director; St John's Abbey and University, Collegeville, Minnesota 56321, USA; and from ISTI's site on the World Wide Web – http://www.osb.org/isti. A new Orthodox Internet ministry has also been established for "victims of abuse in the Orthodox church" – the "Protection of the Theotokos Survivors' site". The address is www.angelfire.com/bc/orthodoxsurvivors/index.html.

5 Sexism may also be expressed towards men by both men and women. Often this is linked with some form of chronic abuse. In my own clinical experience, I have observed women's sexism towards men as initially expressed towards "the other", while the sexism of men towards men appears to be expressed towards the "self". Therapy would need to proceed differently in each of these general situations.

About the Authors

Nicholas K. Apostola (Romanian Orthodox Church) is the Chancellor of the Romanian Orthodox Archdiocese in America and Canada. He has taught at Holy Cross Greek Orthodox School of Theology in Brookline, Massachusetts, and at St Vladimir's Orthodox Theological Seminary in Crestwood, New York.

Marie Assaad (Coptic Orthodox Church) is a former Deputy General Secretary of the World Council of Churches.

Elisabeth Behr-Sigel (Ecumenical Patriarchate) is an author, lecturer and long-time Christian activist. Her areas of interest include theology, the ministry of women and spirituality.

Deborah Malacky Belonick (Orthodox Church in America) is an author who frequently lectures on Orthodox theology, anthropology, spirituality and feminism.

Thamar Dasnabedian (Armenian Apostolic Church) is a professor at the Université St Esprit in Kaslik, Lebanon.

Sophie Deicha (Ecumenical Patriarchate) is a professor at St Sergius Theological Institute in Paris, France. She recently has been a Visiting Lecturer at the Catholic Institute in Paris.

Thomas FitzGerald (Ecumenical Patriarchate) is a professor at Holy Cross Greek Orthodox School of Theology in Brookline, Massachusetts, USA, and former Executive Director of the Programme Unit on Unity and Renewal at the World Council of Churches.

Kyriaki Karidoyanes FitzGerald (Ecumenical Patriarchate) is an author and lecturer on theology and spirituality. She has been a professor at Holy Cross Greek Orthodox School of Theology in Brookline, Massachusetts, and at St Vladimir's Orthodox Theological School in Crestwood, New York.

Aruna Gnanadason (Church of South Africa) is the coordinator of the Women's Programme and the Justice, Peace and Creation Team of the World Council of Churches.

Dimitra Koukoura (Church of Greece) is a professor at the School of Theology of the University of Thessaloniki, Greece.

Leonie B. Liveris (Ecumenical Patriarchate) is the founder and editor of the journal *MaryMartha*.

Mother Maria [Rule] (Russian Orthodox Church) writes and speaks on the questions of women and ecumenical relationships and translates the works of Bishop Nikolai Velimirovich. She has lived in Serbia and now resides in London.

Constantina Peppa (Church of Greece) is an instructor of religion for secondary schools in Athens, Greece.

Teny Pirri-Simonian (Armenian Apostolic Church) is executive secretary for Church and Ecumenical Relations of the World Council of Churches.

Despina D. Prassas (Ecumenical Patriarchate) is a doctoral candidate in historical theology at the Catholic University of America.

Christina Shaheen Reimann (Patriarchate of Antioch) is a retreat leader, lecturer and educator in Orthodox communities in North America.

Ekaterina Shibayeva (Russian Orthodox Church) is a student in the Moscow Theological Institute.

Shanti Verghese (Malankara Orthodox Syrian Church in India) is an advocate for women's concerns in India.

Maha Milki Wehbe (Patriarchate of Antioch) is the coordinator of the women's programme of the Middle East Council of Churches, Beirut, Lebanon.

Constantinos N. Yokarinis (Church of Greece) is a professor at the Department of Education at the University of Athens.

Valerie Zahirsky (Orthodox Church in America) is a writer of Orthodox religious education materials and curricula; she also writes and speaks on topics concerning families and women in the church.